D0038845

Praise for First Folio:

"Four centuries after Will Shakespeare's death, the Bard still manages to create murder most foul when a professor gets his hands on what appears to be Shakespeare's original, handwritten plays. In Scott Evans's fast-paced literary murder mystery, ***First Folio,*** Joe Conrad is sent a mysterious package and is struck dumb by its contents. The documents appear authentic, but it's not clear if they're in Shakespeare's own hand. Conrad begins the hunt to determine the true author, putting himself and his family at risk of death from Benedict, a sadistic mercenary bent on recovering the same documents for his boss, a ruthless collector. It's become a cliché to say, "I couldn't put it down," but in this case, it's true. Unless you have a forgiving boss, don't start reading this late at night as you'll show up at work the next morning bleary-eyed from staying up all night to finish reading it." Les Edgerton is the author of nine books, including the story collection ***Monday's Meal*** and the writing text, ***Hooked: Write Fiction That Grabs Readers at Page One and Never Lets Them Go.***

"With ***FIRST FOLIO***, Scott Evans takes readers hostage in his compelling, page-turning mystery that gives us an intriguing twist to detective literature." Rick Mofina, author of ***If Angels Fall, Now Way Back, Vengeance Road,*** and ***Six Seconds***.

Scott Evans has maliciously dropped another tightly coiled mystery on the protagonist he introduced in his suspenseful first novel, ***Tragic Flaws***. He has added a great deal of throat-clutching action and, unbelievably, more tension. Readers will be seized with the dangers Joseph Conrad must again overcome, this time to solve the slaying of a beloved mentor and answer the mystery of who actually penned the works of Shakespeare. Dealing with intergenerational greed and historical literary fraud, ranging over two continents, ***First Folio*** is an unmissable addition to a series of literary mysteries that will keep us enthralled for years. David Lloyd Sutton, Book Reviewer, the ***Sacramento and San Francisco Book Reviews*** and ***Reason Magazine.***

First Folio

A Literary Mystery

Scott Evans

authorHOUSE®

AuthorHouse™
1663 Liberty Drive
Bloomington, IN 47403
www.authorhouse.com
Phone: 1-800-839-8640

Cover photo by Cynthia Cooper Evans

First published by AuthorHouse 11/20/2010

ISBN: 978-1-4520-7737-6 (hc)
ISBN: 978-1-4520-7738-3 (sc)
ISBN: 978-1-4520-7739-0 (e)

Library of Congress Control Number: 2010914203

Printed in the United States of America

This book is printed on acid-free paper.

Part I:
Love's Labour Lost

CHAPTER 1

For aught that I could ever read,
Could ever hear by tale or history,
The course of true love never did run smooth.
From *A Midsummer's Night's Dream*

As he tore through the wet streets of Baton Rouge, tears of anger streamed down his face. Jack Claire had hoped to authenticate the Shakespeare manuscripts before he died. *But now?* Now that the documents had caused Maggie's death, he wanted nothing to do with them. If only he'd taken the stranger's first calls more seriously, Maggie might still be alive. He slammed the palm of his hand against the steering wheel. The surge of anger caused his heart to pound fiercely and brought a sharp pain to his chest.

Calm down, old boy.

Even at sixty-six, he had been in remarkable shape, tall and fit and feeling well. Until now. Now the image of the slender stranger he'd first seen at Maggie's funeral made him regret ever finding the manuscripts in the office of an old friend, Phil Owens, who had been a visiting professor from Wales.

Years earlier, Jack had taken Phil under his wing at LSU, so when Phil died, he left his books and papers to Jack. Jack arranged one more sabbatical to England, ostensibly to interview new Shakespearean scholars at Oxford University, but in reality to visit his old friend's widow.

Buried among stacks of loose papers inside a massive wooden bookcase in Phil's dark, musty office at Swansea University, as if hidden decades ago, was a metal box, the size of a file cabinet drawer. Jack hauled it out and lifted it onto Phil's desk. Inside was a cache of handwritten manuscripts, written on sturdy cotton stock he recognized as the type of paper used in the sixteenth century, and, in superior condition, a leather-bound copy of Jaggard and Blount's *First Folio*. How many copies of the first collection of William Shakespeare's plays had Isaac Jaggard printed? Five hundred? *This* copy had all the hallmarks of an original 1623 volume!

Staring at the manuscripts, Jack instantly recognized their value. A good copy of the *First Folio* was worth over $500,000. But the handwritten manuscripts? As literary artifacts, they'd be worth a fortune, equivalent to an undiscovered Van Gogh painting.

Sitting in his dead friend's office, Jack had stared in awe at the neat, uniform penmanship—it was *not* the same as William Shakespeare's. Could this be the proof that Will Shakespeare was *not* the author of the plays after all? If so, why hadn't Phil Owens exposed the manuscripts? Afraid he'd become a laughing stock if the papers were fakes?

Jack remembered leaning back in Phil's old chair, wondering why Phil hadn't given them to the world?

What if you had proof Melville hadn't written *Moby Dick*? Or Milton wasn't the author of *Paradise Lost*? Should he expose such a truth?

No. Not without absolute proof.

Now with the Louisiana rain slapping the windshield, Jack parked on the street, looking behind the car to see if the other man had followed. Seeing no one out of the ordinary, he hurried into the post office, carrying the heavy box, only the second person in line.

A simple cardboard box filled with four-hundred-year-old documents recording history's greatest achievements and most profound tragedies. The irony of it stabbed his heart like the memory of his wife's death.

A heavy-set clerk waved Jack to his window.

"What's in the box?" the clerk asked.

"Books," Jack answered.

"You want to send it book rate or priority mail?"

Jack hesitated.

"You can send it priority and have it tracked," said the clerk. "Cost a little extra, but you'll be able to check its progress."

Jack considered the suggestion. *If I can track it, then maybe the killer could, too.*

"No, just book rate will do. I'm in no rush now." Jack looked over his shoulder.

The clerk put the postage tag on the box and pulled it from Jack's hands.

"Anything else?"

Jack couldn't believe it. In the time it took to glance over his shoulder, the box of Shakespeare's manuscripts had been taken from him—papers that could change the world of literature, now in the hands of postal workers.

What have I done?

"Sir," the clerk said. "Anything else?"

Jack turned and reluctantly walked out of the Post Office building. When he stepped outside, nearly blown down by gusts of wind, he pushed through the slanting rain toward his car and threw open the door. As he backed up, he saw the lean stranger, dressed in black, dashing toward him. The man stopped in his tracks. Under the rim of a dripping wet, black baseball cap, the man's sharp eyes peered through the fogged windshield at Jack. For a few seconds, the two men just stared at each other.

Then Jack peeled out of the parking space so quickly that the driver behind him laid on the horn. He drove around the corner and headed to the capitol.

He and Maggie had taken visitors to the Huey P. Long state capitol on many occasions, showing them the observation deck at the top of the tower. The thirty-four story limestone-clad building, a shining example of neo-classical architecture with quirky Art Deco details, looked like a phallic symbol to him—with the two lower chambers, the House and the Senate, on either side of the tower. It was the tallest state capitol in the U.S. The observation deck on the twenty-seventh floor encircled the rest of the tower and, on clear days, offered impressive views. Louisiana lay out flat, green and lush in all directions. You felt as if you could see New Orleans to the southeast, and Jackson, Mississippi, to the northeast.

He pulled into a space directly in front of the building and walked as quickly as he could through the downpour.

Lightning exploded nearby, followed by the kettledrums of thunder. Jack shook off the rain as he scurried through the ornate Memorial Hall to the elevators. The large bronze relief map of Louisiana looked dim and unimpressive in the dark lobby, as did the two large oil paintings that served as murals depicting idealized scenes of life in Louisiana. A couple of security guards stopped talking long enough to watch Jack cross the empty lobby. When the doors of one elevator opened, Jack immediately stepped inside.

He got off at the highest floor the elevator reached in order to walk up two more narrow flights of stairs to the observation deck on the twenty-seventh floor. A maintenance man was unlocking a door to the janitor's closet when Jack, out of breath, finally reached the last step. The man watched as Jack tried the handle of the door that led outside.

"Why is this door locked?" Jack asked, looking at the door.

"Ain't nobody goin' out in this storm," the worker answered.

Jack turned to look at the man. "But I must get outside. I won't be long."

The worker shook his head. "It's a damn hurricane out there, mister."

Jack studied the janitor's face. "You don't understand. I'm a meteorologist at LSU," he said. "I've been appointed by the Governor to study this storm. We've got to be prepared for another Katrina, don't we?"

The worker cocked his head and gave Jack a skeptical look.

"You got identification?"

"Of course." He retrieved his wallet, which fell open to reveal both his driver's license and his LSU faculty ID card. He placed his thumb over the "lish" in "Department of English" and showed the ID to the worker. "See? Just as I said. Dr. John Claire, Department of Engineering, Louisiana State University."

The man inspected the laminated ID card.

"You said you was in the weather department?"

"My good fellow," Jack explained, "the meteorological department is a division of the Department of Engineering."

"I guess that makes sense." He clutched his keys and walked over to the door. "Now ya'll be careful out there."

"Don't worry. I'll be off that roof before you can say, 'to be or not to be'."

Even with concern in his eyes, the worker unlocked the door and held it open.

Jack pushed around the corner of the building, but he was knocked backward momentarily, squinting as wind-whipped rain pelted his face. About as wide as a sidewalk, the deck went around all four corners of the inner part of the tower that rose another seven stories above him. To his left, the walls of the building; to his right, the short guard wall and railings through which visitors could look.

But not today. The clouds and sheets of heavy rain obscured Jack's view. He staggered forward. At the southwest corner of the observation deck, he could climb up on the telescope platform and reach the low bars, which curved inward at the top corner.

Jack struggled, not having counted on the wetness. He placed a foot inside a brace—it provided a foothold that allowed him to straighten up and straddle the barrier. In throwing his right leg up over the high railing, he caught a glimpse of the dark figure rushing toward him. Jack used all his strength to swing the rest of his body over the railing. He slid down on the other side, but his right foot slipped off the edge. Regaining his foothold, he gripped the wet bars tightly.

Jack stared into the killer's face. Shortly cropped black hair framed the man's sharp features under a baseball cap. The man's blue eyes squinted in the wind and rain, under thick black eyebrows. A few pockmarks scarred the hollows of his cheeks. His nose dripped with rain over thin lips and straight white teeth.

"What are you doing, Dr. Claire?" yelled the killer over the roar of the wind. "Climb back over, old man." He pointed a black pistol at Jack's heart.

Jack glanced at the gun and smiled. "All morning, I've been trying to think of the right thing to say. 'Once more into the breach!' doesn't seem to fit. 'How weary, stale, flat, and unprofitable seem to me all the uses of this world.' That doesn't seem quite right, either, does it?"

"Tell me where the papers are, and I'll let you live."

"'What an ass am I?'" Jack roared. "'Prompted to my revenge by heaven and hell, must, like a whore, unpack my heart with words and fall a-cursing.'"

"WHO DID YOU SEND THOSE PAPERS TO?"

A shard of lightning cut through the boiling clouds overhead as thunder exploded around them.

"Do you know Dickens?"

"What?"

"You must know *A Tale of Two Cities*?"

"Is this some sort of clue?"

Jack smiled broadly, staring into the quizzical eyes of Maggie's murderer.

"Yes, a clue. Listen carefully."

The man turned his ear toward the old professor, who said, "Tis a far, far better thing I do than I have ever done before. A far better rest I go to than I have ever known."

The killer switched the gun from his right hand to his left, then grabbed Jack's raincoat and tugged him hard against the wet iron bars.

Stunned by the impact, Jack's heart exploded with pain. His vision blurred. His knees weakened. When he looked up, he could not see the man's face clearly. A sudden urge to reach through the bars welled up inside him. But everything darkened.

Jack released his grip on the cold, black iron and twisted, slipping his arms out of his raincoat. For a moment, he stood in place watching the other man grab for him. Then Jack leaned back and disappeared from the killer's view.

The professional let the rain pelt his back as he walked to the door. He pushed the door open and went inside, stepping over the body of the janitor who had tried to stop him. A wide pool of blood ebbed from the man's body, forming a circle on the marble floor. The killer holstered his gun inside his dark jacket, hurried down the stairs and pushed the button for the elevator.

On the first floor, several people rushed to the windows to look at the large, lifeless body that had landed with a sickening thud on the sidewalk just outside.

No one paid attention as the dark figure walked in the other direction.

The rain fell softly. To the south, the edge of the clouds became visible. On the horizon, a thin ribbon of blue sky and orange sunlight revealed itself. This tempest soon would pass.

CHAPTER 2

What a hell of witchcraft lies
In the orb of one particular tear.
From A Lover's Complaint

Joseph Lawrence Conrad sat in his office at Central Lutheran University in Stockton, California, stunned by the message he'd just heard. Jack Claire, dead. He replayed the voicemail and listened to the somber voice of Hayden Crawford again. "I know you were close to Dr. Claire, so I'm sorry to have to tell you this. He committed suicide a few days ago. There will be a funeral next Saturday at The Cathedral of St. Joseph Catholic church. I hope you can attend, but of course we'll understand if you can't, it being such short notice. Sorry to be the bearer of bad news."

Joe stared at the photo of Jack he kept on his desk. Dr. Claire had been more than a mentor; he'd been like a second father. It had been Jack who had recommended him for his teaching job at CLU. Tears welled up in Joe's eyes, but he wiped them away and prepared to face his students. It was the day of their mid-term exam. Jack would want him to go on with work.

Inside a wood-paneled classroom, Joe turned his back to the students, hoping they would not see his bloodshot eyes, and wrote the exam prompt on a whiteboard. When he finished, Joe brushed strands of light brown hair off his forehead and faced his class. The students in his summer course groaned.

"No complaining," he said, forcing a grin. "You knew what to expect."

They dutifully began writing. The reading list for the popular course, titled "Criminal Intent in Literature, Past and Present," included *Hamlet, Crime and Punishment, In Cold Blood,* and *A Lesson before Dying.* Two nonfiction works were also required for the course, John Grisham's *An Innocent Man* and his own autobiographical book, *Tragic Flaws*, which he'd written after being accused of several murders. The book had sold well during the real killer's trial, but sales had dropped off and he'd just received a letter from Random House that there wouldn't be a second printing—news he'd taken in stride.

As the students wrote furiously, Joe lowered his 6'2" frame into a chair and looked out the classroom window, losing himself in flashes of memory as he stared at the tall redwood trees outside. He recalled his first meeting in Jack's office when he interviewed to become Jack's research assistant.

While eating his lunch, Dr. Claire seemed to delight in feeding the gray squirrels. One by one, they climbed down the branches of the massive old oaks along the ledges outside his window, scampered right inside and made themselves at home, eating the peanuts Jack set out on his cluttered desk. His secretaries—Agnes, older, plump and white, Missy, younger, skinny and black—stood in the doorway to the office and cringed as Jack fed a bushy-tailed creature from his hands.

"One of 'em 's gonna bite you one day, Dr. Claire," Agnes warned in her mild Cajun accent. "Gonna bite the hand that feeds it, for sure."

"That will be the day I wring its tiny neck," Jack cautioned, wagging a finger at the squirrels.

Joe had cleared his throat and lowered himself into an oak chair well away from the squirrels. Agnes and Missy closed the door and let the two men have privacy. Jack had given him a sideways glance.

"You're specializing in American lit, Joe," Dr. Claire had said. "Why do you want to work with me? You know I specialize in Elizabethan authors."

"Yes," Joe had admitted, "but I read your book. I like the way you compare Shakespeare's themes and characters to modern novels."

"Oh?"

Dr. Claire, who later insisted that Joe call him Jack, had seemed skeptical, which compelled Joe to continue.

"The way Faulkner incorporates Shakespearean tragedy in *The Sound and the Fury*, and the way Tennessee Williams makes his women seem like Lady Macbeth and Ophelia in *A Street Car Named Desire*."

After taking a bite of his ham and Swiss on rye, Jack fed a peanut to a frail squirrel and quietly mulled Joe's comment.

"I think I will learn a lot from you," Joe added feebly.

"What do *you* think?" asked Jack of the creature stealing food from his fingers. The indifferent old squirrel ignored the question as it furiously gnawed away the shell of the peanut.

Joe cleared his throat again. "Have you named them?"

Jack forced a smile. "That young couple on the bookshelf is Ophelia and Hamlet. They always eat together, but sometimes Ophelia looks a little melancholy."

"How 'bout the old guy on your desk?"

Jack chuckled. "Oh, my. That's Lear. Getting a bit feeble, I'm afraid. Almost can't make the leap to my desk."

"And his daughters?"

Winking at the younger professor, Jack said, "Skulking about, I suspect, plotting to see who'll take over the prestigious desk once the old man has kicked the bucket."

Jack had cocked his head and flashed his knowing smile at Joe, saying, "You've got the job."

Joe had leapt to his feet and shook Dr. Claire's hand enthusiastically, smiling then as he was smiling now at the memory.

Suicide?

That didn't sound like the Dr. Claire Joe remembered. The man he knew was cheerful and energetic, never morose. Jack's enthusiasm for Shakespeare had been contagious. At times, Dr. Claire read lines from the plays, acting them out, really, in front of the class, changing voices as he read Ophelia's lines, making her sound more like Scarlett O'Hara than a Danish teenager.

Two hours later, after his students had finished their exams, Joe took the bluebooks to his office, sat down and looked at Jack Claire's photo, next to a picture of his wife and their two children. They had discussed going back to Baton Rouge to visit Sara's parents, but had decided it would be too expensive. Now it was different.

Joe picked up the phone and called his wife. "I guess we're going to Baton Rouge after all, Sara."

In Baton Rouge, Sara's parents, Ruth and Paul Taylor, met them at the airport. With a full head of white hair and a deep tan, Paul Taylor was a handsome man. Sara's mother Ruth still bleached her hair.

Joe and Sara's eight-year-old daughter Katie ran and hugged both of them enthusiastically, but their two-year-old son Brian clung to Sara's neck. He hadn't seen his grandparents since Christmas.

Riding south from the airport through the muggy Louisiana heat in Paul's gold Chrysler Concord, Joe pointed outside.

"There it is, Katie. The great Mississippi."

"Dad," she groaned. "You show it to me every time we come here."

He smiled patiently at his precocious daughter. "A lot of famous writers like Mark Twain and Kate Chopin have written about that river."

Sara patted Katie's knee. "It's twice as wide as the Sacramento River, Katie."

"Much deeper, too, I imagine," Sara's father Paul added.

Paul pulled off the highway and dropped down onto tree-lined Highland Road. The shade of the old oaks, laced with Spanish moss, provided a canopy blocking the scalding sunlight.

Sara's mother turned back to look at Joe.

"We were sorry to hear about Professor Claire's death. Everyone was surprised by his, um, suicide." She sneered when she said "suicide."

Sara's father glanced at Joe in the rearview mirror. "Poor man certainly had some misfortune at the end, his wife being killed and all."

Sara asked, "Where did Dr. Claire's wife have the accident, Mother?"

"Right around here, I think," Ruth answered. "I guess she was driving home from the J. C. Penney's store when someone ran her off the road." She glanced at Paul. "Or was it a Piggly-Wiggly?"

Without taking his eyes off the road, Paul answered, "I don't recall, dear. She ran into one of these trees alongside the road here. Steering wheel crushed her chest. Police don't know that she was run off the road, though. That's just a rumor."

Ruth looked at her husband. "Someone saw her being forced off the road, according to the newspaper."

Sara's father tilted his head back toward Sara, saying, "You Southern women love your conspiracies."

"Well," Ruth sighed, "I'm just passing on what I heard."

Joe pictured frail Maggie Claire smashed up in her car. He looked out the window at the old oaks to hide his face.

"My daddy says Dr. Claire was a great man," Katie announced.

Sara's mother reached back to touch Katie's arm. "Why, I'm sure he was, darlin'," she said. "I'm quite sure he was."

The next day, Joe borrowed Paul's Chrysler and drove to campus. He strolled under the sprawling oaks, through the oppressive heat. How little the campus had changed since he'd been a student here. Eventually, he drifted into Allen Hall and climbed the stairs to the English Department office.

"Well, hello there, Joe," Missy said. "Or can I finally call you Dr. Conrad?"

Missy, a slender woman in her mid-thirties, had been hired at about the same time Joe had started at LSU. She was the youngest secretary the English Department had seen, and the first black woman to work in the office.

"I'm afraid not."

"Oh?" she said. "I thought you'd go out there to California and tear it up."

Joe laughed. "Yeah, well, I guess California and I sort of tore up each other."

"I guess you did at that, Joe," Missy said. "I did hear about that trouble ya'll got into out there. I even saw you on the *Today* show."

"Oh," Joe said, blushing. "You saw that interview?"

"Yes, I did. Nobody around here missed it. We had a few copies of your book in the office, too, but they disappeared."

"Did you read it?" Joe asked, blushing.

"I most certainly did. It was very interesting. Those detectives sure got it wrong at first, didn't they?"

"Yes, but they got on the right track eventually."

"You were quite the hero, the way you saved Sara's life. I wish I had my copy now. I'd get you to autograph it."

"I'll send you a copy, a signed one, when I get back home."

"Oh, that'd be wonderful, Joe."

For a moment, Joe and Missy stared into each other's eyes, smiling. Missy's tight yellow dress seemed custom-fitted for her good figure. They looked each other up and down, and Joe felt the old spark of attraction that neither of them had acted on in the past. Then Missy seemed to remember why Joe was back, and her smile faded.

"It's just so sad, Joe," she said. "He was the nicest man I've ever known. And I know how much you loved him, too."

Joe nodded. A countertop separated them, but Missy walked around it, her high heels clicking on the linoleum, and she hugged Joe warmly. Still holding her, Joe asked, "You have any idea why he did it?"

Missy pulled back so she could look up into Joe's eyes without letting go of his arms. "I guess he was just heart broke about Mrs. Claire, is all I can figure."

Joe nodded.

Missy finally pulled away and stepped to her desk.

"I guess you'd like to see Dr. Crawford, wouldn't you?"

"Is he in?"

"Yeah, he's in Dr. Claire's office going through things. You know," Missy said, nodding toward the closed door, "he's finally got what he's wanted all these years."

"He's a good man, Missy."

"Oh, I know. I just wish he'd wait until after the funeral on Saturday to start tearin' things up in there."

Joe smiled as Missy picked up the phone.

"Dr. Crawford? Joseph Conrad's here to see you."

Missy frowned as she listened, rolling her eyes at whatever was being said.

"Okay, sir." She hung up the phone, making a face. "He says you have to wait. Says he'll come out in a minute."

Joe leaned against the counter and thumbed through the summer school schedule on the counter top.

"How's Sara and your baby, Joe?"

"Sara's doing fine, still teaching math. She has the summer off. You know Katie is eight years old now."

"No, she's not!"

"Yep. Smart as her mother and just as beautiful. I'll bring her up here tomorrow, so you can get a look at her."

"Oh, I'd love to see that sweet little baby again."

"Speaking of babies, did you hear Sara and I had a little boy?"

"Yes," Missy said, "I do remember hearing about it, now that you mention it."

"That's why that mess in California was so bad. Sara was pregnant at the time."

"What did they call that guy again?"

"The I-5 Strangler," Joe answered. The memory of tracking the killer and Sara through the rain that horrible night flashed into Joe's mind. Maybe it was just the over- air conditioned office, but he suddenly felt chilled. Even now, two years later, he could feel the cold water of the place called Lost Slough, where he had found the first body.

The door to Jack's office opened and out stepped Dr. Hayden Crawford.

"Hello, Joe," Dr. Crawford said walking over to shake his hand. "Glad you made it. I know Jack would be pleased."

At over six feet, Hayden was an imposing figure. His wavy dark hair and thick eyebrows made his face stern, more like a military officer than a humanities professor. His crushing grip told Joe that Hayden Crawford was now in charge.

"Do you have a few minutes?" Joe asked.

"Sure. Come on in."

Joe was shocked. Although the large desk and bookshelves were in the same place, Dr. Claire's office looked stark and cluttered. Half of the books were off the shelves, either in stacks on the floor or already packed into cardboard boxes. The surface of the desk had been cleared of Dr.

Claire's reading lamp with the green shade, the pictures of Maggie, Hank, and the granddaughters. All the hanging pictures, framed awards and certificates, as well as other artwork, were missing, leaving dozens of bare spots that made ghostly impressions on the walls.

"Wow," Joe said. "It looks so different, so barren."

Hayden walked around the large wooden desk and sat down. "I'm trying to decide which of Jack's books to keep. So many are outdated."

Joe settled into the chair in front of the desk where he had sat so many times before. Somehow the chair seemed different, stiffer.

"Did your wife come with you?"

"Yes. She and my two children. We're staying at her parents' house."

Joe noticed the closed windows. Jack's gray squirrels were nowhere to be seen.

"So, how are they treating you at that private school? Paying you what you're worth, are they?"

The question sounded like an insult.

"Actually, the notoriety from the murder case has made me a celebrity of sorts. The publicity and my book helped the university. Enrollment is up."

Hayden grinned but shook his head. "Maybe LSU's enrollment will go up now, too, with all the publicity surrounding Jack's death. We had a copy of your book floating around the office for awhile. Jack bought a couple, I think. Never got a chance to read it myself."

If Hayden's comment was an insult, Joe let it go.

"Could you tell me what happened? Sara's parents kept a newspaper article, so I know he jumped off the capitol. But what about the janitor? Do they really think Jack shot him?"

"I'm not sure. Maggie's death just destroyed him. Whether or not he shot the maintenance man is an open question. The police didn't find a gun on the roof of the capitol or on the ground near Jack's body."

"Did Jack leave a note?"

"Nothing at the capitol building, as far as I know. I'm not sure what the police found at Jack's home, although I do know they searched it."

"The newspaper said they found a box of cartridges for a pistol but not the gun itself. That does tend to make Jack look guilty of shooting the janitor."

Hayden Crawford leaned forward. "Except for one important detail. I happen to know the janitor was shot with a 9 millimeter. The cartridges they found in Jack's house were for a .22."

"That wasn't in the article I read, Hayden."

Hayden leaned back in Jack's old chair. "I probably shouldn't have said anything, but I have a friend on the police force. I'm sure you can appreciate how valuable a friend on the force can be."

Joe nodded, thinking about Detective Ryan Dunn. If Dunn hadn't followed Joe the night he went after Sara…

"Well, if Jack didn't shoot the janitor, who did? Could someone have pushed him off the building?"

Hayden laughed. "You've been up there, Joe. There's a wall with iron bars on top. It would be impossible for one or even two men to lift a big man like Jack over that railing."

"Maybe someone forced him to jump, you know, at gun point."

"That's possible," Hayden said, nodding, "but you have to wonder why Jack went up there in the first place. I mean, we were being hit by damn near a hurricane that morning. No one in his right mind went outside. The streets were all but empty."

Joe fidgeted in the uncomfortable chair.

"You want my theory?" Hayden rocked back and put his hands behind his head. "I think Jack went up there to kill himself and someone followed him, to rob him maybe. Jack foiled the robber's plans by jumping. But when the janitor showed up, the robber was scared he'd be blamed for Jack's death, so he shot the only witness."

Joe nodded. "As good an explanation as any, I guess."

"Especially when you consider the fact that Jack's home and this office had been broken into earlier in the week."

Joe leaned forward. "*That* wasn't in the paper."

"The police don't see a connection, but the coincidence is too great."

"You're right. Much too coincidental." Joe felt a nagging sense of danger, the same feeling he had had before. "But what was the robber after? Did Jack carry a lot of cash?"

"Not that I know of. We keep a little petty cash in the office here, but nothing worth killing for."

"Then what did the robber want?"

Hayden leaned forward again, the chair creaking under his weight. It was growing dark outside, a typical mid-day thunderstorm rolling in.

"Jack was up to something. He'd made some odd requests in the last year and tried to keep something from the rest of us."

"What kind of odd requests?"

"He ordered some old books from England."

Joe laughed. "For an Elizabethan scholar, that doesn't seem odd at all."

Hayden frowned at the rebuke. "The kinds of books he requested made me think he'd found something quite valuable, an old document of some kind, maybe a decree from Queen Elizabeth herself."

Joe studied Hayden's face. Something didn't feel right. "What kinds of books?" he asked.

Hayden looked uncomfortable. He obviously did not like being grilled by a former student. "Oh, various things. Some quite rare. Texts dealing with British aristocracy." Hayden glanced at his watch.

"I've kept you too long," Joe said.

"It's just, Jack's granddaughters are in town for the funeral. They want to look through his office later today. I have quite a bit to do to get ready for them."

"No rest for the wicked, I guess."

Crawford forced a polite chuckle and rose to his feet.

Over Hayden's shoulder, Joe could see the rain beginning to fall in the quad outside. He stood, too. "Well, maybe Jack's granddaughters know what was going on."

Hayden walked around the desk to escort Joe from his office. "They're in shock. Just lost their grandmother. Now this. Dreadful."

Joe walked toward the door. "It's all very troubling," he said.

"True, but at Jack's age and after the loss of his wife, taking one's life is not entirely unexpected."

Joe nodded. Reaching for the door, he added, "Still, as Jack himself might say, something's rotten in the state of Denmark."

CHAPTER 3

Give sorrow words: the grief that does not speak
Whispers the o'er-fraught heart and bids it break.
From Macbeth

Built in the mid-1800s, the Cathedral of St. Joseph was a traditional gothic cathedral-style church with blood-red doors. It was dark and cool in the back, but in the front, the white marble of the altar glowed brightly under spotlights. Morning sunlight slanted in through tall stained glass windows, bathing the pews in shades of orange, red and purple. Layers of thin smoke from the candles and incense hung in the air over the front rows, creating an ethereal atmosphere.

Joe had hoped to get to the church early enough to sit close to the front with faculty from the university. Now he and Sara were seated in one of the back rows surrounded by people Joe didn't recognize.

Halfway through the service, in a loud, clear Irish voice, Father Mitchell read Psalm 140 to a quiet congregation. Joe hadn't been in a church since his parents' funeral a dozen years ago. He listened to the priest's vivid words.

"Deliver me, Lord, from the wicked; preserve me from the violent, From those who plan evil in their hearts…"

It seemed a strange choice of prayers to Joe, until he realized that the Church had to assume Dr. Claire had been the victim of a murder. If the Church acknowledged that Jack had committed suicide, they would be admitting he had committed a mortal sin.

"Keep me, lord, from the clutches of the wicked; Preserve me from the violent, Who plot to trip me up…"

The words forced Joe to remember the killer who had nearly taken his life and Sara's almost three years ago.

After finishing the prayer, the priest invited others to offer their thoughts on Dr. Claire's life.

Hayden Crawford was the first to walk to the pulpit. After clearing his throat and making a show of arranging the pages of his speech, Hayden scanned the crowd, knitting his bushy black and gray eyebrows.

"Dr. John Claire was a remarkable man, an excellent Elizabethan scholar, a terrific editor, a wonderful teacher, and a good friend. He fell in love with Shakespeare in college and even performed on the stage from time to time. He told me once that his biggest regret was never being allowed to play a lead because of his size. He played Lenny in *Of Mice and Men* and Falstaff in *Henry, the Fourth*, but he yearned to play Hamlet."

Crawford spoke with the strong, clear voice of a trained orator. He described Jack's career and noted all his achievements.

Joe nodded as he listened, his eyes filling with tears. Sara squeezed his hand and slipped a Kleenex into his fingers.

"Maggie and Jack met at Duke University. In those days, young unmarried faculty often dated students, so it was not viewed with suspicion. Maggie would have earned an 'A' in his course no matter what, Jack told me." He paused, as if expecting the crowd to chuckle. When they remained silent, he continued. "They travelled everywhere together, including their trip to Wales just last year to attend a friend and colleagues' funeral. Jack credited Maggie with helping him dress the part, as he would say. Their close and loving relationship was rare, especially these days. I know Jack mourned the loss of his dear wife more than he could let others see, which might explain…well… Now they're together again, re-united for eternity, we hope."

The feeling of loss overwhelmed Joe for a moment, the loss of his parents, the loss of his mentor. He sighed deeply, fighting back the tears.

Hayden Crawford finished by saying, "LSU has lost a great man, and we all have lost a great friend."

A few people sitting near the front of the church nodded politely as Hayden walked slowly, deliberately back to his pew. Two other professors spoke briefly, noting that Jack's granddaughters and great-grandchildren were his only surviving relatives. Joe strained to see the granddaughters, but he and Sara were sitting too far back.

Father Mitchell took the pulpit again and invited more speakers, but no one else rose. "Doesn't anyone else want to say a few words?"

Mustering the courage to speak, Joe stood. Sara squeezed his hand before letting go and Joe walked down the aisle and up to the podium as quickly as he could. Staring at the congregation, he took a deep breath and tilted the microphone up.

"My name is Joseph Conrad," he said, but the microphone squealed for a second and he leaned back, adjusting it down a little. "Jack Claire was my adviser when I was in graduate school. Even though my field was American Literature, he helped me gain an appreciation of British authors. Of course, he really pushed Shakespeare on me—"

The chuckle from the crowd surprised Joe, and he noticed several people nodding.

Former students, no doubt.

"Ernest Hemingway said we should face life with grace under pressure. Well, I'm not sure what kinds of pressures Dr. Claire faced as Chair of the English Department—I'm sure they were many—but I never met a man who lived—" his voice cracked--"who lived with more grace."

Joe glanced up to see a few women in the front rows dabbing their eyes.

"Now as I think about Jack's death, I keep remembering lines from the final scene in *Hamlet*." Glancing up at the ceiling, Joe said, "Forgive me, Jack, if I butcher these words from your favorite play, but here goes." He looked down, closed his eyes, and said, "Now cracks a noble heart. Good night, sweet prince, and flights of angels sing thee to thy rest...."

Joe stood silent for a few seconds, then opened his damp eyes and stepped away from the pulpit. As he walked back to his seat, he stared at the floor until he looked up at Sara's sympathetic face and sat down beside her.

The remainder of the mass was a blur.

After the service, Joe and Sara filed in behind other attendees, walking through a hallway to a reception hall. The line proceeded slowly toward Jack's granddaughters. When Sara finally stood in front of the first granddaughter, she said, "My husband was enormously fond of your grandfather. Dr. Claire was like a second father to Joe."

Joe blushed. "Yes, your grandfather was very supportive. I don't think I'd be where I am today without his help."

"Thank you," one of the women said. "Your words at the service were very kind."

"I could have said much more."

"Do you teach at LSU?" the first granddaughter asked. Joe couldn't recall their names.

"I used to, as a grad student. Your grandfather helped me land a job in California."

"Oh, I see," the woman said. "I have offices in California, too."

Joe nodded. "I'm sorry," he said, "but I've forgotten your name."

"Deirdre," the woman replied. "This is my sister Melinda."

Sara shook Melinda's hand, while Joe held Deirdre's. He looked at Deirdre again. She was only a few years older than he was, in her mid-thirties, with a good figure, dark, inviting eyes and thin lips parted in a knowing smile. Joe noted her sweet, musky perfume. *Red.* Sara had worn it before they were married.

The resemblance between the sisters was obvious, but Melinda looked older, heavier and weary. Deirdre finally gave Joe's hand a squeeze and pulled away.

"Did you and your wife come all the way from California just for this?" Melinda asked.

Joe nodded as Sara leaned in and said, "Well, we also wanted to visit my parents."

"Oh," the woman replied, a polite smile on her face.

They moved away from the sisters and followed others to find a table laid out with plastic wine glasses filled with white and red wine. Joe picked up two glasses and handed one to Sara. Then he took a sip and looked around the crowded room. Hayden Crawford was easy to spot.

"I see Dr. Crawford," Joe told Sara. He started toward him, but Sara tugged his sleeve.

"Are you going to be very long?"

"Probably not. Why?"

Sara frowned. "It's just that, when you get with those people, I feel left out."

Joe touched her arm. "There's no reason you should."

"Go ahead. I'll mingle."

She picked up another glass of wine and walked away.

Joe found a circle of younger faculty members hanging on Hayden Crawford's every word. Clearly, the brown-nosing had begun. Joe listened in on the conversation, some of which was in French.

When there was a pause, Hayden turned toward Joe, explaining, "We were just discussing an article in last January's *PMLA* titled 'Mallarme's Cinepoetics.' Did you read it?"

Joe felt himself blush. "No."

Hayden nodded.

"Does everyone know Joe Conrad?" Hayden asked his disciples. "Joe was a grad student here, but now he teaches out in California at a small, private university called Central Lutheran."

One woman in the circle leaned closer, as if to get a better look at him. Her dark hair was tied up in a bun and her glasses had slid down her nose. She was wearing a long, black skirt and a black blouse, which fit much too snugly. Joe could see a bit of her black bra and a mound of pink flesh bulging between the buttons of her blouse.

"I know who *you* are," she said. "You're the one who was arrested for those rapes and murders last year. I read your memoir. What was it called? *Character Flaws*?"

Joe's face turned hot. "*Tragic Flaws*. It happened a few years ago actually," Joe said, trying to smile. "And I wasn't guilty of those crimes."

"What crimes *were* you guilty of?" Hayden asked.

Everyone laughed.

The young teacher in the tweed jacket asked, "How in God's name did you get yourself into that kind of hot water?"

"Actually," Joe began, "by falling into cold water."

The man in tweed chuckled. "What do you mean?"

"One morning on my way to work, my car overheated. It needed water and I was at a place called Lost Slough. It had been raining a lot and I ended up slipping into the water right next to a dead body."

"How horrid!" one of the others said.

"The woman who'd been murdered graduated from CLU, where I teach."

"Quite a coincidence," the woman in black noted.

"That's what the police thought."

"At any rate," Crawford interjected, "that's all cleared up now, and we can rest assured that Mr. Conrad is *not* a murderer."

"Or a rapist?" asked one of the others.

Everyone laughed again as Joe tried to smile, his face still burning.

"Joe used to be Dr. Claire's research assistant, Janice," Crawford said to the woman dressed in black. "Though I don't think Jack kept Joe as busy as he kept you last year." He turned to Joe and said, "Meet Dr. Janice Wilson, Jack's latest assistant."

Joe looked at the woman again. "What kind of research was he having you do?"

Everyone turned their attention to Janice Wilson.

"He swore me to secrecy," she said, a smile stretching across her full, red lips.

Crawford grinned condescendingly, and said, "What difference can it make now?"

She turned away from Crawford and looked up into Joe's eyes. "He had me looking for handwriting samples."

"Handwriting?" asked Joe. "Whose handwriting?"

"Well, Queen Elizabeth's, for starters."

"Interesting," said Joe.

Janice nodded. "I gathered samples of handwriting from members of the royal family and some of the courtiers from the sixteenth century.

I've looked at the handwriting of more earls and lords than I care to remember."

"What do you suppose he was up to?" Joe asked.

Crawford cleared his throat. "I suspect Jack found a writ or decree from the Queen that somehow related to Shakespeare, maybe a letter expressing her desire to knight him. Who knows?"

"Could it be connected with his death?" asked Joe.

Hayden shrugged. "Maybe."

Everyone in the circle fell silent.

Then Hayden Crawford broke the silence and began discussing the article about French poetry again.

Joe turned to walk away. As he scanned the crowd looking for Sara, he felt a hand on his arm.

"Your name really is Joseph Conrad?" asked Janice Wilson.

"Yes. Mom was a fan of Conrad's *Heart of Darkness.* And as a Catholic, she found Joseph to be a suitable name."

"*Was* a fan?"

"Both of my parents died when I was a senior in high school."

"Oh, I'm sorry." She touched Joe's arm.

"My full name is Joseph Lawrence Conrad."

"Lawrence?"

"Yes," he said. "Mother also liked D. H. Lawrence."

"Lawrence is one of my favorite authors." She drained her glass. "Have you read *Women in Love*?"

Joe smiled. "Years ago. Good book."

"Yes," Dr. Wilson agreed, stepping closer. "I particularly liked the descriptions of fig eating."

Joe blushed.

The woman laughed. "You remember the scene, I see."

They walked together to the buffet table, but no glasses of wine remained.

"Well," Janice Wilson said, "time to find a nice bar and continue our mourning."

Joe saw Sara a few feet away, her back toward him, talking to an older woman. "It was very nice meeting you," he said politely. He held out his hand. "I see my wife."

Janice Wilson shook his hand. "Nice meeting you."

Joe grinned politely. "Good luck with Crawford as your new chair."

The woman turned toward the young scholars fawning over Hayden Crawford's every word. Then she glanced back and smiled at Joe, saying, "Oh, Hayden? Why he's just a big ol' teddy bear."

Joe shook his head, watching as she walked away. A few minutes later, Sara found him.

"I was talking to one of Dr. Claire's neighbors. She told me that Mr. and Mrs. Claire's house had been burglarized shortly before his death."

"Yeah," Joe said. "We talked about that yesterday, remember?"

"She also said that lots of people think Dr. Claire was murdered."

"That's what your mother said, Sara."

"I know. But I didn't really believe my mother. She *is* a rumor mill, after all."

Just then, a man in a gray suit addressed the crowd. "I'm sorry, I'm sorry to interrupt," he said, his voice booming over the din. "But we've lost the guest book."

Several people piped up again, asking, "What did he say? What was lost?"

"It seems that somebody removed the guest book from the foyer, and now it's missing. Does somebody have it? Please, does somebody have the guest book?"

"Who in the hell would steal the guest book?" Joe asked.

"I can't imagine," Sara said. "A reporter, maybe."

"Maybe," Joe said.

An hour later, as they left the reception hall, a gentle rain began to fall.

Across the street from the church, the wipers of a dark sedan swiped the raindrops off the windshield. The man inside the dark car was photographing each person as they stepped out, though no one leaving the reception noticed.

CHAPTER 4

Delays have dangerous ends.
From *King Henry VI, Part I*

Sunday morning, Sara's parents drove Joe and his family to the airport and they flew back to Sacramento. During the flight, Joe read an article about Jack Claire from the Sunday newspaper Sara's father had given him.

"You'll find this interesting," Paul Taylor had said. "A big story about your friend Claire. All his accomplishments. Something curious about his death, too."

A photo of Jack and Maggie, though grainy, captured the gleam in Jack's eyes, that mischievous, inquisitive light that drew people in. Near the end, Joe found what his father-in-law had mentioned.

> **Although police initially ruled Dr. Claire's death a suicide, the murder of the Janitor, who had worked at the Capitol for over thirty years, raises questions in the mind of at least one detective. "The Janitor was shot, but we didn't find a weapon on the Professor's person," Detective Laffite said. "So what I'd like to know is, where's the gun?" The police urge anyone with information to call immediately.**

Joe stared out the window of the plane, wondering what had actually happened to his mentor.

Monday morning, Sara and the children slept in while Joe dressed for work. The hour drive from their house on Tenth Street in Davis to the CLU campus in Stockton took him past Lost Slough where he and his wife had almost lost their lives. Now, lush green vegetation on both banks of the slough reminded Joe of Mark Twain's description of the Mississippi River. But Joe knew that in the middle of winter, the leaves would fall again, and, with the rain, the gnarled branches of the valley oaks would darken.

Joe's office on the third floor was illuminated by one small dormer window. He turned on the desk lamp and surveyed the scene. His oak desk, piled with book boxes and strewn with papers, almost filled the space. Next to it, an old oak file cabinet showed its age, books and papers stacked on top. Against one wall stood shelves filled with more books of all sizes, their colorful bindings reflecting the lamplight warmly.

Joe plopped his briefcase down on his desk and grabbed the coffeepot. After he made coffee, he glanced at three book boxes stacked on his desk. The one on the bottom was the size of a microwave oven, larger than any he'd received from a publisher before. Most boxes contained no more than three or four books. This box could hold twenty or thirty.

Joe set the boxes on the floor and pulled papers from his briefcase. After reviewing his lecture notes, he was ready for class.

"I hope all of you read *Julius Caesar* while I was gone. What was the motive for his murder?"

An older Hispanic student named Marco raised his hand but spoke before Joe had a chance to call on him. "It was a power grab, pure and simple."

Joe faced the student and smiled.

"Is it really that simple?"

An African-American girl name Darlene shook her head. "Well, no power grab is simple," she replied.

"Yeah," added Marco. "Like the play shows, it's got to be planned."

"Whether you're a senator like Brutus or a corporate executive," Darlene said.

Or the assistant chair of an English Department? Joe wondered.

"Right, Professor?" Darlene asked.

"Sorry?" Joe pushed his suspicion about Hayden Crawford aside.

"You've got to plan these takeovers ahead of time, right?"

"How is that shown in the play?" asked Joe.

And with that, the discussion ignited.

After class, Joe popped into his office long enough to check email. Before turning off the light, he glanced at the boxes, briefly considered opening them, but he was anxious to get home.

As Joe passed Lost Slough, driving north on Interstate 5, he opened his phone.

Sara answered. "How'd it go today? Did your students mutiny?"

Joe laughed. "Funny you should ask. We *are* reading Julius Ceasar."

"When will you be home?"

"Thirty minutes."

"We'll be at the pool."

"I'll join you there. I might take a jog first."

Joe started to hang up, but Sara spoke.

"By the way, you got a message from Dr. Crawford. He must have called when the kids and I were at the store."

"What'd he want?"

"Just asked you to call him. Maybe he wants to offer you a job."

Joe considered that for a minute. The prospect of teaching at his alma mater excited him, but the idea of being around Sara's parents did not.

"I doubt it. See you at the pool."

As Joe continued toward Sacramento, his thoughts turned toward LSU. Maybe his status as a minor celebrity at CLU had made it possible for Hayden to hire him, despite his lack of a Ph.D. Maybe he *should* finish his doctorate.

When he got home, Joe listened to the message: "Joe. This is Hayden Crawford. Please give me a call as soon as you can. I'll be in the office until four. I need to discuss something with you." He sounded serious.

Joe checked his watch. It was 3:30 in California, which meant it was 5:30 in Louisiana. The offices would be closed.

He decided to call Hayden in the morning and changed into jogging shorts. He ran through the green belts for thirty minutes, then circled back toward the community pool.

At the pool, Sara was lying on her side, reading. Brian was asleep on a towel under the shade of an umbrella and Katie was standing in the shallow end of the adult pool watching the older children roughhouse. She observed them as a scientist might observe monkeys—with clinical disdain.

Sara, reading a novel, looked up and wiped a tear from the corner of her eye as Joe took a seat beside her.

"How's the book?"

"Not as good as *The Notebook*, but I'm enjoying it."

"Can I guess the plot?"

She put the book on her lap.

"Go ahead, Professor Snob."

"Someone dies before their time and the person who loved the dead person is searching for someone new. Is that about right?"

Sara stuck out her tongue. "You got one thing wrong. The person who lost a loved one wasn't looking for a new love. It just sort of happened."

"Ah," nodded Joe. "How original."

Sara glanced over at Katie to make sure she was okay.

He saw a lane open up in the pool. "I'm gonna swim a few laps," he said, standing. He looked down at Sara. She leaned back on her elbows and smiled up at Joe, her eyes shielded by his shadow.

She was getting a good tan. With the bleaching of the pool water and the sun, her straight shoulder-length hair looked blonde. Even her thick, arched eyebrows were lighter, helping to frame her green eyes. Joe ran his eyes over her body. The turquoise bikini lifted her breasts together and her slim waist disappeared into the narrow V of her bikini bottom. Her long toned legs led Joe's eyes past the gold chain on Sara's right ankle to her deep red toenails. Sara raised one knee as if to draw

Joe's gaze back up to her face. When he looked at her mouth, she ran her tongue across her upper lip and broke into a smile.

"You'd better cool off," she laughed.

Joe smiled down at her.

"What stroke would you like me to do?"

"Shh," she scolded, looking around.

Joe walked over to the edge of the pool and hopped in next to Katie.

"Hi, daddy. Are you going to play with me?"

"Yes, honey. Right after I swim a few laps."

Before he slipped into the cool water, Joe breathed a sigh of satisfaction. *Only a cold Corona could make this better,* he thought. *Life is good.*

CHAPTER 5

Tomorrow, and tomorrow, and tomorrow...
From *Macbeth*

On Tuesday morning, Joe pulled the boxes out from the corner of his office. He hoisted the large box up onto his desk and noticed it didn't have the usual label from a publishing company. The address had been written out by hand. And the handwriting looked like Jack Claire's.

Why hadn't he noticed that on Monday? He'd just assumed it was from a publisher.

Joe took his letter opener, slid it inside the flap of the box and cut the clear plastic packaging tape. The very act of slicing the tape made Joe imagine someone slashing a person's throat. He pulled the letter opener out and put it down.

The loose flaps looked like the two sides of a draw bridge. Darkness underneath, like the dark water of Lost Slough where he'd found Patricia Miller's body.

Gingerly, Joe bent back the flaps one at a time. As he did so, the contents on top became visible in the harsh florescent light.

Four wooden file boxes, slightly larger than a ream of paper, were stacked inside, three on their sides and one on end. Joe removed the top wooden box and tugged some of the sturdy cotton pages out. The oddly shaped pages were wider than normal but not as long, not the usual 8 ½ by 11 but closer to 9 by 9 ½, Joe guessed. At first Joe thought the faded handwriting was a different language, the neat letters looked almost Arabic.

Joe leaned down and looked more carefully. Obviously handwritten, not printed, and the lines of writing were difficult to read, crowded together on the page. Some words looked German, others like French. Parts of words were obviously in English, but the penmanship was too slanted to make out at first.

Joe spotted two words he recognized, and they made his heart stop. Although the "s" was written like a lower-case "f", Joe recognized the title of the work written neatly at the top of the page:

The Tempeft

No mistaking it. *The Tempest.* One of Shakespeare's earliest plays. But if Joe remembered correctly, Jack Claire had told him and the other students that no hand-written manuscripts of Shakespeare's plays existed.

This fact had always troubled Joe. As prolific as Shakespeare was, one would assume that volumes of his works had survived the past four hundred years. After all, far older writings had survived the ages—Homer's *Iliad* and *Odyssey*, the gospels in the Bible, the works of Plato.

Were these the lost original works of William Shakespeare? This must be what the burglar had been searching for in Jack's office at LSU. Had Jack Claire been murdered for this? If so, this box also put Joe in danger. And his family. That thought made Joe's heart skip a beat.

He stared at the object. It was Pandora's Box. If he opened it, what plagues would fly out?

Should I call Dunn?

Detective Dunn had become a friend after the Lost Slough incident. Joe's sister-in-law, Susan Taylor, was another possibility. A corporate attorney, she'd found Bill Morgan, the defense attorney who'd helped Joe make bail. Suzy lived and worked in Sacramento.

Joe plopped down in the chair. At this level, he could no longer see inside the box, he could only stare at the side of it.

For all he knew, the papers were forgeries, part of some elaborate hoax.

But if they were real, how much would they be worth? Thousands of dollars. Millions, maybe.

After sitting for several minutes, his mind whirling with questions, he forced himself to take a few deep breaths to calm down. He checked his watch. Two hours before his class started.

What should I do? Call Sara?

She'd be terrified. Being in possession of these papers would definitely make Joe a suspect in the burglary at LSU. No. Sara had already left Joe once when he'd been suspected of a crime.

He needed an expert, someone like Jack Claire, who could tell him whether or not these documents were real.

But who? Jack was the only Shakespearean scholar Joe knew personally, and he was dead.

A relatively new hire at CLU, a young woman named Leah Strickland, taught the Shakespeare courses, but she was on sabbatical, studying somewhere in England.

Whom had she replaced? Joe remembered. He grabbed the university telephone directory and looked up the man's name.

Jonathan Smythe had retired six years earlier. He'd been one of the most popular department chairs in the history of CLU's English Department. Joe had gotten to know him a little in person, but mostly by reputation. When Joe first arrived, he repeatedly heard other professors refer to someone named Smitty. "What would Smitty do?" someone was bound to ask at a faculty meeting when a particularly challenging conundrum presented itself. "What would Smitty do?" became a popular refrain around the department.

Smitty was a Shakespearean scholar of, if not the first order, at least the second, which was several "orders" ahead of Joe's level of expertise. If anyone might know what these old manuscripts were, it was Jonathan Smythe. Joe found his home number and called it.

The telephone rang repeatedly. Finally, just as Joe was thinking about hanging up, a gravelly voice came on the line.

"Hello."

"Dr. Smythe," Joe began, "this is Joseph Conrad from the English Department at CLU."

"Who?"

"Joe Conrad. We talked quite a bit at the last department Christmas party. You encouraged me to include Macbeth in my course, the Literature of Murder."

"Oh, you're *that* Joe," Smitty responded, his voice lightened. "Call me Smitty."

"Sorry to disturb you at home, but I have some papers I'd like to show you."

"What sort of papers?"

"Well, that's just it. I'm not sure. They look like copies of some of Shakespeare's plays."

"I see," said Smitty, sounding skeptical.

"The papers seem very, very old," Joe added. He felt inarticulate, incapable of describing the true condition of these manuscripts. Was "very old" the best he could do? "The paper quality isn't like anything I've handled before."

"That's interesting."

The phone stayed silent for a few uncomfortable seconds.

"Yes. I'd like to see these papers of yours."

"Are you coming to campus any time soon?" asked Joe.

"Coming to campus? Hadn't planned on it."

"Maybe I could bring the box to your house, then."

"The box?"

"The papers arrived while I was in Louisiana attending a funeral. You knew Jack Claire, didn't you?"

"Oh, yes, yes. I heard he'd died. Very sad."

"These papers actually were sent by him."

"From Claire?"

"Yes," said Joe.

"That's *very* interesting."

Joe could almost hear Smitty's mind working, putting the pieces together. Shakespearean manuscripts sent by a well-known Shakespeare scholar shortly before his death. Yes, thought Joe. This *is* interesting.

"I'd like to examine those papers, lad. Can you bring them to my home?"

"Sure."

"You haven't handled them, have you? The manuscripts, I mean." The old professor sounded annoyed.

"Not many. I opened the box and took a few papers off the top."

"If they're authentic—but what are the chances of that? I mean, honestly?"

"I'm not sure, Professor. That's why I'd like your opinion. When can I bring them?"

"How about tomorrow morning? You can stop by here for coffee before your class."

Joe thought for a second. "Tomorrow morning will be fine. Eight o'clock all right?"

"Eight o'clock? Yes, yes," said Smitty. "See you at eight. You have my address?"

"It's in the university directory."

"Fine, fine. See you tomorrow."

With that, Smitty hung up. He hadn't remembered Jonathan Smythe being as impatient as he now seemed. Joe hung up and resealed the box carefully. The secrets of Pandora's Box would have to wait.

Part II:

A Midsummer Night's Dream

CHAPTER 6

Put out the light…
From *Othello*

Benedict found the woman passed out in her studio apartment, the sliding glass door to the small patio already open, only the screen door latched. But after slicing through the screen, he simply lifted the latch and quietly slid the screen door to the side just enough to step into the one room apartment.

She lay on her stomach on the tousled bed in a skirt and nothing else. The young woman snored heavily, the ashtray on the nightstand overflowing. The smell of liquor strong.

In the dim light, he inspected the woman's bare back. A large mole on her right shoulder blade stood out, even in the darkness. An image—perhaps a sunflower—was tattooed on her lower back, just above her skirt.

After searching the English Department offices again, he still hadn't found the documents he'd been hired to steal. Benedict was sure the old man had mailed them that last morning before he fell to his death. *But where?* The Directory in the old professor's office had pointed him here, to Dr. Claire's "Research Assistant."

He'd been stupid to let the old man get away. He should have gone into the professor's home the night before and tied him up. He could have taken his time. Benedict had always gotten what he was after when he had taken his time with an informant in the past.

This job was a little different. He'd been instructed not to injure the old man, if he could help it. That had been his mistake. Taking the advice of an amateur. *He* knew how to do the job.

Stay focused. Don't dwell on past errors.

He stood over the woman on the bed and surveyed the simple apartment. To the right, a small kitchen with a table and two chairs. On the table sat a laptop, another over-flowing ashtray, and stacks of books and papers. Only a few cabinets on the walls and under the counters. Easy to search. Directly behind him, the front door. To the left, four makeshift shelves—planks of wood between cinder blocks standing on their ends, packed with books. No TV. A beanbag chair languished in the corner to the left of the shelves and a loveseat rested against the wall.

He turned once more to look at the woman and the bed. Small matching nightstands stood on either side—the only furniture in the place that matched—a cabinet door on the bottom of each.

On the wall to his left were two doors, one partially opened. He could see the edge of a toilet. Maybe in the vanity under the sink.

The other door was closed. A closet that separated the bathroom from the kitchen. The small walk-in closet was easy to search. It yielded nothing but clothes, an opened box of condoms, hats, fake feather boas, Mardi Gras masks.

Next he searched the bathroom. The vanity cabinet under the sink was filled with cans of hairspray, cleaners, nail polish, but no papers.

He tugged at the mirror. Sometimes people hid things in the wall behind the medicine cabinet, if it lifted out of the wall easily. This one did not. He checked the heater vent over the shower. Using a screwdriver on his Leatherman knife, Benedict unscrewed the two screws holding the screen over the heater vent. Nothing.

He rinsed off his hands, which were covered by surgical gloves.

The kitchen proved more challenging. Pots and pans in the lower cabinets had been stacked so randomly that it was nearly impossible to remove them quietly. Once, after he had made a slight clinking noise with the pans, he heard the woman's snoring stop, so he waited.

She rolled onto her back and the snoring started again. Benedict glanced at the woman's large bare breasts. *She might be fun*, he thought.

Have to keep my mind on my work. His client was already displeased with the "mess" he'd made of the old man and his wife.

The oven held a pan of old lasagna, half eaten, but nothing else.

Now it got tricky. The bookshelves were time consuming. Nothing behind the stacks of books except more books and magazines that had fallen.

He unzipped the beanbag chair and quietly poured out the pellets until he was satisfied that nothing else was inside. Now the little sofa. The cushions were too light to hold the documents. He tipped the loveseat over. The bottom was covered in a sheer black fabric. Lifting the torn edges of the black fabric, Benedict shone the light inside the base. Nothing.

Too bad. This meant that the manuscripts could be under the bed or between the mattress and the box spring. Or that she had hidden them somewhere else, in a storage unit, perhaps.

Or she didn't have them.

Working quietly, he righted the little sofa and replaced the cushions. Wiping sweat from his forehead, he stepped closer to the sleeping woman.

Taking a small bottle and a handkerchief out of the pocket of his dark jacket, he poured ether on the cloth, then, holding it away from himself, he leaned over the sleeping woman. He gently placed the cloth over her nose and mouth.

Her face twitched. Then she shook her head from side to side, still asleep. Her eyes were closed as she lurched forward and sat up in bed.

Benedict took his other hand and held the back of Dr. Janice Wilson's head, pressing the handkerchief more firmly against her lips and nose. Suddenly, her eyes opened and she reached up with both hands, trying to tear away the man's hands.

He knew what she was feeling. Nausea swelled in her stomach. She felt dizzy. Then everything would go cloudy and black for her. Ether induced a deep sleep but not as peaceful as surgical anesthesia.

Her head lolled in his hands and her body went limp. He allowed her to breathe in the ether a little while longer, watching her chest rise and fall until her breathing became labored. He knew he could not keep the cloth on her face any longer if he wanted her to live.

And Benedict did want the woman to live. At least for now.

He picked up her limp body and carried it over to the sofa, stretching her out as carefully as a lover might place his mistress on a bed. Then he went back to his work.

First, he tipped the mattress up against the wall. He shone his penlight on the box springs, spotting something. Two magazines. A *Penthouse* and a *Playgirl*. Both old and well worn. *Bisexual?* He shook his head. *People always surprise you.*

He tipped the box springs up against the mattress. The thin dust cloth under the box springs was torn and hanging in several places, making it easy to see inside. Nothing.

Under the bed between the edges of the cheap blue metal bed frame were only shoes, panties, a pair of stockings, a few half-smoked cigarettes and dust balls. No manuscripts.

Benedict lowered the mattress on top of the box springs and opened his knife. He cut three long slits in the mattress and pulled them open, feeling inside each one. Again, nothing.

He lowered the mattress onto the box springs, the sheet, pillow and blankets having slid off onto the floor where he left them. Then he stepped back to the girl and lifted her onto the bed. She was still in a deep sleep.

But he knew her sleep wouldn't last much longer.

Laying her out on the mattress, Benedict went to work tying her wrists and ankles to the bed frame with electrical cords he pulled off the lamps. Janice Wilson lay spread eagle on the bed.

As an after-thought, he grabbed the sheet and tossed it over the woman's exposed breasts. He turned on the bathroom light and adjusted the door so light fell across the woman's face. Then he sat on the sofa and smoked a cigarette, waiting for the ether to wear off.

While he was smoking his second cigarette, the young woman began to pull her arms and legs against the cords. He stubbed out his cigarette and shoved the butt into his pocket, as he had the first cigarette, not wanting to leave any DNA behind. The woman's face twisted in pain, her eyes still shut.

"Ouch," she said, her eyes still closed.

She was coming out of the foggy darkness. It would be another few minutes before she would be conscious enough to question.

"Ouch!" she said louder. Now her head rolled back and forth, as though she were trying to wake herself up. "What the hell?"

Benedict stood up and walked over to the bed. From his jacket pocket, he took out a roll of duct tape and tore off an eight-inch strip, placing it over the woman's mouth. He hadn't done this sooner in case she had vomited, but now it was okay.

She struggled as he watched, and then her eyes opened. She tried to scream, but it was muffled by the tape. Her eyes widened with fear. Benedict grinned.

"Listen," he whispered. "I don't want to hurt you. Understand?"

She struggled harder, tugging at the bindings on her wrists and ankles, jerking back and forth, which only made the knots tighter. She looked terrified.

"I don't want to hurt you," he whispered in her ear, bending closer. "I just want you to answer a few questions."

She would not stop struggling. He slapped her across the face.

"Listen to me," he whispered. "Settle down and answer my questions. Then I'll leave and you'll never see me again."

Janice Wilson nodded. Benedict knew she was trying to calm herself. He knew she felt sick. Drunk. Dizzy. He knew her arms were in pain.

"I know this is uncomfortable for you. I apologize for that. If you answer my questions quickly, then I can leave. All right?"

She nodded again. A tear rolled out of the corner of her right eye.

"Here's what I need to know, and you must answer truthfully. If you don't tell the truth, I'll hurt you. Do you understand?"

The woman nodded again. Even in the dim light, he could see fear in her eyes.

"Did Dr. Claire send you a box of documents?"

She looked confused. He could tell she was trying to make sense of his question. Finally, she shook her head, "No."

"Dr. Claire gave you papers to take care of. You know how valuable they are. But ask yourself if the papers are more valuable than your life."

Fear flashed in her eyes again.

"Do you understand?"

She nodded.

"Did Dr. Claire send you the papers?"

She shook her head.

"Are you sure?"

She nodded.

Benedict smiled. "I don't believe you." He took out his knife and opened the blade in front of her face.

Janice Wilson's eyes widened with fear and she began to sob. He put his lips close to ear.

"Do you have a hiding place in the apartment? A loose floorboard, maybe?"

She shook her head.

"Do you have a storage room here at the apartment complex?"

She seemed confused again, but then shook her head.

"I've already searched your office, so I know the papers aren't there. Do you have another hiding place?"

She shook her head.

"A friend's house?"

Her head jerked back and forth.

"I know you wouldn't want to put a friend in danger, but I can assure you, I won't harm your friend," Benedict whispered. Then he put his face directly in front of Janice Wilson's face. "Just tell me where the fucking papers are!"

Janice Wilson cried, closing her eyes and shaking her head from side to side.

"This is your last chance," he told her. "Tell me where the Shakespeare papers are or die. Those are the only two choices you have."

She cried harder, but suddenly she jerked and pulled at her bindings, straining to get loose. The sheet slid away and her breasts wobbled as she struggled. He could tell she was angry.

Benedict grinned at the futility of her efforts.

"Tell me now," he said calmly. "Where are the Shakespeare papers?"

She shook her head violently from side to side.

"Do you know or not?" he asked again.

Again, she shook her head. Then she closed her eyes and wept, her chest heaving with deep sobs. He knew he'd broken her. "Do you have the papers or not?"

Weakly, she shook her head from side to side, utterly defeated.

"Okay," Benedict whispered. "I believe you." He stroked her cheek with his gloved hand. "It's all right, now. I believe you."

Her sobs softened to whimpers and her muscles relaxed.

"There, there," he cooed. "Better?"

She stopped moving and opened her eyes.

With his finger, he wiped the tears away from both eyes. He knew, with the surgical glove on his hand, the finger would feel odd to her. But he remembered the box of condoms he'd found, and he grinned as he moved his finger down to her chin and traced the smooth edge of her jaw.

"Here's what's going to happen. I'm going to put you to sleep for a little while and then I'll leave. You'll sleep for about twenty minutes and then you'll wake up, just as you did before. Do you understand?"

She nodded.

"I'm afraid I have to leave you tied up. Is that okay?"

Again, she nodded.

"Of course, you don't have much choice, but I just wanted you to understand. I'm not here to hurt you. I'm just looking for those papers."

He could see her eyes studying his face. Maybe she was trying to determine if he was sincere. Maybe she was trying to memorize his face for the police. It didn't matter.

Benedict removed the small bottle of ether again and poured a little on his handkerchief.

"This will just help you sleep."

He could see her begin to cry again.

He smiled. "It's just ether. It will put you to sleep. Then I can leave. It's almost morning. Eventually, someone will find you and free you."

Tears rolled out of Janice Wilson's eyes as she listened.

He placed the cloth over her nose and mouth and watched her eyes. At first, she didn't struggle. But as she began to feel the effect of the ether, she resisted it, as he knew she would. Of course, resisting only caused her to breathe in more deeply, which allowed the ether to work more rapidly.

Her eyes fluttered and closed, even as she fought to keep them open.

Soon she was breathing steadily, even beginning to snore again.

Benedict looked down at her. He wrapped his gloved hands tightly around her neck and depressed her trachea slowly with his powerful thumbs. The crushed windpipe allowed no air, and soon he felt the woman tense and stiffen under his grip. Finally, the heaving chest stopped. The eyelids failed to move. He clutched her throat for another minute to make sure. Then he relaxed his grip and air escaped from the dead woman's nostrils.

CHAPTER 7

Every subject's duty is the king's; but every
Subject's soul is his own.
From *King Henry V*

Wednesday morning, as instructed, Joe took the documents to Jonathan Smythe's house, a modest three-bedroom ranch-style home only a few blocks from campus, in an older, staid neighborhood where mature trees shaded the streets and front lawns. Joe rang the bell, struggling to keep the box in his arms. He glanced into a window and saw a woman peeling cucumbers at the sink. She glanced up at him.

Smitty's wife Alicia was tall and slender, about sixty, but she looked older and more frail than Joe remembered from the Christmas party. She managed a reluctant smile, dried her hands and stepped around the corner. A few seconds later, the door opened and he stepped into the modest foyer.

"Hope I'm not being too much of a bother," he said.

"No. Not at all." Dressed in a short-sleeved white and blue striped blouse with a pink sailboat on the front and dark blue shorts, Alicia seemed polite, if reluctant to host strangers. "Jonathan will be out in a moment. We're just back from our walk."

"Is there someplace I can put this?" Joe asked.

"Of course. Just follow me."

Joe walked behind the frail woman into the sunken living room and then up a step to the dining area, which had been converted to a large study. A massive mahogany table stood in the center of the room under a modest chandelier. The surface of the table was covered by neat stacks of books and papers. There must have been some method to the madness, but Joe couldn't at first glance discern what it was. The far wall was covered by tall bookshelves, filled top to bottom with books, many crammed in horizontally on top of the upright stacks. A mahogany desk faced a large window, which looked out onto the backyard. The window afforded Joe a quick look at the well-manicured shrubs and flowers outside.

"Just put the box down here." Alicia pointed to two short, even stacks of paper.

Joe carefully placed the box on the papers as instructed and breathed a sigh of relief. "Thanks," he said, his arms starting to tingle.

He glanced around the room. "What a great idea," said Joe. "Turning the dining room into a study."

He peered out the window at the back yard. To the left was a four-foot statue of Buddha sitting on a mound adorned by flowers. Stepping stones led from in front of the statue to a kidney-shaped swimming pool to the right, but the pool looked dark.

"Is that a swimming pool?"

"It used to be. Now it's a fishpond. We keep Cohoes."

"A lovely yard. You keep it up nicely."

"We used to be able to take care of it ourselves. Now we have a Japanese man who comes once a week. He's also a Buddhist, so he and Jonathan chant together before he does the yard work."

"I didn't know you were Buddhists," Joe said.

"Jonathan's been one since college. I tried for awhile when we were first married, but my heart wasn't in it. My first husband and I were Lutherans."

"Quite a difference, I imagine."

The woman forced a grin.

Joe turned his attention to the living room. A white brick fireplace with a wide stone hearth dominated the eastern wall, with long vertical windows on either side. In the far corner, an antique cabinet. A long white sofa took up most of the wall that faced Joe, and between the sofa and two large easy chairs was a heavy glass coffee table with a bare surface. Between the two easy chairs was another antique cabinet that seemed to be the mate of the one in the corner. The odd mix of dark antique cabinets and modern off-white furniture gave the room an austere feel.

"I was just making some coffee. Would you like some?"

"That would be great," said Joe, stepping down into the living room. He sat in one of the overstuffed chairs and crossed his legs.

Joe heard footsteps and turned to see Jonathan Smythe step out of the darkness of the hallway into the light of the living room. He too was tall and thin, taller than his wife and in excellent shape. His short white hair framed his tanned, kind face, and his dark eyebrows caused his blue eyes to stand out, making him look, to Joe, at least, like Paul Newman.

"Good morning, good morning! Nice to see you." He held out his hand as Joe rose from the chair. "Remember, call me Smitty. You found us all right?"

"Yes."

"Good, good. Did Licia let you in?" Joe started to answer, but was interrupted. "Well, of course, she did. You wouldn't just barge in someone's home unannounced, would you?" Joe tried to respond again, but Smitty said, "I'm sure you're not in the habit of just walking into other people's homes, are you, lad?"

"No," Joe finally managed.

"Well, where is it? Where's this box of mysterious papers?"

Joe gestured toward the large table in the dining room behind him.

"Your wife had me set it down there."

"Good, good. Let's take a look, shall we?"

Smitty stepped down into the living room and then back up into the dining room. He switched on the overhead light.

"This is just an ordinary book box! You'd expect something special if they really contain documents from the sixteenth and seventeenth centuries, wouldn't you, lad?"

"Well, I suppose, but—"

Smitty opened the lids carefully, bending each one backward to keep each lid out of the way. He lifted the first wooden box out and withdrew a sheet a paper from it.

"Ah, yes," he said, almost whispering. "I see why you worried so." He gingerly held the paper. "My word! This does look authentic! Yes, yes, I'd say you were quite right to bring them to me. Do you recognize this page?" he asked without turning toward Joe.

"No, I'm afraid—"

"This is a handwritten first page of a comedy, one of Will's first plays. *The Two Gentlemen of Verona*. Do you know it?"

"Haven't read it in years."

"This tell-tale S is the first letter of 'Sylvia,' the object of affection in *The Two Gentlemen of Verona*. That happens to be the first name of a good friend of mine at Berkeley. How exciting this is!"

"I didn't really study the documents closely, once I realized how valuable—"

"Look how surprisingly sturdy the paper still is." Smitty took the wide, yellowed paper over to his desk and laid it down flat. He turned on the lamp and pulled open the top drawer of the desk, his fingers searching for something as he stared at the paper. "Damn it. Where is it?"

Joe stepped forward. "I'm not sure what—"

"Ah-hah!" Smitty removed a large square magnifying glass from the drawer and began inspecting the paper closely. "Look at this."

Joe stepped closer, peering over the other man's shoulder. Smitty pointed to the shaky, capitalized S at the top left corner of the page.

"Yes," said Joe.

"This S does not look like the one Will used to sign his name." Jonathan swung around and retrieved a book from the shelf. He thumbed through it and found the page he wanted. "Look here."

Joe followed his finger to the bottom of the page. It showed a reproduction of a handwritten document.

"What's is it?" Joe asked.

"It's a copy of Shakespeare's Will. Look at the signature."

Joe didn't need to use the magnifying glass that Smitty held out for him as he examined the shaky, uneven signature.

"So you think this isn't Shakespeare's handwriting?"

Smitty used the magnifying glass to peer closely at the entire document, bending over it like Sherlock Holmes, his head bobbing up and down as he scanned. Joe could see the look of delight on his face.

"Fascinating," Smitty said. "Simply fascinating. Look at the penmanship of the title and the cast of characters."

Joe read the first line. The neat, even handwriting looked almost like printing.

Enter Valentine and Proteus

Even with his untrained eyes, Joe could see obvious differences between the awkward, irregular penmanship of the signature on the will and the neat, steady hand of the dialogue. "Yes," he said. "The title and stage directions look different."

"Keep reading," Smitty encouraged.

Joe read the first few lines of Valentine's dialogue:

> *Cease to persuade, my loving Proteus.*
> *Home-keeping youth have ever homely wits.*
> *Were't not affection chains thy tender days*
> *To the sweet glances of thy honoured love,*
> *I rather would entreat thy company*
> *To see the wonders of the world abroad*
> *Than, living dully sluggardized at home,*

Joe straightened up. "I'm not sure I understand. What's it mean?"

"Hard to say with any certainty, lad. If these pages are authentic, not old reproductions, it could mean that Will had help writing this play. Or, as was often the case with early plays, he had help in rewriting it. Someone may have taken Will's rough draft and cleaned it up. Do you know much about the good quartos and the bad ones, or the way playwrights made copies of their plays for the actors?"

Joe blushed. He'd forgotten much of what his old mentor, Dr. Jack Claire, had taught him years ago.

"I have to admit, I haven't been keeping up with the history of the plays."

"Unfortunate. Such an important piece of the puzzle with Shakespeare, the history of his life and work and the way society functioned in his age."

"I teach *Macbeth* and *Hamlet* every year," said Joe. Somehow, he sounded like a bragging schoolboy, in front of this Elizabethan expert.

Smitty smiled. "Good lad."

At first, it seemed a condescending grin to Joe, but then he observed the patient, almost serene expression on Smitty's face. Was this the face of a Buddhist attempting to reign in his superior knowledge?

"First, it's important to keep in mind that not a single manuscript written in William Shakespeare's handwriting has survived, as far as we know. Of course, this fact fuels the fires lit by skeptics who claim that Shakespeare is not the author of many—or, indeed, most—of his works."

Joe watched as Smitty seemed to slip into his professor's robe and begin a lecture which, Joe assumed, he'd given dozens of times.

"You see, we have the Orthodox believers—the Stratfordians, as they're called—because they believe the man from Stratford-upon-Avon, Will Shakspear, wrote the works attributed to Shakespeare."

"Shack-spur?" repeated Joe.

"Yes. Shakspear, as opposed to Shake-speare, the name we've come to know. Those who are skeptical of the uneducated rustic fellow from Stratford are known as the Heretics."

Joe laughed. "You make it sound like a religion."

Smitty smiled. "In a way, it is, for to believe in the man from Stratford requires quite a leap of faith. But let's get back to examining these wonderful papers."

Smitty waved his hand over the top of the opened box as if to bring Joe's attention back to the matter at hand.

"In Shakespeare's era," Smitty continued, "it was common for playwrights to write out a first draft of their plays for the actors to use as they started to rehearse. Sometimes an Elizabethan playwright like Shakespeare or Christopher Marlowe would also provide prompt books.

Anyway, these rough drafts are referred to as "foul" papers. Sometimes after complaints from the actors themselves, the playwright would go back and produce clearer copies, which we refer to as 'Fair Papers.'"

"Yeah," said Joe. "I recall Dr. Claire telling us that."

"Now, here's where it gets interesting. These Fair Papers would then be given to others to transcribe. The people who wrote out these copies were called what? Do you know?"

Joe could only think of the story by Herman Melville, "Barttleby, the Scrivener."

"Scriveners?" Joe replied.

"Yes. Or simply scribes. Today we'd refer to them as copyists. Since printing presses were relatively scarce in those times, the fastest way to make several copies of a play was to hire scribes. They worked cheap, but you got what you paid for."

Joe turned his attention back to the document resting on Smitty's desk.

"Then you think this is just a copy made by a scribe?"

"Ah! There's the rub! No. This doesn't look like that type of copy. We'd expect folded papers. The next step in producing scripts was to print the plays as Quartos. This is definitely not a Quarto!"

"But it could still be just a copy of something Shakespeare himself wrote?"

Smitty nodded. "Yes, yes. It could merely be a copy of a foul paper written by someone in Will's company at the time. Lots of different kinds of copies were made in those days, lots of plagiarism going on, too, you know."

"What do you mean?"

"Plays were big business in London. And throughout England, for that matter. In fact, it may have been a traveling troupe of actors at Stratford-upon-Avon one summer that captured Will's interest. When William's father, John Shakespeare, was a glove maker and later a Bailiff at Stratford, the Queen's Men played there routinely. We know they were paid nine shillings for their performance in 1569."

Out of the corner of his eye, Joe noticed movement and turned to see Smitty's wife carrying a tray with two coffee cups and a plate of sweet rolls. A small white pitcher and bowl also rested on the yellow tray.

"Would you boys like some coffee?"

"Oh, yes, dear. How thoughtful."

"Thank you, Mrs. Smythe," said Joe.

She placed the tray on the coffee table between the sofa and the two chairs. She winced as she straightened up.

"You didn't have to go to all that trouble, Licia," Smitty said.

"Can I get you anything else?" she asked.

"No, thanks, dear. This is wonderful."

"In that case, I'm going into the bedroom to lie down and read."

"Fine, fine. You do that."

Joe watched as Alicia turned and stepped into the hallway, disappearing into its cool darkness.

"She hasn't been feeling well," said Smitty.

"Maybe I should come back another time?"

"No, no. Let's finish our discussion."

They stepped into the living room and fixed their coffees. Then Joe followed Smitty back to his desk where they could see the document again. They stood well back from it though, careful not to spill coffee on the paper.

"Where was I?" Smitty asked He took another sip of his coffee. "Oh, yes. The business side of plays. When young William was married to an older woman—a forced marriage at that, since he had gotten Anne Hathaway pregnant—and at a time when John Shakspeare's business was slipping, Will might have joined one of the company of actors just to get away from Stratford. He probably joined Lord Leicester's Men, who passed through Stratford in 1587, on their way back to London."

"So that's how Shakespeare became a playwright?"

"Well, he probably joined as a stage hand or an actor initially and later tried his hand at writing. In time, he might have discovered his talent."

Joe glanced at the papers on Smitty's table.

"I'm still unclear. If this isn't a copy produced by a scribe, then who wrote it?"

"The answer to that question, my young colleague, is difficult and complex. It might have been any number of people, including a scribe, perhaps an older, more experienced one. Of course, boot-legged copies of plays were worth money to other playhouses, so this copy could have been done by an actor. Rival theatre companies would send members of their company in to see a play and copy the dialogue as they watched."

"My God!" laughed Joe. "Like people today sneaking video cameras into movie theaters?"

"Yes, quite so. And for the very same reason—greed!"

"Incredible."

"Of course, there are lots of other possibilities. Many skeptics over the years have argued that Will Shakespeare was merely a front for other authors."

"I've heard one possibility is Christopher Marlowe."

"Yes. Marlowe was a contender. Sir Frances Bacon was another. The truth is, about half a dozen names have surfaced."

Joe sipped his coffee and turned to look at the box on the library table. What possible secrets might be contained within, he wondered.

"What next?"

Jonathan sipped his coffee, looking at the box with Joe. A wide smile lit up his face.

"I think we should take everything out and survey our treasures."

Joe almost spit out his coffee.

"Should we? I mean, the papers aren't as delicate as I thought they'd be, but still."

"Oh, we'll be careful, very careful," Smitty said. "The paper is a sturdy rag bond. It survives as well as it does because it hasn't been acid washed, the way today's paper is. Of course, it's your call. Jack Claire sent the papers to you, after all."

"True," Joe said. "But I'm sure Jack knew I'd find someone like you."

Smitty smiled. "Jack and I knew each other, you know. Not as well as he and Thorne knew one another."

"Oh?"

"I heard Jack present a paper at a conference years ago. Actually, it was about twenty years ago, come to think of it, in Chicago. He and I corresponded a few times."

"Interesting," Joe said, checking his watch. He had an hour before his class.

"Am I boring you, lad?"

"Not at all. It's just, I've got to get back to campus to meet my students."

"Oh, yes, of course. Right you are. Mustn't keep young minds waiting."

"Well, I don't have to leave this instant, but..."

"But shortly. Of course. Then we must decide our next course of action."

"Yes, I guess—"

"Here's what I propose, Joe. If you leave these papers with me, I'll keep them just as they are until you come back. Then we can go through them together."

Joe was torn. Should he leave the box of papers with this man he knew mainly by reputation, or should he carry the box back to his office? And then what? Carry it back and forth between his office and Smitty's home until they had more answers?

"Can I ask you a rather crass question?"

The older professor smiled. "How much are they worth?"

Joe nodded.

Smitty's expression turned more serious. "Very difficult to say. If these are true copies of Shakespeare's plays, written in his own time, and if some of the handwriting is actually his, then, who knows? Hundreds of thousands of dollars, at the least."

"And, again, not to be crass, but at most?"

Smitty shook his head, as he gazed at the simple brown box. "Literally invaluable. Several million dollars. Perhaps much, much more."

Joe put his coffee down. "I'm just not sure what I should do. The truth is, I'm not sure why Jack would trust me with these papers. Don't get me wrong. I loved him as if he were my own father. And I know he was fond of me. But I also know that...."

"What, Joe? What were you going to say?"

"Well, he must have realized that I've been a bit of a screw up. I mean, let's face it, two years ago, I was in jail."

"Yes, true, but I'm sure he knew you'd been cleared of all that."

"I know, but—"

"And from what I've read, you're actually something of a hero. I did read your book. Liked the title, found it very apropos. *Tragic Flaws*. Referring, of course, to your own and the flaws in the police investigation, which had tragic results. I'm sure Jack was impressed. You saved your wife and helped capture the real killer."

"That's all true, but—"

"Those are important accomplishments, you know, out in the real world. Out there where evil doers dwell."

Joe laughed. "'Evil doers?' Sounds like Bush."

Smitty picked up his coffee cup and took another sip as Joe studied his face. "There are people who follow no path, no moral code. *You* know that better than most people, after *your* trials and tribulations."

Joe allowed the smile to leave his lips as he reflected on the older man's comment. "I know, but I'm no Shakespeare scholar. He should have sent the papers to someone like you."

Smitty's eyes brightened. "I think I have the answer, if you're willing to hear it."

"Fire away. Why did an esteemed scholar like Jack Claire entrust me, a lowly, untenured English instructor, with these sacred documents?"

"Ah. You've already guessed the answer yourself, haven't you."

"What do you mean?"

"You called these 'sacred' documents."

"So?"

"Don't you understand, Joe? You're on an errand, lad, sent on an errand by a king in his realm. You are by definition an errant knight."

"An errant knight?"

Smitty laughed out loud. "Yes, lad. You are one of the Knights Templar! You've been entrusted with a sacred duty."

Joe laughed. "But I don't want to be a knight!"

CHAPTER 8

How poor are they that have not patience!
From *Othello*

The same morning, Benedict awoke early in his hotel room, made coffee, and lit a cigarette, smoking as he watched the coffee drip into the small glass pot. This errand had gone on longer than he'd expected. He didn't mind killing, but he regarded each unplanned death as sloppiness on his part. He had made a display of Claire's home and office to frighten the old professor, but the man had proven to be more obstinate than he'd counted on. Old fool.

He'd searched all the places in Baton Rouge where the papers might be hidden. Time to widen the search.

He stubbed out his cigarette and examined the photocopied pages of the guest book from Claire's memorial service, along with the photos he'd taken. He'd ruled out members of the Administration at LSU. Claire would not trust them. His read of the old professor convinced him that Claire didn't care as much about the University's reputation as he did about the documents.

For the same reason, he'd ruled out people in the general community. These were not people Claire would trust with documents of such great literary merit.

Several out of town visitors remained on the list, including Jack Claire's granddaughters. Dr. and Mrs. Jacob Sloan lived in Columbus, Ohio, and Deirdre Claire lived in Marin, California. Who else on the memorial list lived in California? Benedict scanned the pages. Only one couple. Mr. and Mrs. Joseph Lawrence Conrad.

He drained the last of his bitter coffee. It made sense to travel north first. By ten, he was on a flight to Ohio.

Benedict lit a cigarette after driving his rental car out of the airport at Columbus. Using the rental's GPS, he found Melinda Sloan's handsome Tudor-style home. He parked on the street. At the front door, he rang the doorbell and waited. No sounds came from inside. He rang again, peering into one of the long, narrow windows on either side of the front door. He knocked again. Still no response.

After pulling on a pair of gloves, he picked the lock and slipped inside. On the wall to his right was an alarm keypad. The alarm hadn't been set. *Typical.*

Benedict stood in the foyer and listened. He moved through the downstairs room, looking for people but also searching for a box or papers mailed by Dr. Claire. Nothing. The lush carpet on the staircase enabled him to climb the stairs without making a sound. He searched the linen closets. No box. No papers. He padded down the hall to a child's bedroom. The bed was made and the room was tidy, with the exception of a few dolls and a Barbie dollhouse on the floor under the window and a massive stuffed animal at the foot of the bed. He doubted Jack's granddaughter would have put the papers in a child's room, but to make sure he opened the closet door and inspected the contents. Nothing.

The next room obviously belonged to a boy. Toys of every kind strewn across the carpet, the bed unmade, and the closet door open, additional toys making it impossible to close. He made a quick inspection.

The Master bedroom was spacious. On his knees, he looked under the bed, using his pen light to inspect each pair of shoes and a folded rowing machine. No boxes. No papers.

He opened the door to the walk-in closet. A few office style file boxes were easy to examine, but they only held old household records. On the shelves above the hanging clothes were shoeboxes, which he opened one at a time and placed back exactly where he'd found them.

On the floor in the corner stood a small fire safe. Testing its weight, he found that it had not been bolted down to the floor. As he leaned it forward, the door swung open. Benedict laughed. He knelt and examined the contents. The jewelry and the limited coin collection were tempting, but were not what he was after. Insurance papers and other documents—exactly what he'd expected.

To be thorough, he checked the master bathroom, but found nothing.

The guest bedroom was next. A handsome double bed with a Mahogany frame occupied the center of the main wall. He knelt down and looked underneath the bed. A long, flat box. He pulled the box out but could tell by its weight that it probably didn't hold heavy stacks of papers. Removing the lid, he saw a white wedding dress folded in half in a clear plastic garment bag. He smiled, then put the lid back on the box, slid it under the bed and stood up, moving toward the desk.

The papers on the desk had something to do with the partnership of the husband's medical practice. Sitting down at the desk, Benedict opened each drawer and fingered the files. All seemed to concern either household bills or the medical practice. As far as he could tell, there were no trick drawers in the desk. The papers weren't there.

Opening the closet, he found a locked wooden file cabinet. The little push-in lock was a type he'd had trouble with before, but after working it for several seconds, it popped open and Benedict completed the search. Each drawer deserved careful inspection, but his efforts again yielded nothing.

In the hallway ceiling was a trap door with a cord hanging down. He pulled the door down and unfolded the ladder. After climbing the steps, he turned on his penlight. Fortunately, the attic was empty. Pink insulation and air ducts. Still, he climbed the steps and walked along the planks, ducking between the trusses. He lifted the long sheets of insulation and looked underneath. Sometimes people cut part of the insulation away, he knew, and hid a box of valuables underneath. Breaking a sweat in the heat, he walked the length of the attic on the wide planks, lifting the sheets of insulation between each pair of two-by-fours. Unless the box had been shoved far over to the edge of the roof, there was nothing under any of the rows of insulation.

After brushing himself off, he climbed down and closed the attic, checking the carpet for debris.

Downstairs he made a room by room search that was equally meticulous. Nothing. He finished his inspection of the kitchen before moving into the garage. If Dr. Claire's granddaughter did not appreciate the value of the papers, she might have put them out there.

An older two-door BMW sat on one side of the garage. The other space, closer to the door into the kitchen, was empty. The garage didn't take long.

The BMW?

The interior was clean. He picked the lock to the trunk. A black medical bag, an emergency road kit, an Army blanket, the spare tire and jack.

He went through the side door of the garage to the backyard. The garbage cans were empty. A small doghouse was empty, too. The backyard was dominated by a swimming pool. Lawn chairs and a Weber gas grill on the patio. A small fence in the back corner probably hid the pool pump from sight, but Benedict walked back to check. Nothing.

Standing under the shade of the roof over the patio, he contemplated his next move. Melinda might have turned the papers over to the family lawyer. Benedict went back inside the house and found an address book in the cabinet under the telephone. The attorney's phone name and number were under the letter "A" with the word "Attorney" written first:

Attorney Mark Andersen

"Jesus, these people are predictable," he said out loud.

He called the number and asked for the attorney whose name was in the address book. His call was transferred to a secretary.

"May I help you?"

"Yes," said Benedict. "This is Dick Edwards at Klein, Hudson, and Pitkin. I'm calling on behalf of Dr. Sloan."

"Yes."

"I just wanted to confirm that the box of documents from Melinda Sloan's grandfather, Dr. Claire, arrived safely. We're contacting another expert."

"I'm sorry, what box? What documents?"

"Maybe I should speak to the attorney of record," Benedict said in his most condescending voice.

"Well, he's in a meeting, but I can assure you, any documents he receives would go through me. What documents are you referring to?"

"This would have been a large book-sized box full of papers. Probably arrived within the last week."

"Well, sir, I can assure you, nothing like that has arrived here lately. We've had a few contracts delivered by courier, but no large boxes."

Benedict hung up. He scanned the kitchen and the dining room again. What had he missed? Nothing. But he'd learned to be thorough. "Measure twice; cut once," he said aloud, smiling as he remembered the throat of his first victim.

He walked back toward the staircase, glancing around as he walked to take in the Gestalt of the rooms, to see if there were an obvious hiding place he'd neglected. The Master bedroom deserved one more quick inspection. So did the office. Repeating steps he'd taken before, he both duplicated and then altered his search, trying to see the rooms from different angles.

In the child's room, he examined the enormous stuffed lion on the end of the bed. Something stopped him dead—the sound of the garage door going up.

Benedict dropped the stuffed animal and stepped out into the hallway. The door between the garage and the kitchen banged open, and he heard small feet and a little girl's giggles.

"Lydia," a man's voice ordered. "Let Major out before you go upstairs."

Benedict stood in the hall and glanced at the little girl's bed.

Downstairs, young Lydia Sloan reluctantly changed course and walked to the sliding glass door.

"C'mon, Major," she called. The German Shepherd was sniffing new scents throughout the room. "Major, come!" the girl repeated. But the dog followed the scent toward the front door and looked up the staircase.

"What's wrong?" Melinda asked.

"He won't obey me!"

"Major, go outside!" Melinda commanded. "Major, now!"

Reluctantly, the dog turned toward the little girl and ran to her, licking her hand.

"Go outside, boy." She slid the door open.

But the dog turned and looked back toward the stairs, whimpering.

"Major, go now!" Melinda commanded again.

His brow furrowed. Unsure what to do, the large dog stood his ground and looked back over his shoulder at the two females. He turned and walked toward them slowly, and then turned back around to face the stairs. Then he barked.

"What's wrong with the damn dog?" asked Dr. Sloan, carrying two suitcases in from the garage.

"I don't know," Melinda said. "He's not obeying."

The doctor put the suitcases down and clapped his hands together.

"Major! Go outside now!"

The dog sat and focused on the staircase, barking sharply once again.

The doctor walked over and slapped the dog's snout.

"Daddy!"

"Well, the dog has to mind. Major, go outside."

Confused, Major whimpered and turned reluctantly. He padded outside, but then he turned and watched as Lydia closed the sliding door. She waved at Major, then turned and walked toward the staircase.

After running up the stairs, she stopped at the door to her room and looked at the stuffed lion. It was on the floor, not on her bed where she always left it. The sight produced a chill down her neck and back.

Then she felt the presence of someone standing behind her and she spun around.

"What is it, honey?" Her father was holding the two suitcases, standing behind her in the hallway.

"Oh, daddy. You scared me," she said, clutching her heart. "Timba moved."

"What?" Her father chuckled.

"My Timba. He's been moved."

"You just forgot where you left him."

Lydia remained standing in the doorway. She shook her head. "No I didn't," she said. "Timba moved."

Then she heard a creak from the timbers above her room.

"Daddy," Lydia called. She heard another groan from the wood above her room. "Daddy! Someone's in the attic."

Benedict stepped as gingerly as he could through the cobwebs toward a large slatted vent under the apex of the roof. He knew this vent would let him out onto the roof of the garage, and from there it would be an easy drop to the side yard. He heard the muffled voices below, despite the German Shepherd's relentless barking.

As he neared the vent, he could see the perfect outline of a large spider web that stood between him and the vent. At the center of the web waited one large, black spider—bigger than any he'd ever seen, in this country or any other.

Benedict froze.

Spiders! He'd learned to control his fear of them, but the effort took a few seconds. He reached out slowly and brushed the lower strands of the web. The large spider simply rotated in the center of the web.

Using his gloved hand, Benedict destroyed more of the web on the right side. The spider scurried up one strand toward the ceiling and disappeared into a crevice between the skip-sheeting of the roof and the tar paper. Benedict stepped through the remaining web and tested the slatted vent. Nailed tight.

He switched on his small flashlight and found several nail heads, running his finger over them.

Below in the hallway, Dr. Sloan put his hand on his daughter's shoulder and turned her around so she was looking up at him instead of at the ceiling.

"Go downstairs to your mother and tell her to let Major back inside."

"But, daddy. You come, too."

"Go on, honey."

Lydia's face wrinkled with fear and her eyes began to water, but she walked quickly to the stairs and ran down as fast as her little legs could carry her. Dr. Sloan reached up for the handle of the folding attic stairs.

Just as he was about to seize the handle, a noise startled him. He jerked his hand away.

Major! The volley of barks echoed in the narrow hallway.

Major stood at the man's knees barking furiously at the ceiling.

Dr. Sloan looked over to see Melinda holding Lydia at the corner of the staircase.

"Be ready to run downstairs and call 9-1-1," he told his wife.

He reached up and jerked the handle. The staircase swung down and with it something he didn't recognize until it was too late.

The dark object hit the doctor's face. He screamed, as did his wife and daughter. A large rat caught in a trap hit the floor.

Major barked and sniffed the dead rat on the carpet.

The doctor wiped his face spastically with both hands.

Melinda giggled.

"Oh, God, honey. Are you all right?" she asked, unable to stop laughing.

"No!" he said. Instead of pulling the folding ladder open and checking the attic, Dr. Sloan hurried into the bathroom to inspect his face in the mirror, sure the dead rat had left blood on his mouth.

Benedict used the time to pull a few nails with a small crowbar from his burglar kit. He removed as many nails as needed in order to pry the vent open at the bottom. Then he wriggled through and stood on the slanted roof. He pushed the vent back into place and walked nonchalantly down the garage roof to a corner hidden behind a tree. He sat on the edge and dropped to the lawn, having to roll once to absorb the impact of the fall.

On his feet, he walked briskly to the car and climbed in.

Melinda Sloan, still giggling, patted her husband on the shoulder as he inspected his face in the mirror. Lydia stared down at the rat, its neck crushed by the trap, its body as stiff and dry as a stale dinner roll.

Major sat beside her, staring up into the darkness of the attic.

Calmly, Benedict sat in the rental car and pulled a briefcase from the backseat. He lit a cigarette and unlatched his case, pulling out a list of names and addresses. The next name on his list was "Mr. and Mrs. Joseph Conrad" of Davis, California. He started the car and drove to the airport.

A few hours later, he was on a flight to California. Davis was a twenty-minute drive from the Sacramento Airport. He would continue the search early Wednesday morning. He stared out the window of the jet. Below him, through layers of thin, broken clouds, the world appeared neat and orderly. Unlike landscapes pockmarked by bomb craters like those he'd flown over in the past.

CHAPTER 9

The little foolery that wise men have makes a great show.
From *As You Like It*

Joe left Smitty's house and drove to campus. The potential value of the papers unnerved him. Shouldn't he give the papers to one of Jack's granddaughters? Or should he take them back to Louisiana and give them to the University?

Maybe the papers should be taken to England. Dr. Claire had always encouraged him to go to Europe. "See where western literature was born," the old professor had advised. "See where the arts thrived. Get a feel for the world."

Perhaps this was one last lesson from the old mentor.

During class, Joe was so preoccupied that he had trouble leading the discussion, but he muddled through.

After class he went to his office and checked his voicemail. There was one message from Sarah: "I called twice already. Where are you?"

He hadn't told her about going to Smitty's house. That would mean telling her about the papers, and he hadn't wanted to do that until he had a better understanding of what they were. Now he was afraid to tell her how valuable they might be. But he knew he had to call her.

She sounded irritable. "Where were you this morning?"

"I went to visit Jonathan Smythe. You met him at the Christmas party, remember?"

"No, not really," Sara said, sounding annoyed.

"He retired about the same time I was hired, but he's the one everybody talks about. You know. 'What would Smitty do?'"

"Oh, yeah. His wife's name is Alice?"

"Alicia."

"I remember her. Quiet, a little nervous. I could relate. Why'd you visit *them*?" asked Sara.

Joe debated whether or not to tell her.

"I didn't mention it, but when we got back from Louisiana, there was a box waiting for me at the office. I didn't think much of it at first, just books from publishers. Anyway, I opened it Tuesday."

"Okay. I'll bite. What was in it?"

"The box was from Jack Claire. He must've mailed it just before he died. It's filled with old manuscripts."

"Manuscripts?"

"Yeah."

Now Sara stayed quiet. He visualized the troubled look on her face.

"What kind of manuscripts, Joe?"

"I'm not sure. Probably from the seventeenth century. That's why I visited Jonathan Smythe. He's an Elizabethan scholar. I thought he might know something that could help me decide what to do."

Sara remained quiet, but then said, "I'm getting a bad feeling about this."

"These papers could be worth something."

"That's why I'm getting a bad feeling." She waited for him to respond, but he didn't. "What did you and Dr. Smythe decide to do?"

"We haven't decided anything yet. We barely had a chance to examine the contents. I'm going back there this afternoon and I guess we'll look at all the papers. Then we'll decide."

"Do you think this is connected to those burglaries at LSU?"

Joe was afraid even to think it, let alone say it out loud.

"I don't know. Could be, but I just don't know."

"Damn it, Joe! Don't you see? It's starting again."

"What?"

"You know what the hell I'm talking about."

"Jack wouldn't have sent these papers to me if he thought they could hurt me, Sara. Or you. He loved both of us. You know that."

"I'll tell you what I know. I know Jack Claire is dead. Whether he jumped off the tower or was pushed, he's dead. And so is his wife."

"But Sara—"

"If the person who killed Jack Claire is looking for those papers, then get rid of them."

"Calm down, Sara."

"Do you remember what happened the last time you got yourself involved with this kind of—of intrigue?"

Joe rubbed his forehead. "Of course I do."

"I almost got killed."

"I know."

"And we almost made Katie an orphan."

"I remember."

"Get rid of those damned papers."

"I'll call you after I meet with Smitty."

Sara hung up without saying goodbye. He held the phone to his ear for a few seconds. Then he gathered up his students' essays, closed his briefcase, and left his office.

In fifteen minutes, he was standing at the front door of Jonathan Smythe's house ringing the doorbell.

Smitty opened the door looking troubled. "Hello, lad, hello. I'm afraid this isn't a good time. Alicia's napping."

"Oh?" Joe already had one foot inside the door. "Then maybe I should take the box with me and come back later."

"Take the box?" Smitty glanced over his shoulder toward the dining room. "I'm not sure you need to do that. Can't you come back tomorrow morning? We can look through the papers then."

Joe felt torn. If he left the papers with Smitty, then he'd gotten rid of them like Sara wanted. On the other hand, if they were as valuable as this old scholar thought they were, he might miss out on a fortune. Jack had sent the papers to him, after all, not to Jonathan Smythe.

"I don't know, Smitty. I think I should keep the papers, at least for the time being."

"But—"

Before the old professor could protest too much, Joe pushed into the foyer.

"Let me just check on 'Licia."

With that, Smitty closed the door, locked the handle, and walked down the hall. He went around a corner and out of Joe's line of sight.

Joe stepped into the living room and then up to the dining room floor. What he saw made his jaw drop. The large library table had been cleared of the stacks of books and papers that had previously covered its surface. In their place were twenty or more stacks of the old brownish parchments from the box. The box itself was lying on its side on the floor, empty.

"Damn it!" Joe said. He stepped around to look at the papers more closely. They were covered with handwriting. He could barely read the titles, but the few he could were titles he recognized. *Measure for Measure, Much ado about Nothing, The Comedy of Errours, Love's Labour Lost.*

"Unbelievable," Joe whispered. He looked up in anger when he saw Smitty step down into the living room out of the hallway. "Smitty, you promised."

"Sorry, lad. The temptation was too great." He walked over to the table and held out his hands in front of Joe. "I just couldn't help myself. This is the find of the century!"

Joe stepped closer to the massive table on which the papers were displayed. "Is it?" he said, trying to control his anger.

"The find of the last four centuries!"

Joe took a deep breath and turned away from Smitty's nervous face to scan the stacks of pages. "You think they're authentic then?"

Smitty threw up his hands, giggling. "I don't know what to think, to tell you the truth. There are at least three different kinds of penmanship here. And the hand that you and I would recognize as being most like Will Shakespeare's isn't on many of the papers. In the few places where his handwriting *does* show up, the penmanship halting, ragged, unpracticed. Not a smooth, flowing cursive at all. Shaky and uncertain. As if he were being coached in how to write. I'm completely perplexed!"

He motioned toward two short stacks of manuscripts at the corner of the table.

"Look at the handwriting here, Joe. Completely different from any of the others."

Joe read the titles out loud: "*Venus and Adonis*," he said slowly, "and *The Rape of Lucrece*. These are the long poems."

"Right you are. Two of the earliest works attributed to Shakespeare." Smitty took an antique wooden letter opener and pointed to the first sentence of the poem *The Rape of Lucrece*. "Look at the way the *F* and the *R* in the first word are written larger and bolder than the rest of the letters in the first line of the poem."

Joe read the line out loud: "**Fr***om the besieged* ***A****rdea all in post*."

"Now look at the B in the second line."

"***B****orne by the trustless wings of false desire*."

"Okay," said Joe, trying to make sense of the clues. "F-R-B. What's it mean?"

"Francis Bacon!"

Joe examined the handwriting again.

"But those three letters aren't the only capitalized or bold letters on the page."

"True, true," agreed the old professor, smiling. "What other letter is capitalized?"

Joe looked again. "Well, the *A* in Ardea, for example."

"Exactly! Put F-R-A together, followed by B, and you have Fra. B., is exactly the way Francis Bacon abbreviated his name."

Joe looked at the page more closely. Then he stood and faced Smitty. "Why wouldn't Bacon simply write his name on the page?" he asked. "Why be so cryptic?"

"Bacon was fascinated by anagrams and ciphers. He had to be as one of Queen Elizabeth's spymasters. In fact, he invented a system for coded messages called the Bi-literal Cipher. He described it in a book titled *De augmentis scientiarum*, published in 1623. That was the same year the *First Folio* was published, by the way."

Smitty's excitement was contagious. "An intriguing coincidence," remarked Joe. "But why hide his identity as the author of the poems?"

"Well, one reason could be that, as a member of Parliament and an advisor to the Queen, he probably wanted to hide that part of himself that could be viewed as less than serious. While the nobles secretly enjoyed poems and plays in Elizabeth's court, these were guilty pleasures, like a professor of British Literature admitting he enjoyed watching soap operas on television."

Smitty turned to his bookshelf and ran his index finger across the backs of several books before finding the one he wanted.

"Here," he said, opening a handsomely bound old text. "Listen to this quote from a book titled *English Poesie* published in 1589: 'in these days (although some learned Princes may take delight in Poets) yet universally it is not so. For as well Poets as Poesie are despised, and the name become honourable infamous, subject to scorn and derision, and rather reproach than a praise...' Guilty pleasures are kept secret, Joe," Smitty concluded, winking. "*You* know that better than anyone, I suspect."

Joe blushed. Smitty knew about his own guilty pleasures—his visits to a strip club in the past, which had made him a good candidate for the Lost Slough murders.

"I suppose," Joe admitted. "No one wants their private lives exposed." Joe eyed Smitty as he spoke.

"Now imagine you're an English professor or better yet, a politician, and the public learns that you actually write the scripts for a soap opera. Or worse, the scripts for porn films. That might be more equivalent by today's moral standards—or lack thereof," Smitty added.

Joe frowned. "Porn? You can't compare the works of Shakespeare to *porn*."

"Standards of decency change, lad. Remember, Joyce's masterpiece *Ulysses* was banned because *it* was considered pornographic. Don't forget Henry Miller's *Nexus* series. Salinger's *Catcher in the Rye* is still banned in some school districts."

"I know, but really. Bacon was a well-known writer of essays. Why hide the fact that he wrote these poems?"

"If Bacon wrote the long poems and the sonnets, he was probably homosexual, a fact he wished to conceal. Especially since the objects of his desire seemed to be much younger men."

Joe nodded. It made sense. An important figure like Francis Bacon would keep his identity as a poet and playwright secret, especially if those works were considered vulgar by the norms of Elizabethan society.

"So what should we do now? What's our next step?"

"If I had a book with a sample of Bacon's penmanship, we could compare, but I can't find the ones I used to have."

Smitty scanned his bookshelves again, and Joe glanced at the wall of books.

"Would the library on campus have what we need?" Joe asked.

"Not to my knowledge."

Joe nodded. The library at Central Lutheran University was not extensive, CLU having fewer than four thousand students.

"I could try the U. C. Davis library."

"True," agreed Smitty. "But we may have a better option."

"What's that?"

"I've taken another liberty, I'm afraid."

"Oh?" Joe's ire rose again. "What?"

"I've called a colleague, an expert. Dr. Sylvia Williamson. She wants to see samples of the papers."

"Samples?"

"I described everything we found inside the box."

"Everything *you* found, you mean."

"Right, right. Deeply sorry, lad, for betraying your trust, but—"

"You're forgiven." Joe put his hand on Smitty's bony shoulder. While Smitty looked fit for someone in his late sixties, Joe realized he was actually frailer than he seemed. "Where is Dr. Williamson? Does she live here in Stockton?"

"My God, no," Smitty laughed. "No, no. She's at Berkeley. She's an Elizabethan scholar like me, but she also specializes in dating old books and documents, verifying their legitimacy."

"She sounds perfect."

A smile lit up Smitty's face. "Oh, yes. She's perfect, all right. Incredibly knowledgeable, a genius, I daresay. And beautiful. You'll see. We're going to Berkeley tomorrow, Joe."

"*Tomorrow?* I have class tomorrow. I can't."

"Sure you can. Cancel class. This is the find of the century!"

Joe studied Smitty's excited face as he considered the proposal.

"Maybe you can take some of the papers to Dr. Williamson, Smitty. I suppose I can trust you with a few sample pages."

The light left Smitty's face. Joe sensed a reluctance he hadn't seen before.

"It's not that I don't think you trust me. It's just that, well..."

"What?"

"I'm not really allowed to drive anymore."

Joe blinked. "Why not?"

"Well, I've had a few accidents in these last few years. Until recently, Licia's been doing the driving."

"Oh," said Joe. "I see. Well, how about Friday? I don't teach on Fridays."

Smitty looked dejected. "I've already told her we'd be there tomorrow."

"I'm sorry. I can't just cancel classes for no good reason."

"If this isn't a good reason, I don't know what is."

"I can't do it. I'm sorry."

"This could *make* your career, Joe."

For Smitty, whose teaching career was over, these must have seemed like trivial concerns, but Joe had already come close to losing his teaching position once.

"And yours?"

The flash of anger was real. "*My* career has already been made, lad. You can be assured of that."

"I know. I don't mean any disrespect." *But this would be quite a feather in your cap, too, at the end of your career.*

Smitty closed his eyes for a few seconds, and Joe watched his lips move. Was he chanting?

"I understand," he said finally. "No, of course. You have a family with young children. Of course you have to think about the immediate future."

"Thanks," said Joe.

"I'll call Sylvia back and ask her about Friday. It's just, she became very excited when I told her about our find."

Joe noted his use of *our.*

Suddenly, Smitty's eyes lit up again. "Oh, my God, lad! I haven't told you about the *Folio.*"

Smitty stepped around the table to the far corner, placing his hands on either side of a thick book but acted reluctant to touch it. Looking down, he said, "I found this in the last wooden box. This is, I think, an authentic copy of Jaggard and Blount's *First Folio.*"

Smitty pointed to the cover. Each corner was protected by triangles of metal. "These are silver, I think. And look at the oval of matching silver in the middle of the cover."

As if afraid to step closer, Joe stood where he was, trying to make out the engraved figure on the silver oval.

"The engraving—is it a fish?"

"No. A wild boar with a crown over it, a five-pointed crown."

"What's it mean?"

"It's probably from a family crest. It might tell us who owned this edition of the *Folio.*"

Smitty carefully opened the heavy dark leather cover of the over-sized book.

Even from where he was standing, Joe immediately saw the controversial Droeshout engraving of Shakespeare on the first page.

Smitty placed his index finger on Shakespeare's neck. "Notice anything odd about Shakespeare's face?"

Joe leaned down and took a closer look. "He's got a double chin?"

Smitty smiled. "Some people believe that double chin, as you call it, or the quite visible line, actually shows the edge of a mask. When you combine that detail with the ambiguity in the last lines of Ben Jonson's verse, it raises some doubts."

Mr. WILLIAM
SHAKESPEARES
COMEDIES,
HISTORIES, &
TRAGEDIES.
Published according to the True Originall Copies.

LONDON
Printed by Isaac Iaggard, and Ed. Blount. 1623.

Joe read the lines out loud: "Wherein the Graver had a strife/with Nature, to outdo the life: /O, could he but have drawn his wit/As well in brass, as he hath hit /His face ; the Print would then surpass/All, that was ever writ in brass. / But, since he cannot, Reader, look / Not on his Picture, but his Book."

To the Reader.

This Figure, that thou here ſeeſt put,
It was for gentle Shakeſpeare cut;
Wherein the Grauer had a ſtrife
with Nature, to out-doo the life :
O, could he but haue drawne his wit
As well in braſſe, as he hath hit
His face ; the Print would then ſurpaſſe
All, that vvas euer vvrit in braſſe.
But, ſince he cannot, Reader, looke
Not on his Picture, but his Booke.

B. I.

Mr. WILLIAM
SHAKESPEARES
COMEDIES,
HISTORIES, &
TRAGEDIES.

LONDON

"What do you make of it?"asked Smitty.

Joe shrugged. "Jonson is telling us to ignore the face and know the author through his writings. Is that what you mean?"

"Some would argue for that interpretation, yes."

"What do *you* think, Smitty?"

"I think we're at the beginning of a long journey." Smitty patted the page gently with the palm of his hand, saying, "Thirty-six plays. Nine hundred pages. It's incredible."

"You honestly think it's an authentic original of the *First Folio*?" He stepped around the corner of the table to get a better look.

"I'm sure of it," Smitty said. "I've seen two others before, one at the Folger in Washington, D. C., and one at the Huntington Library in Pasadena. This copy looks to be in better condition than either of those. In fact, this might be the most pristine copy in existence, thanks to this leather cover."

"How much would it be worth?"

Smitty turned to look at Joe. "To a crude collector, it could be worth two- or three-hundred thousand dollars. But these are the kinds of artifacts from which one does not profit. Something like this must be donated to a library or a museum so the whole world has access."

Joe looked over the stacks of plays that covered the large table.

"But suppose I *am* a crude investor, Smitty. If all these documents are authentic, how much are they worth?"

Smitty grabbed Joe's arm. "You can't possibly be thinking about selling these."

Joe looked down into Smitty's face. "If these documents are as valuable as you say they are, then we have to be very careful."

"Well, of course we do."

"No," Joe said. "Don't you see?"

"What?"

Joe gulped, feeling the blood drain from his face as he realized what they had.

"I think these papers are the reason Dr. Claire was murdered."

"Murdered? I thought it was suicide."

"But a custodian was killed, too. I don't see Jack Claire killing someone else just so he could kill himself."

Smitty stared into Joe, then turned to look over the stacks of manuscripts. "I see what you mean."

"If the custodian had tried to stop him from going out on the observation deck that morning, Jack would've waited and come back another day."

"Yes, that's certainly how I'd handle it." Smitty looked over the papers again. "But of course Jack had recently lost his wife. In his grief, he might not have been himself. Maybe he just didn't care anymore."

Joe shook his head. "No. The Jack Claire I knew would never kill anyone."

Smitty smiled and patted Joe on the arm. "Now *you're* forgetting."

"What?"

"Jack Claire was a veteran, wasn't he?"

"So?"

"He probably did his share of killing in that war."

Joe considered this for a moment. "No, he just wasn't that kind of person. I don't buy it. Besides, I think he worked in an intelligence department."

"So you believe someone killed Claire to get to these documents?"

Joe nodded. "You probably haven't heard, but several offices in the English Department at LSU were burglarized just days before Jack's death. Including his."

The smile left Smitty's face.

"That *does* make a difference," he said. "If someone was searching the offices of LSU faculty, that explains why Claire mailed the documents to you, in order to get them out of Louisiana, out of harm's way."

Joe nodded. "Yeah. I guess I'm not the knight in shining armor after all. Just somebody Jack knew who lived far away. But why not mail them to a library or a museum? Hell, why not give them to the police?"

"The police! Can you imagine your average policeman handling these precious papers, Joe?"

"*You* seemed to handle them okay."

"I was careful. And the papers are sturdier than you'd expect. They're really in superb condition." Smitty reached over and touched Joe's hand. "Please don't be angry with me. We had to examine these papers eventually."

"What should we do, then?"

The older man offered a sympathetic smile. "It's your call."

Joe tried to think. "I still know Ryan Dunn pretty well, the detective who helped me last time I was in trouble."

"You aren't in trouble, lad."

"If these papers turn out to be evidence in a murder investigation, we're both in trouble, if we keep them to ourselves."

The expression on Smitty's face told Joe he understood. "Let me think." He closed his eyes. "Besides me, who else knows you have these papers?"

"Only my wife."

"Is there any way for someone in Baton Rouge to trace the papers to you?"

Joe thought for a moment. "I'm not sure."

"But has anyone contacted you, someone out of the ordinary? I mean, do you have any reason to believe someone might be able to trace these to you?"

"Maybe. I spoke to Hayden Crawford, the assistant chair under Jack, and several people at the funeral."

"The service for Jack—was it well attended?"

"Oh, yes. Hundreds of people were there."

"Did you stand out? Did you speak?"

"Yes, briefly."

"But no one has contacted you?"

Joe blushed. "Actually, the police did want to talk to me about the burglaries."

Smitty stepped back. "You're a suspect in the burglaries?"

Joe shook his head. "No. There were other break-ins after we flew home, so that pretty much ruled me out."

Something happened to Smitty. It was as if the wind shifted and he could not catch his breath for a minute. He stared at Joe suspiciously, then stepped around to the other side of the table, putting the table between Joe and himself.

"Did you *steal* these papers, Joe?"

Joe's heart sank. It *was* happening again. Just as Sara had feared. He was being accused of a crime, a terrible crime, if you added in the murder of Jack Claire and the custodian at the state capitol building.

"No, Smitty. I did not steal these papers. You saw the box. It was addressed to me, and it was sent from Baton Rouge!"

"That proves nothing. You could have mailed them to yourself to get them out of your possession, in case the police searched you while you were still in Baton Rouge."

The same sickening feeling he'd felt two and a half years ago washed through him again. He *did* look guilty. Two men were dead and he was now in possession of documents that might be worth millions. He'd been in Baton Rouge. True, he was there days after the murders, but police might think he'd gone earlier, committed the murders to get his hands on the papers, then mailed them to himself, and made a showing at Jack's funeral just to keep up appearances. Or to tie up loose ends? Who knows what the police would think…

"Smitty, it was my idea to call the police, remember? If I were guilty of these crimes, why would I suggest calling them?"

Smitty had gone pale. Joe could see the suspicion in his eyes.

"To throw me off. To make yourself seem innocent. Maybe that's why you suggested calling the police. There's a line in Hamlet you may remember. 'You can smile and smile and smile, and still be a villain.'"

Joe took his phone out of his pocket and opened it. "If you'd like, we can call the police right now." He punched in 9-1-1 and handed the phone to Smitty. "Just push the 'Send' button. I'm sure the police will be here in five minutes."

Smitty took the phone from Joe's hand and looked at the number on the screen. He put his thumb over the "Send" button and looked up into Joe's eyes.

"Maybe we *should* call the police," Smitty said. "Maybe it's time."

CHAPTER 10

We must take the current when it serves,
Or lose our ventures.
From *Julius Caesar*

Regretting his decision to bring the papers to Smitty, Joe studied the older man's expression as Smitty decided whether or not to call 9-1-1 on Joe's cell phone. Involving the police would confirm Sara's worst fears. Would she leave him again? His stomach churned, remembering how it had felt last time. Glory among the literati had soured into a nightmare. Then he chuckled as he asked himself, *What will Smitty do?*

"Why are you laughing, lad? What in God's name do you find humorous about this?"

"No," said Joe. "It's just that, well, you must know you have a reputation for solving problems in the department. 'What would Smitty do?' I'm sure you've heard that."

"Yes. Go on."

"It's just, I'm beginning to think I made a mistake in bringing *this* problem to you. Instead of solving it, you're about to create a slew of new problems."

Smitty studied Joe's face for a few seconds longer. He moved his thumb over to the "End" button and cancelled the call to 9-1-1. Then he punched in a new number and hit the green "Send" button.

Joe's heart stopped. "Who are you calling?"

Smitty smiled and winked.

"No, really. Who the hell are you calling?" Joe asked again, stepping closer.

"Hello, Sylvia? It's Jonathan."

Joe exhaled a sigh of relief.

"I'm fine," Smitty said into the phone. "But I'm afraid Alicia's not well. Yes, thank you. Listen. Would you be free on Friday instead?"

Joe smiled and nodded at Smitty, who winked back.

"Oh? That's great. Then Joe and I will come over Friday morning, say about ten o'clock? Yes, we'll bring some sample pages. What? Oh, let me ask Joseph. He's standing right here." Covering the mouthpiece of the phone, Smitty said, "She wants to see the copy of the *First Folio*."

"I don't know. What do *you* think we should do?"

"I think we should take it to her. We don't have to leave it there. Let's get Sylvia's opinion and then we can decide."

"Sounds good."

Uncovering the mouthpiece, Smitty said, "Yes, we'll bring it with us. Should make your day to see it." He laughed, telling Joe, "Sylvia says it will make her *year*."

He ended the conversation and handed the phone back to Joe.

"Then it's decided?" Joe asked.

"Yes. We'll take some randomly chosen pages from a variety of these manuscripts and the copy of the *First Folio*. That should give her enough to work on for quite awhile."

Joe scanned the stacks of manuscripts covering the tabletop.

"Which pages should we take?"

Smitty walked to his desk and opened a drawer. Removing two pairs of white gloves, he said, "Let's decide that together, shall we?"

For the rest of the day, Joe couldn't stop thinking about the Shakespeare papers. That night after doing the dishes together, Joe and Sara sat down on the sofa with fresh coffee, and, after taking a sip, Sara asked again what he'd decided to do.

"Well, Smitty's keeping the papers at his house."

Sara nodded. "Good."

"He wants to take some of them to an expert at U. C. Berkeley."

"Take them all, as far as I'm concerned."

Joe swallowed a mouthful of coffee, and then said, "Jack *did* send them to *me*, Sara."

"I don't care." She held his gaze and raised her eyebrows. "Those papers are trouble. Keep them away from me and the kids."

"I'm driving Smitty to Berkeley on Friday. We'll give some samples to his expert and see what she says."

Sara put her cup back down into its saucer. "This expert is a woman?"

"Yes. Dr. Williamson. Funny, huh?"

"How is that funny?"

"Well, she's an expert on William Shakespeare and her name is Williamson. Don't you find that coincidental?"

"No. She's a woman, right? So she can't be anyone's *son*."

"Anyway, we'll let her examine the papers and then we'll decide what to do with them."

"Good," said Sara. "Just keep them away from us."

"I will, Sara. Besides, the things that happened, they happened in Louisiana, not here. I'm sure we're safe."

Sara lowered her head and gave him a skeptical look, but dropped the subject when Katie came in.

On Thursday, as soon as he stepped into his office, he froze after turning on the light. The hair on the back of his neck bristled. Something seemed out of joint.

Joe put his briefcase down on the desk and looked around. He opened the file cabinet drawers. The files were in place, yet someone might have rifled through them. He opened the drawers of his desk. Everything was there. Yet the items—paper clips, postcards, envelopes, extra pens—looked rearranged somehow. He stood up and inspected the bookshelves.

He hadn't dusted his shelves in a year, and the janitor never did, yet the dust was gone. He laughed nervously. Had someone broken in just to clean?

Joe picked up the phone and called the department office.

"Has anyone complained that their offices were broken into, Molly?"

"Why? Was yours?"

"I'm not sure," Joe admitted. "Maybe the janitor just cleaned better than usual."

"You're the second person to call. Dr. Richmond thinks his office was broken into as well, but nothing was taken."

"Is Craig here?"

"He was earlier, but he and his wife left for Yosemite."

"But he said nothing was stolen?"

"Said the same thing you did, that maybe the janitor cleaned better than usual. That's what we think down here. Somebody moved things around in our offices, too."

Joe's heart skipped a beat. "Anything missing?"

"No. The janitors probably went through things when they cleaned. That's all."

He shut his eyes and tried to think. "Have you told Dr. Thorne?"

"He's on vacation, Mr. Conrad. We don't bother him unless it's serious."

It might be serious, thought Joe. He switched the phone from his right hand to his left and asked, "Should you call the campus police?"

"Why?" huffed Molly. "Get those poor janitors in trouble for nothing?"

"Maybe it wasn't the janitors. Maybe someone else broke in looking for something?"

"Who?" asked Molly, chuckling. "Looking for what?"

Joe didn't want to explain. "I don't know, Molly. I can't say."

She said goodbye and he hung up.

Someone had searched his office—he wasn't imagining it, was he? Just as someone had searched the offices at LSU. Was it just a coincidence? If he told Sara, she'd say it was all happening again. The last time, she'd left him and taken Katie.

The excitement he'd been feeling about the Shakespeare papers was now tempered by the fear of losing Sara and the children.

What about Smitty?

Joe picked up the phone and dialed Jonathan's number. Smitty answered after several rings.

"It's Joe."

"Yes, lad. Looking forward to tomorrow?"

"What?" asked Joe. "Oh, yes. Tomorrow. Yes, of course."

"You'll be quite impressed with Dr. Williamson."

"Yes, I'm sure I will. Listen. The reason I called is, we've had some break-ins here at campus."

The phone stayed silent for a moment and Joe wondered if he'd lost the connection. Then Smitty said, "Break-ins?"

"Yes. Someone searched my office and a few others."

"Anything stolen?"

"No, but the same thing happened at LSU before Dr. Claire was killed. I think someone's after the Shakespeare papers."

There was another pause. He could picture Smitty piecing it together.

"And you think they somehow traced them to you?"

"I suppose. Maybe." Joe closed his eyes, trying to sort it out. "I'm not sure. It could just be a coincidence, I guess, but—"

"But that's one hell of a coincidence, don't you think?"

"Yeah. Don't you?"

Smitty stayed silent. Joe pictured him contemplating, finding a Zen state of emptiness, perhaps. Then he said, "We need more time. We need to get these papers to Dr. Williamson."

"I'm worried. I think whoever is after those papers may have killed Jack. If they're capable of killing Jack, then—"

"Then they're capable of killing you…or me, I suppose. Is that what you're worried about?"

"Yes. That's why I called. To see if you were okay. No one's broken into your place?"

Smitty chuckled. "No. We're safe as two bugs in a rug."

His stomach churning, he asked the older man a question he didn't want answered: "Should we go to the police?"

"Look, Joe. If they didn't find the papers in your office, maybe they'll move on and search someone else's place."

"I'm not sure who else...." He paused, remembering his encounter at Jack's funeral with the granddaughters.

"What is it?"

"Well, one of Jack's granddaughters lives out here in California. At least, she has offices in San Francisco and San Diego, I think."

"You should call her. Maybe they'll search her offices next."

"Maybe," said Joe.

"You should warn her, anyway. Do you have her number?"

"No. I'd have to look it up."

"If she's in danger, lad, you must."

Joe nodded, but worried about the frail old professor and his wife. "Be careful. I've had a little experience with the rougher side. I don't want anything to happen to you or Alicia."

Smitty was silent, but Joe could visualize him closing his eyes and smiling his Buddha smile.

"Thank you, lad."

After hanging up, Joe dialed information. The automated voice asked, "City and state?"

"San Francisco, California."

Then the female version of *2001*'s Hal asked him what name.

"Deirdre Claire."

A real operator came on. "Can you spell the last name, please?"

Joe spelled it slowly and waited.

"I have twelve listings for D. Claire or Deirdre Claire. Do you have an address?"

"No," said Joe. "Can you try a listing for an antique store, Claire Antique's maybe?"

"Checking," the woman said, annoyed. "I have nothing under Claire Antiques."

Joe closed his eyes and thought for a second. "Can you give me the listings of all the Deirdre Claires, then?"

"No, sir. I need an address."

He hung up and tried to think. He should have asked for a business card when he was at Jack's service. He called LSU.

"Missy? This is Joe Conrad."

"Oh, my word. How *are* you?"

"Fine, I think. How are you?" asked Joe, detecting her concern.

"Oh, lordy. We had some terrible news here."

"What is it, Missy?"

"One of our young female faculty members was murdered in her sleep. Strangled to death."

Joe's heart sank. "Who was it?"

"Dr. Wilson."

"Janice Wilson?" He closed his eyes and visualized the young woman with the dark hair and the tight black blouse smiling up at him, seductively sipping her wine.

"Did you know her?"

"I met her at Jack's service."

"The police found her yesterday afternoon."

"Yesterday?" Joe asked, trying to make sense of the time line.

"I'm not sure what's going on around here, Joe." Missy sounded as if she was about to cry. "First, Mrs. Claire dies, then Dr. Claire. Now this. It's a nightmare."

"Does Dr. Crawford know?"

"I tried to call, but they're not answering." Her voice cracked as she tried to explain. "It's so hard to reach them. When I do get him, it's usually the middle of the night over there in France and Dr. Crawford is so rude, I just don't feel like explaining anything. They go off on these day trips, he calls them, but they last more than one day."

Joe would have laughed, if he hadn't been so worried. "I need the phone number for Dr. Claire's granddaughter here in California. Do you have Deirdre Claire's number?"

"Why in the world do you need that?" She had recovered and the tone of her voice changed.

"I just need her number, please."

Away from the phone under her breath, Missy said loud enough to be heard, "It's like nobody cares a young woman is murdered in her sleep."

"Here it is."

He wrote as she read the number, and he read it back to her.

"You sound tired, Missy. Maybe *you* should take a vacation, too."

"Vacation!" she huffed. "I can't take a vacation 'til Dr. Crawford gets back!"

After hanging up, he dialed the number for Deirdre Claire.

"French Quarter Antiques," a female voice said.

No wonder the operator couldn't find the damn number! he thought.

"Is this Deirdre Claire?"

"No, this is her assistant. May I help you?"

"I met her at her grandfather's funeral, and I have some information for her."

"I'm afraid she won't be in the rest of the week, but I can leave a message to have her call you."

"Do you have a home number or a cell number? It's very important."

"I'll be happy to give her the message. She just got back from Louisiana. She and her sister were closing down their grandparents' house. Ms. Claire has some other business out of town today and tomorrow, so I know she's quite busy."

"I see." Joe wasn't sure what to say next, but he wanted to offer some kind of warning. "Tell me, have you had any burglaries?"

"Burglaries?" asked the woman. "No. Why? Are you planning something?" she chuckled.

"No," laughed Joe.

"Who is this again?" asked the woman.

"I'm a former student of Jack Claire's, an English instructor at CLU in Stockton."

She remained quiet, as if writing down the information. Then she said, "I'll give Ms. Claire your message." She hung up without saying goodbye.

Joe sat back and tried to think. The last time something like this happened, the more he tried to help, the more suspicion he cast on himself. Smitty didn't seem that concerned. But Smitty didn't know about Janice Wilson either.

If she had been killed in Baton Rouge the previous day, was it even possible the killer was now in California? Maybe he was imagining things. Looking around his office now, it seemed all right. Nothing out of the ordinary.

But Molly had said things in their offices had been disturbed. Craig Richmond had mentioned it, too.

Joe grabbed his coffeepot. Good, fresh coffee would help him sort it out.

When he got back, a student named Amanda was waiting outside his office. She wanted help with her research paper, an uninspired treatise on the use of foreshadowing. She'd identified some obvious symbols in Macbeth—the blood, the dagger—but had ignored more subtle ones. By the time he finished helping her, he had just enough time to grade the previous day's quizzes before heading to the classroom.

After class, Joe went back to his office and looked around. The janitors had cleaned. So what? "I'm being too paranoid," he said out loud.

But driving by Lost Slough that afternoon on the way home, Joe shivered at the memory of falling into the cold, dark water near the dead woman's body—the unnatural stiffness of the woman's corpse as he tried to pull it to shore. He suddenly imagined Janice Wilson's face on the half-nude body he'd found in the slough.

On an impulse, Joe stopped at The Ardent Reader, a bookstore in Davis, and looked for books on Shakespeare. He found a hardback that looked promising.

The clerk, a slender bespectacled man in his forties, was reading and seemed annoyed when Joe interrupted him. The clerk took his money, made change and handed him a receipt. Then the clerk perched on his stool without saying a word, and opened his book.

"Your store is well named," Joe said before turning to leave.

That evening, he did not tell Sara about the murder of Janice Wilson. Or about his suspicion that someone had searched his office.

Sara climbed into bed beside him.

"What are you reading?" she asked sleepily. Joe showed her the cover of the hardback and she yawned. "Looks pretty dull."

"Well, it's not Nicholas Sparks."

She feigned a smile and rolled over.

After reading for another hour, he turned off the light and tried to drift off. But he slept fitfully. Nightmarish visions of Janice Wilson's full red lips and seductive green eyes bulging in death interrupted his sleep.

As he rolled over and faced the digital clock, reading the numbers 3:27, he remembered a line from Hamlet's famous soliloquy—

"For in that sleep of death what dreams may come?"

Part III: The Two Gentlemen from Verona

CHAPTER 11

Present fears are less than horrible imaginings.
From *Macbeth*

Friday morning, Joe awoke a little after 7:00 to the smell of French toast. He found the children already eating when he stumbled into the kitchen, Katie at the table under the window and Brian in his highchair squeezing a soggy piece of syrup-covered toast.

"Good morning, daddy," Katie said. "Are you coming to the pool with us today?"

"No, honey," he said, pouring himself a cup of coffee. "I'm taking a colleague to a big fancy college today."

"You're taking a Collie to college?" asked Katie.

He chuckled and sat down next to his daughter "Not a Collie. A col-league."

"What's a call-league?"

Joe stirred creamer into his coffee. "A person you work with," Joe explained. "Sort of a professional friend."

Sara put a plate of French toast in front of Joe.

"A 'professional friend'?" she asked, cocking one eyebrow. "Down on Bourbon Street, they have another name for that type of friend, and it's not colleague. It's call girl."

"Sara!" laughed Joe. "Show some respect. I'm taking Dr. Jonathan Smythe, Professor Emeritus, to U. C. Berkeley today."

"I know, I know," she laughed, sliding pieces of toast onto her own plate.

Katie asked, "What's a call girl?"

Joe and Sara looked at each other, Sara almost spitting out her first bite of toast.

Before Joe could ring the doorbell, Smitty opened the door and hurried Joe inside.

"I expected you an hour ago."

"Sorry," Joe said. "I didn't sleep well last night."

"I want to show you something."

Smitty led Joe over to his large worktable and pointed to an opened book.

"What's this?"

"This, my fine lad, is a book by Nathan Drake. *Shakespeare and His Times*. I'd forgotten I had it!"

Joe bent down and looked at the page. It was filled with six scrawled signatures. Joe had seen the last one—the one from the Will—many years before in Jack Claire's class.

The others were almost unrecognizable.

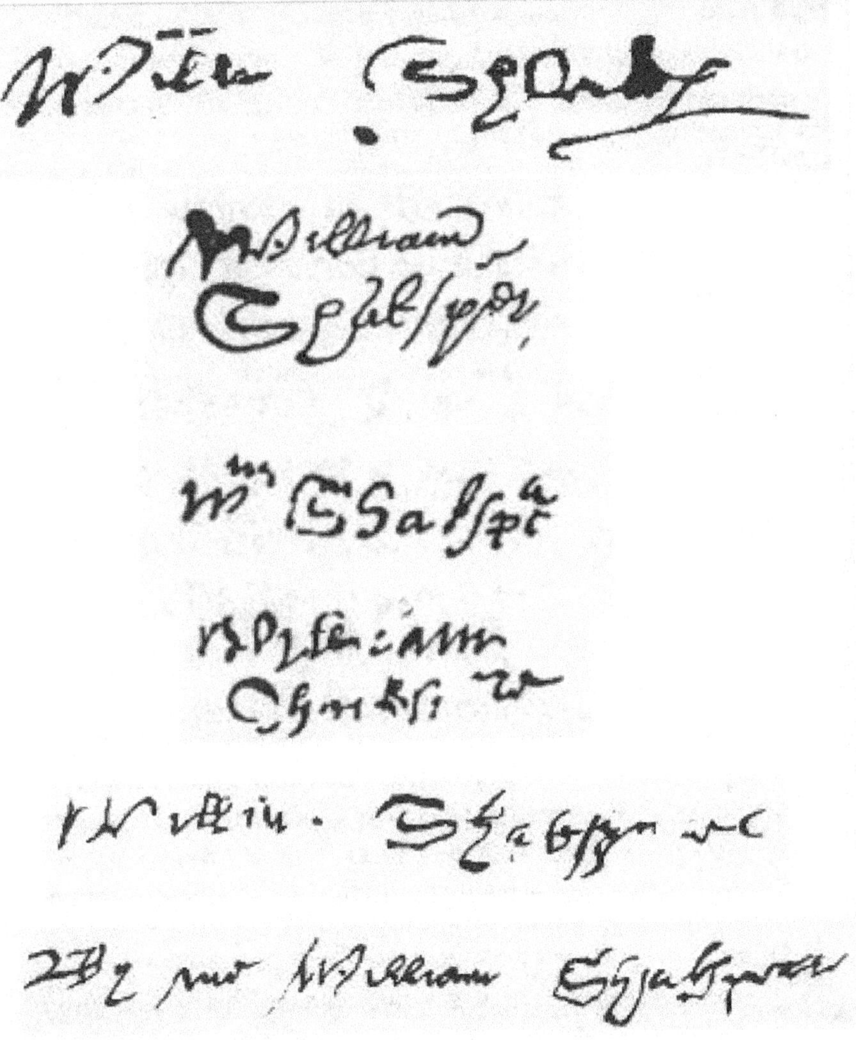

"The clearest one is obviously from Shakespeare's Last Will and Testament."

"These are the only examples of Shakespeare's handwriting. All are from legal documents William Shakespeare was required to sign."

"But they look like, I don't know, like they were made by someone who couldn't—"

"Who couldn't even sign his own name?"

"Yeah," agreed Joe. "As though they were made by a child or someone with cerebral palsy, maybe."

"Yes, exactly. Someone unaccustomed to writing."

Joe looked at Smitty. "What's it mean?"

"It means that whoever signed these legal documents had trouble writing anything by hand. Yet I recall reading a note written by Ben Jonson and found after his death that praised Shakespeare's penmanship. How the players admired it."

"How'd he do it then? Write volumes and volumes of plays? He certainly didn't have a typewriter."

"Clearly not," agreed Smitty. "But he was compelled to sign these legal documents in front of witnesses, so he couldn't have someone else do it for him."

"Someone else?"

"Joe, it's clear. Shakespeare didn't write these manuscripts." Smitty waved his hand over the papers spread out across the table. "He couldn't even sign his own name clearly."

"If he didn't write these plays, then who did? Marlowe?"

Smitty smiled. "No, not Marlowe. I'm sure of that. But some people think Christopher Marlowe faked his death and started writing under the penname William Shake-speare. But if you compare Marlowe's style to Shakespeare's, you find too many differences."

"If not Marlowe, who?"

"At one time I was sure it had to be Francis Bacon. We can be fairly certain from our earlier examination of the handwriting that Bacon wrote the long poems. But not the plays. They were written by someone else."

Joe looked at the book again, and then bent down and looked at the pages of manuscripts next to the book. The halting handwriting in the book was clearly not the elegant, flowing penmanship on the pages and pages in front of him.

Joe and Smitty gathered the sample sheaf of papers they'd selected earlier and placed them carefully inside a sturdy, new-looking leather briefcase Joe had brought.

"A gift from my father-in-law when I finished my Master's," he explained. "I never use it."

"Why not?" asked Smitty. He seemed to admire the bright gold silk interior, running his fingers over the smooth material of the lining. Yellow light reflected up, highlighting his features.

Joe shrugged. "I don't know. Too pretentious. Looks like something a stock broker would carry."

As he drove to Berkeley, Joe sipped his coffee while Smitty dozed. When they started the climb up the hill out of the valley heading for Livermore, Smitty sat up and looked around. The hillside west of Tracy was cluttered with dozens of giant modern windmills used to generate electricity.

"These God-awful windmills." he said.

"Like something out of H. G. Wells' *War of the Worlds*," said Joe.

"Terribly ugly. I know it's clean energy, but aesthetically dreadful."

"Tell me, Smitty. You said you once believed Francis Bacon had written plays. Why is that?"

Smitty rubbed his eyes and looked at the road ahead of them.

"Many people have wondered how someone with Shakespeare's limited education could have known about so many different subjects."

Joe glanced at Smitty as they ascended the hill.

"Didn't he get what we'd call a classical education?"

"Yes and no," said Smitty. "He probably had the best education available in Stratford at the time. There's no record he attended the grammar school there, but assuming he did, he would have learned grammar, rhetoric, logic, Latin. Have you seen the schoolhouse in Stratford? It's still standing."

"I've never been to England."

"Oh, lad. You must visit England. You must see Stratford-upon-Avon."

"You've been there, I take it?"

"Oh, yes. Twice. Anyway, Shakespeare did not go to university, nor did he ever travel outside England."

Joe looked over at the other man in disbelief. "He never went to Europe?"

Smitty shook his head. "You're surprised?"

"I've read enough of his plays to know they include detailed descriptions of European cities. Verona, Venice. It's hard to believe he hadn't visited those cities himself and wasn't writing from first-hand knowledge."

Smitty nodded. "Yes, that's a point his defenders have trouble with. Clearly, one doesn't have to walk the streets of a town to write accurate descriptions of it, especially if one were able to pick the brains of people who'd been there. But there are some specifics that give even his staunchest supporters pause."

"Like what?"

"Well, in one play, Shakespeare describes a flooded plain in Spain that had to be crossed by boat. Modern scholars who visited the location found it dry and concluded that this was proof Shakespeare had gotten his facts wrong, reinforcing their assumption that his knowledge was second hand."

"Okay," said Joe, checking traffic as he merged into another lane.

"The problem is, there was a year in the late 1500s when the rain in Spain fell mainly on the plain, and travelers could cross only by boat. Whoever knew that had to have first-hand experience."

Joe thought about it. "I suppose."

"Before now, while I had my suspicions, I accepted the idea that Shakespeare was simply a genius. Maybe in talking to other people who had traveled abroad and by reading accounts of other people's travels, Shakespeare *was* able to acquire enough knowledge to make the settings of his plays come alive. London was a thriving, international city filled with travelers from all over the world."

Joe nodded.

"But Shakespeare also lacked knowledge of the inner workings of Queen Elizabeth's court, he lacked knowledge of hawking, of military affairs."

"Hawking?" asked Joe. "Is that the same thing as falconry?"

"Yes, more or less."

"But did you have to be a nobleman to know about falconry? I thought commoners took part in the sport as well."

"Oh, that's true, but it was discouraged by the nobility. Anyway, there's no evidence that Will Shakespeare ever participated in hawking. Unless it's something he did during the so-called lost years."

"But aren't the plays themselves evidence that Shakespeare had some knowledge of falconry?"

"Yes, but there are other problems with Shakespeare's credentials. He had to read Latin and Greek fluently, for example, since so many of the source works were available only in those languages. But he had 'little Latin and less Greek,' and having left school by fifteen or so, Shakespeare could not have been well educated in ancient Greek and Roman history or their mythologies, yet his plays are rife with allusions to classical works."

"I have to confess something," said Joe.

Smitty perked up, grinning. "Oh, really? Sounds intriguing."

"On the way home yesterday, I bought a book on Shakespeare, *Will in the World* by Stephen Greenblatt. Have you heard of it?"

Smitty smiled. "Oh, yes. Read it when it first came out in 2004. What of it, lad?"

Joe glanced over at Smitty. The small car struggled to reach the summit.

"Well, Greenblatt's a pretty impressive scholar, Smitty. A professor at Harvard, editor of *The Norton Shakespeare*."

"True enough, lad. All true."

"Do you remember the subtitle of his book?"

"I do. *How Shakespeare Became Shakespeare*. So what?"

The car had reached the summit and Joe pulled out of the slow lane to pass a truck. Ahead, clear blue sky rose above rolling hills of dry golden grass.

"So what?" repeated Joe. He nodded his head toward the back seat. "It's back there. Can you reach it?"

Smitty turned and saw the book laying face down on the seat. He grabbed it and held it up. The greenish gold cover showed an engraving of Shakespeare by E. Scriven, a rendering of the Chandos portrait.

"I read the first hundred pages last night. He makes a pretty strong case for Shakespeare as the writer of the works that bear his name."

Smitty opened the book. "I beg to disagree, young Joseph. He *presumes* Shakespeare is the author and then supports that presumption with guess work."

"Guess work?"

Smitty smiled and opened the book to the Preface. "Just listen to Greenblatt's own words: '…there are huge gaps in knowledge that make any biographical study of Shakespeare an exercise in speculation.'"

"Yeah, I read that, too, but…"

Smitty thumbed through the first chapter. "Listen to this about Shakespeare's father: 'John Shakespeare himself seems to have had at most only partial literacy.' And this about his mother: 'Judging from the mark she made on legal documents, Mary Shakespeare, the mother of England's greatest writer, also could not write her name…' Couldn't write her name, Joe! The greatest writer of all time grew up in a house of illiterates? Damn unlikely."

Joe was surprised by the contempt in Smitty's voice.

He turned the page. "Oh, listen to this," said Smitty. "This is typical of Greenblatt's so-called evidence: 'Though the Stratford school records from the time do not survive, Will almost certainly attended this school, fulfilling his parents' desire that he learn Latin.' Don't you see, Joe?"

"I guess so."

"Greenblatt falls into the same fallacy as other Shakespeare biographers."

"What do you mean?"

"Begging the question. He assumes Shakespeare is the author and then works backward from that assumption. He searches for any evidence that supports his supposition instead of looking at the evidence objectively to see where it leads."

Joe looked forward. The hazy air of the valley was behind them now, cleared by the breezes that came in from the Pacific Ocean, just over another set of rolling hills. Sprawling below them was the city of Livermore, with two of the most important scientific laboratories in California, Lawrence Livermore and Sandia. The air of scientific thinking infiltrated the car.

"I see what you mean, Smitty. It's like bad police work."

"How so?"

"The police arrest someone for a crime. Believing he's guilty, they build the evidence to make it fit their suspect instead of looking at it objectively."

Smitty nodded. "You've had a little experience along those lines, haven't you?"

Joe glanced over again at the older man, whose eyes showed sympathy.

"I have."

The traffic thickened as Joe drove through Livermore. A BART train was pulling into the station. They drove on in silence as Smitty thumbed through the Harvard scholar's book.

"Listen to this," said Smitty in a softer voice. "'Dogged archival labor over many generations has turned up contemporary allusions to him, along with a reasonable number of the playwright's property transactions...but no immediately obvious clues to unravel the great mystery of such immense creative power.'"

"A great mystery, all right," added Joe.

"It's as if Greenblatt is hedging his bet, giving himself an out in case someone comes along later and proves that Mr. Shakespeare was a fraud."

"Is that what we're doing, Smitty? Proving Shakespeare was a fraud?"

"Perhaps," the older man answered quietly.

Joe looked at Smitty, whose expression had grown solemn. "You're worried?"

"It's just that, well, I had put this entire matter out of my mind years ago. It was a frustrating debate and there seemed no real answer, so I focused on the works themselves. What difference did it make who wrote them? But now..."

"But now what?"

"Now these documents raise all of the old questions again. And I, for one, want to know the truth. If a terrible hoax has been perpetrated..."

"You sound a little sad, Smitty."

He nodded. "It's a sad duty to take down a titan, but it's also thrilling. 'The truth shall out.' We must search for the truth." Smitty's eyes brightened again as he turned and smiled at Joe. "Wait until you meet Sylvia. You'll love her."

Traffic on the 580 thickened in Dublin, and by the time they reached Interstate 880, they were forced to crawl until they were north of Oakland. A trip that should have taken one hour took almost two. Joe concentrated on his driving while Smitty dozed again, until they exited on University Avenue, where Jonathan Smythe woke up, as if by some instinct. He smiled as he gazed upon the unmistakable landmark of the Berkeley campus, the Renaissance-style clock tower that rose above the city, shimmering in the afternoon heat.

CHAPTER 12

He that is robb'd, not wanting what is stolen,
Let him not know't, and he's not robbed at all.
From *Othello*

Two days earlier on Wednesday morning, after watching the young instructor leave, Benedict observed the house for several hours. He saw Conrad's wife push a stroller down the sidewalk with a little girl holding on. Their clothing and beach towels suggested they were headed to a nearby pool. He'd have a few hours.

As thorough as ever, Benedict first searched the one-car garage behind the house, but it held a lawn mower and a few garden tools. Three boxes in the rafters held Christmas decorations.

The Conrad home was too accessible. The woman had left a window open in the small master bedroom. If he had to, he could slit the screen of one of the windows and climb in. The back door was easy to pick, though, and he preferred not to dirty himself or leave a shoe smudge on the exterior wall.

The home itself was small, with only two bedrooms. He searched it in less than an hour, including a brief look into the small attic. But he found nothing except a lead—the location of Mr. Conrad's work. Pay stubs in the top drawer of the desk in the master bedroom told Benedict that Joseph Lawrence Conrad worked at Central Lutheran University.

Wednesday evening after dinner, Benedict found the University's website and searched for information about Joseph Conrad, learning the campus layout and the location of Joe's office. Benedict had no trouble searching the building late Wednesday night and early Thursday morning. Campus security was light. No cameras. A security car drove around the outside of the campus every hour. Very predictable.

Joseph L. Conrad's office was in the English Department on the third floor. He checked other offices first, before Conrad's. An old strategy. Check the perimeter first. If he got caught, he wouldn't give away the real target. He'd be arrested on a simple B and E charge, and in a few hours, he'd be free to return.

By three a.m., he was ready to search Conrad's office.

He started with the desk. A few reference books leaning against a paper tray that held student papers, but nothing more. The drawers contained the usual papers teachers thought were important. Benedict fingered through them, but the valuable documents weren't there.

The file cabinet was next. He went through each drawer. Nothing. Usually, he could find what he was commissioned to find in a few hours or a few days. In and out, fast and clean. That's how he liked it. But this job had grown unpredictable. And messy. Killing the young woman had been satisfying. He'd considered raping her—she had plenty of condoms—but something about her had turned him off.

And the old bastard on the tower. *Jesus, he'd been difficult.*

After the file cabinet, Benedict searched the bookshelves. Standing on the chair, he used his penlight to search behind the stacks of books, pulling them away from the wall five and ten at a time. Nothing.

Everything was so damn dusty. Even in the dim light from the desk lamp and from the penlight in his mouth, Benedict saw the marks in the dust that indicated someone had searched the shelves. He used a cotton rag to wipe the shelves down—he'd learned long ago to bring one to wipe away handprints and fingerprints. Even though he wore gloves, the prints left behind would show the police the size of the burglar's hands, and from that information they could estimate his height.

Benedict was almost ready to move on when he noticed a photograph on Conrad's desk. Behind color photos of the young teacher's wife and children stood a black and white photo of Dr. Claire with his right arm around Joseph Conrad. Conrad was dressed in a cap and gown, a somewhat embarrassed expression frozen on his young face and Dr. Claire was smiling broadly, beaming with pride, it seemed to Benedict. It was a father's look of pride for a son.

He held that photograph under the light and studied that expression. Claire obviously had a special feeling for this young teacher. He'd have to search the house again. Maybe he'd missed a key or a bill to a storage locker.

He drove back to Davis, stopped at a cafe near the hotel, ate Eggs Benedict, smiling at his private joke, and made it back to his room by 7:30, hanging a Do Not Disturb sign on his door.

The rest of Thursday had been spent sleeping late, working out in the gym, and checking email. Another potential client had contacted him with an intriguing offer that involved travelling to Buena Aires to recover money embezzled from an accounting firm. Benedict researched timelines and expenses before sending the client an estimate.

Friday morning, he worked out again, showered, dressed and went downstairs to Café Bernardo for an early lunch. He ordered a small salad and ate outside, watching the breeze blow the branches of the trees across the street, watching the young people, college students, talking at the tables around him. Wearing a short-sleeved, light green dress shirt and black slacks, he hoped he gave the impression of a businessman from out of town, dressed casually for a few Friday meetings.

And in fact he *was* a businessman, of sorts. That's how he advertised himself, a "private security consultant specializing in difficult cases requiring great discretion. Satisfaction and confidentiality guaranteed." It didn't take much intelligence to read between the lines. The ad in *Soldier of Fortune* magazine had brought him a steady stream of clients. At this rate, he could retire in ten years, five years ahead of the schedule he'd imposed on himself after leaving the Army.

By 12:45, he was parked on Tenth Street, watching Conrad's house. He'd had time to smoke one cigarette when the front door at 333 opened and the woman with her two children left. She pulled the door closed firmly and jerked at the handle to make sure it was locked. Benedict smiled, watching her. It was amusing to witness civilians who trusted their simple locks.

The slender young woman turned around and smiled at her

daughter, and the three walked briskly down the sidewalk and turned onto B Street. He watched the woman walk, her hips moving nicely as she took each step in her high-heeled sandals. She wore a bright red flowered sundress over her bikini—he could see the outline of her suit through the tight-fitting material of the dress. *She'd be nice*, Benedict thought.

He hadn't had a woman in three weeks. After the mishap with the old lady's car in Baton Rouge, he'd taken a day to visit the French Quarter in New Orleans, surprised by how relatively empty it still was after Hurricane Katrina. He visited a favorite haunt, a massage parlour, where a Chinese girl with hair down to her ass had pleased him. Twice. It brought a grin to his thin lips as he watched the young instructor's wife push her stroller down the street and turn the corner.

That's when Benedict decided he would have this teacher's wife.

He'd take her at some point, maybe after the job was over, a little revenge for the delays they were causing him. He imagined finding her alone, maybe when she went shopping. She was petite, but he knew she'd fight. He could visualize forcing her legs apart, thrusting himself inside her, the surprised expression on her face. He'd seen it before.

Yes, he would wait until after the job, after he was off the payroll. It would be his private perk, his bonus for a job well done.

Benedict climbed out of his car and walked confidently across the street toward the Conrad home. When he reached the driveway, he glanced around. No one was looking. No curtains pushed open across the street. No one walking by. He turned down the gravel driveway to the back door again, and again it opened as easily as he had before.

This time, he searched more thoroughly, looking for a key to a safety deposit box or a storage locker, looking through receipts and bills and check books for payments to a storage facility or a bank for a deposit box rental. Nothing.

He searched the bedroom again, lingering in the drawers of the woman's dresser, touching bras and panties. He checked her bra size, 34 D. *Yum*. He found a newer pair of panties with pink flowers, clean, no stains. He folded the panties neatly and pushed them into the pocket of his slacks, feeling his erection. Then he went back to work. He searched everything carefully, reading notes and papers to find some clue. He was closer—he knew it.

In the kitchen again, he scanned the yellow walls and opened cabinets. Loose photographs lay carelessly in a drawer. One seemed to be of Conrad, whose face Benedict vaguely recalled from the funeral in Baton Rouge. Yes, Conrad had spoken at the service. Benedict slipped the photograph inside his pocket, confident the family wouldn't miss it.

Inside one cabinet door next to the telephone hung a calendar. He noted the date when the flights to and from Baton Rouge were marked, the week before. He looked at the square box for today's date. The words, **Joe-Berkeley** , were written in blue ink, and for a second, Benedict wondered if this was the right house. Was this Joe Berkeley's house? Then he realized his blunder and chuckled at himself.

That's when the telephone rang.

It startled him—the phone hung on the wall beside his ear. Benedict closed the cupboard door and walked back into the master bedroom. A small desk sat under the window, and on the desk sat another telephone with a built-in answering machine. He stood over the machine. After the third ring, a man's deep voice spoke to potential callers, saying, "*We're having too much fun to answer the phone right now, so please leave a message after the beep.*"

There was a beep, and then the same deep voice spoke.

"*Hi, honey. It's me. We finally made it to Sylvia's office, despite the traffic. As soon as we reached Oakland, it was like trying to leave Tiger Stadium after a football game. Bumper to bumper. You should see this campus. It's like LSU on a hillside. It's huge. Anyway, we're all starving, so Sylvia's taking us to an Indian restaurant on Telegraph Avenue. Smitty says it's his favorite spot. Hey, if it's good, maybe we can come sometime. Anyway, I don't think we'll leave here until four of five, so after I drop Smitty off, it'll probably be seven-thirty or eight before I get home. I'll call you later.*"

Benedict grinned. Conrad was up to something. Now he knew the names of the people who were helping him. Someone at Berkeley named Sylvia. Maybe the Shakespeare papers were with her. And someone named Smitty. He could check the telephone book for Smiths, though he knew there'd be a hundred. If he went back to the CLU campus, there would be something to narrow his search.

Benedict turned and saw himself in the vanity mirror hanging above the woman's dresser. The woman's husband wouldn't be home for hours. She would be alone with just the two young children. *Should I wait? Treat myself?*

No. The children would make it messy. *Don't be careless. That's what happened in Baton Rouge.*

He left through the back door, locking it, and walked to his car. In ten minutes he was driving west on Interstate 80 toward the coastal hills. The grasses of California had turned to the color of gold.

CHAPTER 13

From women's eyes this doctrine I derive:
They sparkle still the right Promethean fire;
They are the books, the arts, the academes,
That show, contain, and nourish all the world.
From *Love's Labour's Lost*

After calling home, Joe stepped back inside Dr. Sylvia Williamson's large office. He had left the briefcase on the large work table in the middle of the room, and Smitty and Sylvia were removing one page at a time, holding each document up to the light, examining each paper as if they were surgeons examining X-rays before a major surgery.

Sylvia turned to look at Joe, her beautiful brown eyes bright with light and excitement.

"These are incredible, Joe," she said.

Joe hadn't known what to expect, but Dr. Williamson's beauty was stunning. She stood six feet tall, a well-proportioned woman with deep brown shining skin, smooth as warm honey. She wore a snug burnt orange and yellow-print dress, something that looked like it had come from Africa. Hanging from her neck was a piece of gold jewelry that looked as if it had come from Cleopatra's private collection, a wide serpentine necklace from which hung an S-shaped piece of gold. A matching bracelet dangled from her right arm.

Sylvia's raven-black hair was pulled tightly up and back, and it rested on top of her head almost like a crown. Her eyes were startling. Large areas of white framed large brown pupils. The Chestnut shape of her eyes seemed almost Asian and their keen intelligence and intensity struck Joe. He guessed she was in her thirties or forties, but she could have been sixty or sixteen.

He stepped toward the table to see what had impressed the two scholars so much. "This is the most remarkable find," she gushed. She reached over and held his forearm for a few seconds.

Joe blushed. He looked at the paper Sylvia was holding.

"I'll need to send one sheet of paper to the chem. Lab on campus," Sylvia said. "They've worked with me before, so they know how to test and date the inks and paper. Unfortunately, the process will ruin some of the page, so you need to make the choice, Joe."

He looked from Sylvia to Smitty and back to the page Sylvia held in her hand.

"What about the page you're holding? Isn't it from *Cymbaline*?"

"Yes," answered Sylvia. "This is the one I would suggest. It's a rewrite of the previous page."

"The earlier page will be of more interest to scholars, Joe. They'll want to see what revisions Shakespeare made."

Joe felt out of his depth. "Will it be completely destroyed?"

"No, not completely."

"Test it, then."

"Did you two notice these markings?" Sylvia asked, smiling at Joe.

Smitty stepped around the edge of the table. "What markings?"

With Smitty on her left and Joe blushing on her right, she held the page with her left hand and pointed to a mark in the margin with the long pink fingernail on the index finger of her right hand.

"It looks like a hand," Joe said.

"Yes, a hand with a pointing finger, pointing to something in the text," added Smitty.

"Notice the dots at the end of the wrist," Sylvia said. "There are five dots spaced evenly apart."

"Yes," said Smitty. "I noticed a few markings like that on many of the other pages, too. Rather odd, isn't it?"

"Not entirely," said Sylvia. "We call it a fist. We have the same thing on our word processing programs, Smitty. You know, those wingdings people use to point out something."

"Oh, yes, yes. Of course."

"Shouldn't it be called a pointing fist," added Joe, trying to sound witty.

"Probably," chuckled Sylvia. "What's interesting is the addition of a bit of laced sleeve and the five dots at the end of the wrist."

Smittly leaned closer. "Hard to tell."

Sylvia picked up a magnifying glass from the table and held it over the page. The two men bent forward to look through the glass. The "fist" did seem to have something like a lacey sleeve and five little dots where the wrist ended.

: ☞

Joe glanced at Smitty—their faces inches apart—and then Joe glanced backward, realizing his head was inches from Sylvia's right breast. He lurched back quickly, his face burning red.

"Yes, um, it's odd," he said. "Not really a fist."

"More like the back of a left hand with the index finger and the thumb extended," added Smitty, still looking through the magnifying glass.

Sylvia's perfume filled Joe's nostrils. She placed the page in a large manila envelope and Joe watched as she licked the flap and sealed it.

"Anyone else need some water?" Joe asked. "I could use something cold to drink."

Sylvia smiled. "We should go to lunch."

Smitty straightened up again. "Yes, definitely. I need to eat, I'm starving."

"I'm feeling a little light headed myself," admitted Joe.

"Let's eat," she said. "Bring that." She put her finger on the leather-bound cover of the *First Folio.*

Joe removed the rest of the loose papers from the briefcase and put the book inside. He closed the case and picked it up carefully so the book wouldn't be damaged.

"The rest of the papers will be safe, won't they?" he asked.

"I'm sure they will," Sylvia answered.

They stepped into the hall and waited as Sylvia locked the door to her office. Then she led them through the Berkeley campus gate and down busy Telegraph Avenue, through throngs of people. To Joe, half the people, dressed in tie-died Tee shirts, bell-bottomed blue jeans, wearing beads and peace symbols and sandals, seemed to have stepped out of a time machine, transported from the 1960s. From various doorways drifted incense, cigarette and marijuana smoke. Music from every decade and every region of the world throbbed from other doorways, but east-Indian and Reggae seemed to dominate. People playing guitars and flutes and pipes stood on street corners inviting donations.

The jostling, noisy crowds on Telegraph Avenue reminded Joe of the French Quarter, but the street inspired a different feeling, the tension and excitement of political activism instead of the bawdy partying and drinking and jazz music of Bourbon Street. Carrying the briefcase made Joe feel out of place.

The Indian restaurant was cool and dark, and smelled of curry and lamb. It was 2:00 in the afternoon, so most of the lunch crowd had already left. The low tables were surrounded not by chairs but by stools with pillows of various shapes and colors. Joe followed Sylvia and Smitty to a table in the back corner and sat with his back to the door.

Smitty was already reading the menu, a content grin on his lips, and Sylvia was looking across the table at Joe.

"Tell me again how you came to possess these documents, Joe."

"They were mailed to me," he said, sensing her suspicion. "My good friend, Dr. Claire, sent them to me before his death. Claire was the head of the English Department at LSU."

"Yes, I know his work," said Sylvia. "I read his book years ago, a nice comparison of characters from Southern authors and the way Shakespeare might have influenced them. I should tell you, I'm not a big fan of Southern writers, though."

"Oh?" said Joe. The statement would have been heresy at LSU.

"Too much use of the n-word, for one thing. I'm sure you can appreciate why I'm not fond of that."

Joe nodded. "Of course."

"Especially Faulkner. Every fifth page, there it is. You're just getting caught up in the flow of a story, and it jumps out at you."

"His defenders would probably say he was a product of his times," Joe said, half-heartedly.

"Oh, I know the arguments. Believe me, I know the arguments. Southern authors aren't especially respectful of women, either," Sylvia added.

"Dr. Claire also edited *The Southern Review*, didn't he?"

"Yes," Joe said, grateful Smitty had changed the topic. "Circulation tripled during Jack's reign."

Sylvia shook out her napkin, asking, "Why do you suppose he sent the Shakespeare papers to you, Joe?"

Joe glanced at Smitty, looking for help, but Smitty was scanning the room, looking for a waiter or waitress.

"Honestly, I don't know. I wish he hadn't, really."

"Oh, lad. Don't say that. This is a great adventure. This is potentially the most important thing that's happened in English letters in decades."

"If not centuries," Sylvia added. "You know, I've never been comfortable with the idea that a glover's son, maybe with a grammar school education and without access to a great library, could have written all those works."

Joe chuckled. "But isn't that sort of a, I don't know, a classist way of thinking? I mean, isn't anyone capable of greatness, no matter how poor they were?"

"Oh, of course," Sylvia admitted, "given the right circumstances. But look at it objectively. Whoever wrote the plays of Shakespeare had to have a very comprehensive education in classical literature and philosophy. He had to read Greek and Latin, because so many allusions to works available only in Greek and Latin show up in Shakespeare's plays. Plutarch, Ovid."

"What's the line in the dedication in the *First Folio*?" Smitty asked. "Little Latin and less Greek?"

"Who wrote that?" asked Joe.

"The line is 'small Latin and less Greek'," corrected Sylvia. "Ben Johnson wrote it in his tribute in the *First Folio*."

A waitress finally came and took their orders. Sylvia knew what she wanted and ordered first, and Smitty followed her lead. Joe ordered curried chicken and rice.

"Should we order wine?" asked Sylvia.

"I'll have a glass," chimed Smitty.

"Sure," said Joe. "I'll have a coffee before we head back to Stockton."

Joe excused himself and went to the restroom. After washing his hands, he was tempted to call Sara again, but he knew they would stay at the pool until 4:00 or 5:00. Smitty and Sylvia were sipping their wines when Joe returned.

"Not to mention a thorough grasp of the law," Smitty said.

"The law?" asked Joe. He sipped his wine, a crisp Riesling that slid down nicely.

"Yes, lad. Whoever wrote the plays had a thorough understanding of legal matters and legal jargon. Not the kind of thing a glover's son picks up."

"But Will's father was a bailiff or something in Stratford, wasn't he?" asked Joe. He glanced at Sylvia. "I started reading a book by Stephen Greenblatt."

"*Will in the World*?" asked Sylvia.

Joe nodded as he took another sip of the good wine. The muscles in his neck were beginning to relax.

"Oh," said Sylvia. "Yes, I read it. Not the best scholarship. Much too much conjecture. More like historical fiction, really."

"That's what Smitty said."

"Don't forget hawking?" chimed Smitty.

Joe looked over at him, perplexed. "Hawking?" he asked. Did he mean the physicist, Steven Hawking? Had Smitty had too much wine on an empty stomach?

"Yes," said Smitty. "Several plays make references to hunting with hawks, one of the sports of aristocrats that Will probably didn't know much about. Yet the references display expert knowledge, so again, it makes you wonder. Where did Will from Stratford learn about hawking?"

"Well," Sylvia said, grinning, "the Stratfordians would have us believe he learned everything he knew by doing exactly what we're doing now?"

"Eating at an Indian restaurant?" asked Joe.

"Not in an Indian restaurant," Sylvia replied, "but eating and drinking ale in a tavern, yes."

Smitty grinned. "The argument is that Shakespeare was like a sponge—"

"A genius-sponge," added Sylvia.

"Yes. He simply absorbed knowledge from everyone around him."

"That still doesn't explain a few other areas of expertise," added Sylvia. "Whoever wrote the plays also had expert knowledge of military matters, and not from a foot soldier's perspective. From a general's perspective. I'm not sure there were many generals hanging out with Will at the Inn where he did his drinking."

The waitress interrupted with their plates of food. The steam rising off the hot food made Joe's stomach grumble, and he realized he was even hungrier than he thought. After a few bites, he spoke up.

"Besides military affairs, what else? What other areas of expertise show up in the plays that Mr. Will Shack-spur lacked?" Joe was having trouble getting used to pronouncing the great writer's name the way Sylvia and Smitty were now saying it.

"You've taught Shakespeare, haven't you, Joe?" asked Sylvia.

"Yes, of course."

"Which plays?"

Joe blushed a little, realizing he was no expert.

"I've taught *Hamlet* a few times. I love that one. Best play ever written, I think." He observed Smitty's smile and realized how silly it was for him to say that since it was obvious he hadn't read all the plays ever written. "I've also taught *Macbeth* and *Othello*. And *Juilius Ceasar.*"

"Good," said Sylvia, without a condescending note in her voice. "What do all those plays have in common?"

Joe blushed. It was like going through his oral exams again for his Master's. "They're all tragedies?"

"Yes, of course. They're all tragedies, but what else?"

Joe sipped his wine and closed his eyes to think. He needed fresh coffee to answer exam questions. Suddenly, he could sympathize with his own students when he put them on the spot during class discussions.

"Well, by definition, a tragedy is a fall from height. All of the main characters are noblemen and all of them experience a great fall from grace, as it were."

"Good," gushed Sylvia. "What does that tell us about the author?"

Joe looked at Smitty, who was smiling that annoying Buddha smile again, and then he looked back at Sylvia. He was suddenly reminded of the scene in *Silence of the Lambs* when Dr. Hannibal Lector is coaxing answers out of Clarisse Starling.

"I'm not sure what you're getting at," Joe finally admitted, hoping Sylvia wouldn't eat his liver with a nice Chianti.

"Well, it tells me that the author felt an affinity with high born people, the nobility, and that he knew the inner workings of court life."

"I doubt Mr. Shack-spur rubbed shoulders with Queen Elizabeth and her courtiers. But whoever wrote the plays knew a great deal about how the aristocracy lived and functioned on a daily basis."

Joe blinked as the answers began to sink in.

"So what you're saying is, if we look at the plays as evidence of how the author lived, if we do a biographical interpretation of the literature, then Shakespeare had to have been a member of the aristocracy."

"That's right. Maybe not someone directly in line for the throne, but someone close enough to the Queen to hang around her and be at least on the fringes of court life."

Sylvia nodded, and Joe followed her lead.

"That helps us know where to look for handwriting samples," she added.

Joe smiled, adding, "This is like an episode of *CSI*."

Smitty and Sylvia turned toward him, asking in unison, "What's CSI?"

CHAPTER 14

I am not as I seem to be,
Nor when I smile, I am not glad.
From "Not Attaining to His Desire, He Complaineth"

"You've never heard of *CSI*?" asked Joe.

The two scholars shook their heads.

"It's a TV show. Crime Scene Investigation. There are three versions of the show," added Joe. "It's about the people who collect evidence at crime scenes. You know, all the little details, like hair, blood, DNA, fabrics."

"Like Sherlock Holmes?" asked Smitty.

"Yes," said Joe, grinning. "But much more scientific. It's one of my wife's favorite shows. You feel like you learn about things—biology, chemistry—all sorts of physical evidence."

"Sounds intriguing," said Sylvia. She took a final bite of her meat and rice, and pushed the plate toward the center of the table. "Joe, do you mind if I look at the *Folio* again? All this talk of physical evidence got me thinking."

Joe glanced around the restaurant and then lifted the briefcase onto his lap. After unlatching the lid and opening it, he lifted the heavy, over-sized book out of the case and handed it over to Sylvia.

She didn't open the book. As Smitty looked on, she ran her fingers over the silver oval in the center of the leather book cover. "This symbol intrigues me," she said. "I think I may know where this comes from," she said. Looking at Joe, she asked, "Do you know much about heraldry?"

"Family crests? Coats of arms?"

"Yes, that sort of thing."

"Well, a little," said Joe. "Why?"

Sylvia drained her wineglass. "I think this figure of a wild boar with a crown over it is taken from someone's family crest."

"Yes," said Smitty. "That's what I suspected. As I mentioned to Joe earlier, a leather cover of this quality, with silver reinforcements at the corners and the two silver latches—this had to have been commissioned by a wealthy person. I assume whoever commissioned the cover had that centerpiece of the boar put on to identify the family who owned this copy of the *Folio*."

"Yes," said Sylvia. "But don't you see? In this case, the owner might also be the author? Or at least a member of the author's family."

Smitty tapped his wineglass, which was empty. "But Sylvia, just because this copy of the *First Folio* was with the handwritten manuscripts, that doesn't necessarily prove a link with the author."

"Of course not," Sylvia admitted. "But it's a good place to start." She smiled at Smitty and then at Joe. Then she ran her fingers over the silver boar again. "We have to visit the library before we go back to my office. I want to look at a couple of books I don't have in my office."

"So off to the library?" asked Smitty.

"As soon as I pay the bill," said Sylvia.

"You?" asked Joe. "Shouldn't we go Dutch?"

"I'm not Dutch," Sylvia joked. She pulled a credit card from her purse. "If we have what I think we have, then the University will have made a very wise investment."

Benedict found himself trapped in traffic after the bridge south of Vallejo. Though only thirty miles from Berkeley, he crept along in bumper to bumper traffic for another hour, after driving forty minutes from the Conrad home in Davis. Once he reached University Avenue, it was almost three-thirty. He drove to the U. C. Berkeley campus and, after wasting another thirty minutes, found a parking garage. Using the campus directory, he located the English Department and finally found the office of Dr. Sylvia Williamson, the only "Sylvia" he had seen on the directory of offices inside Wheeler Hall.

He wandered down the dimly lit hallway looking for her office door. When he found it, halfway down the hall, he looked through the screened glass on the side of the door. The lights were off, but sunlight slanted in through the high windows, revealing a large table littered with papers and open books in the center of the room and massive, floor-to-ceiling bookshelves lining the far walls. No one appeared to be inside, so Benedict tried the door handle. Locked, as he suspected.

"May I help you?" A slender young man stood behind Benedict.

"Oh, you startled me." Benedict jerked his hand off the door handle. "I was looking for Dr. Williamson, but she doesn't seem to be in."

The slender young man wearing a tightly fitting black tee-shirt and tight black jeans pointed to a piece of paper hanging under the placard with Dr. Sylvia Williamson's name on it.

"She's not in on Fridays, see?"

Benedict looked more closely at the printed schedule. "Oh, yes. But I was sure she was here earlier. Do you know if she'll be back."

The young man shook his head. "I doubt it. I mean, it's late on a Friday afternoon, man. Who wants to work?"

Benedict turned around and faced the annoying, skinny little twenty-something.

"Well, you're here, aren't you? And I'm here, aren't I? Lots of people work on Friday afternoons, *man*."

The younger man stepped back. "Hey, chill, Rambo. You're gonna blow a gasket if that vein in your forehead pops."

Benedict grinned, showing teeth. He imagined twisting the boy's head around on his long, flimsy neck until he felt the vertebrae crack, the slender body going limp in his hands. "I guess I'll come back later."

"Yeah. Do that, dude. She'll be in at ten o'clock on Monday. Catch her then."

With that, the young man stepped around Benedict and walked quickly down the hall, disappearing around a corner. Benedict turned back to the door, held the handle and peered inside the glass, knowing it would be easy to pick the lock. But the young man might bring a security guard back with him.

No, he would come back later, when he knew the building was empty and he could take his time searching the woman's office. For now, he would simply bide his time by searching the grounds—maybe the people he was looking for were somewhere on campus. Benedict had a photograph of Joseph Conrad he'd taken from the home in Davis. Glancing at it, he strolled casually down the hall to a directory that included photographs of the faculty in the English Department. He examined at the photographs. The smiling face of a beautiful Black woman stared back at him from the wall. Now that he had two clear images of his targets, he would simply walk around the campus, checking the coffee shops, the bookstore, the library… He had a few hours to kill.

Joe found the library on the U. C. Berkeley campus as large and as impressive as the one at LSU. He followed Sylvia and Smitty to the elevators. A few dozen students were studying at various tables on the first floor. None bothered to look up.

On the third floor, Sylvia led her entourage through the stacks to the back of the room where a few tables jutted out from the wall.

"Have a seat here," she instructed. "I want to find a couple of books."

She started to turn, but then touched Joe on the shoulder as he was sitting down. "Let me see the cover of the *Folio* again."

He pulled the briefcase up and placed it on the table. With his thumbs, he unsnapped the latches. The sound of the two snaps echoed. When he lifted the lid, light from the nearby window caught the gold lining of the case and reflected yellow-gold light on the facial features of the three scholars. Smitty smiled.

Sylvia pulled out her phone, focused in on the image of the razor-backed wild boar with the crown over top and a banner underneath and took a picture.

"Good," she said, staring at the screen on her phone. She turned it so Smitty and Joe could see the image. "This will help me find what I'm looking for."

With that, she spun around and walked gracefully away, disappearing between stacks of books. As he watched Sylvia Williamson glide out of sight, her long, toned legs as shapely as any runway model's, Joe noticed Smitty grinning at him, and he blushed.

"You were right, Smitty. Who wouldn't fall in love with *her*?"

Joe turned his gaze toward the leather-bound folio. He was tempted to take the book out of the briefcase and open it on the table so they could inspect it while Sylvia was gone.

Sylvia returned with two average-sized books, but their covers were bright purple. Joe left the briefcase open, but pushed it to the end of the table against the wall. Sylvia placed the two purple books on the table and opened one to a page held by her finger.

"Look at the handwriting in the letter. It matches our manuscripts, I think."

Joe leaned down for a closer look.

"It's much neater than those signatures you showed me, Smitty."

"Whose handwriting is this?" Smitty asked.

"Edward de Vere's." Sylvia turned a few pages. "This is a painting of Edward de Vere, the seventeenth Earl of Oxford. He's been one of the top candidates for years."

Joe looked at the noble portrait. "He looks a little like Shakespeare, doesn't he."

She turned the page. "Now look at this," she said. "Doesn't that look like the boar on the cover of the Folio?"

The ornate coat-of-arms was done mostly in red, gold, and blue. A large blue razor-backed boar stood at the top, its two curved tusks the same shade of gold as the razor-like fur on its back. Joe looked at the banner with the Latin word, "Vero Nihil Verius," above the coat-of-arms.

"What's that say?" asked Joe. "I was an altar boy, but my Latin is pretty limited."

"Vero Nihil Verius," Smitty said. "It means something like, 'no truth but truth, doesn't it, Sylvia?"

"'Nothing truer than truth' might be a more accurate. But look at the image of the boar. Isn't that exactly like the image on the Folio?"

Joe slid the book closer to the briefcase so they could compare the images side by side. "Looks pretty damn close to me, but I'm certainly not an expert."

"Nor am I," said Smitty. "What's this book, anyway." He folded the cover closed to read the title. "Oh," he said, smiling. "It's Looney's book."

Joe read the title out loud. "Shakespeare Identified? Who's J. Thomas Looney?"

"His name was pronounced 'LOAN-knee,' not 'loony'," Sylvia corrected. "He argued that Edward de Vere, the seventeenth earl of Oxford, was the author. That's the Vere coat-of-arms. It's a play on words, don't you see?"

Smitty nodded.

"Wait," said Joe. "I'm not following."

"Vere and vero and verius—they're all variations on the word Truth."

"As in 'verify,' Joe," added Smitty.

As Joe studied the image of the blue boar more carefully, a loud ringing noise made him jump. His cell phone.

"Sorry," he whispered. He fumbled to find the silencing button on the side of his phone and then looked at the screen. "It's Sara. She's probably home from the pool with the kids."

Joe opened the phone and stepped away from Smitty and Sylvia. "Hi, honey. What's up?"

"Hi," Sara's voice said thinly. The reception inside the large building wasn't clear. "I'm not sure, but I think someone's been in our house."

Joe felt his heart skip a beat. "What?"

"We came back from the pool, and something isn't right."

"What do you mean?"

"I can't put my finger on it, Joe, but Katie feels it, too."

"Feels what?"

"Well, first, Katie said it smelled like smoke in the house. Like cigarette smoke."

"Did you leave a window open? Maybe somebody walking by—"

"No. The windows are closed. The air conditioner's on, so—"

"Are any of the windows broken, Sara?"

"No. And the front door was locked when we got home. I let Katie unlock it, and she couldn't get it at first."

"What about the back door. Check the back door."

"Locked. We checked it after Katie said she smelled a smoker in the house."

Joe closed his eyes and tried to think. "Is there any tangible sign of a break-in?"

The silence made Joe think he'd lost the call, but then Sara's voice crackled. "I can't hear you very well. Are you outside or—"

"No, I'm in the library on campus." Joe walked closer to the windows and looked down at the few people strolling on the campus as if nothing was happening. "Did you hear my question?"

"No, nothing tangible. It's just a feeling."

"Maybe you should call the police anyway."

"How soon can you get home?"

He'd have to drive Smitty back to Stockton and then head north. "At least two and a half hours."

"What should I do? I'm worried and Katie's frightened."

Joe shut his eyes again. "Look, call the police and tell them what you've told me. Just ask them to take a look at the house. If someone did break in, if someone's still hanging around, the police will scare him off."

"Okay," Sara said. "But what should I do then? I mean, after the police leave?"

"Call your sister. Go stay at her place until I get back."

"That's what I was thinking."

Joe stared out the window, watching the people walk along the sidewalks and stretch out on the lawns. A couple was playing Frisbee.

"I'll get Smitty right now and we'll head back to Stockton. Call me when you and the kids are headed toward your sister's place, okay?"

"I will." Her voice was breaking. "I hate this, Joe. I hate it."

"I know, I know, but it's probably nothing."

He waited.

"No, it's probably something and you know it. That's why you're down there--you're looking for answers."

All he could think to say was, "See you soon. I love you."

"I love you, too, Joe, but…"

"But what?"

"You know what. I can't go through this again. Not again."

"Stay at your sister's place until I get there."

Silence.

"Call me. Sara?"

The phone was dead. He walked over to Smitty and Sylvia.

"We've got to head back, Smitty," Joe told them. "Sara thinks someone was in our house. She thinks someone broke in while she was gone."

Smitty looked at Sylvia and she looked at Joe.

"Well, of course, you've got to go," Sylvia said.

"I'm sorry," said Joe. "She's pretty worried. It's probably nothing, but…"

"With everything that's happened, we'd better play it safe," agreed Smitty.

Joe spun around and started to walk away from the table.

"Joe," said Sylvia. "Don't leave this." She pointed to the briefcase, open on the table. The gold lining reminded Joe of the silk lining inside Jack's coffin. He reached across the table and closed the lid, locking the latches.

"Maybe I should leave this with you, Sylvia. If they're onto me, then at least these pages might be safer with you."

Sylvia looked at Smitty, searching his eyes for the answer.

"Yes," Smitty said. "Joe's right."

Sylvia reached out and touched Smitty's arm. "What about your place, Smitty? Could they have traced Joe to you somehow?"

Smitty and Joe looked at each other.

"I don't know," Smitty said. "It's possible."

"I don't see how," Joe said. "Unless they tapped my phone at the office or followed me to your house."

Joe handed his cell phone to Smitty. "Do you want to warn Alicia?"

Smitty looked at the phone, his face distorting with concern. "No. I don't see how they could have traced you to me, but if they did, they'll simply take the papers and go, won't they?"

Joe pushed the phone into Smitty's hand. "They killed Jack and Maggie, Jonathan. I think they might have killed a young woman named Janice Wilson, too."

Smitty took the phone and started dialing. "What should I tell her?"

"Tell her to get the hell out of the house," Joe said. "Can she go somewhere? Stay with someone?"

Smitty held the phone to his ear, listening to the rings. "Yes, she can go next door. What about the papers, though? Should I ask her to take them with her?"

Joe and Sylvia yelled, "NO!"

"Her life is more important than these damn papers," Sylvia said.

"I agree," added Joe. "We'll worry about the papers later."

"She's not answering," Smitty said.

"Let it ring," said Joe.

"Don't you have an answering machine, Smitty?" Sylvia asked.

"Yes, we do, but it's not working, I guess."

Joe looked at Sylvia, whose worried expression couldn't be ignored.

"You two need to get back to Stockton as fast as possible," she said.

"Will you take the briefcase?" Joe asked, handing it out to her.

Sylvia started to reach for it, but then drew her hand back.

"No, I don't think I should."

Joe weighed his options, and then grabbed the case and spun around, walking toward the elevator with Smitty and Sylvia following. He pushed the down arrow and its doors opened just after the others reached it. The elevator ride seemed to take forever. All three of them stared down at the briefcase until the elevator stopped and the doors opened.

Joe stepped aside to allow Sylvia to leave first, but as she crossed the threshold, a large figure grabbed her and tugged her out as she screamed. Joe reached out to pull her back inside. She stumbled, and screamed again as the man held her by both wrists, pulling her out of the elevator and out of view.

Her scream echoed in the library as she disappeared.

CHAPTER 15

Shrill trumpets' sound, sharp swords and lances
Strong,
War, blood, and death were matter of her song.
From "An Heroical Poem"

Joe shot a quick look at Smitty, whose face turned white with fear. Then, as the doors started to close, Joe lurched out of the elevator in time to see Sylvia being pulled between stacks of books. With Smitty on his heels, Joe raced around the corner. Sylvia's hand clutched her heart as she turned back toward Joe and Smitty, her mouth twisted in… what? Pain? Fear?

No. Laughter.

She was unable to catch her breath. Her abductor, a tall, slender young man in black clothes, was grinning. And Sylvia was about to burst into laughter, but she threw her hand up over her mouth to keep from shrieking.

"Oh, my gawd! Jason, you scared me to death!"

The good-looking young man struggled to keep himself from laughing.

"I'm sorry," he said, chuckling, "but I've been looking for you for half an hour."

Joe's heart was racing, and when he looked back, he saw Smitty slumped against the bookrack, trying to catch his breath.

"Are you all right?" Joe asked.

Jonathan tried to nod, but he closed his eyes and seemed to stagger back.

"Oh, Jonathan, I'm so sorry," Sylvia said. "Are you okay?"

"I think so," he managed. "I thought…well, you know what I thought."

Sylvia tried not to laugh. She glanced back at the slender young man. "Jason, you have got to stop doing things like that. You're gonna give someone a heart attack."

Joe shot Jason a scowl. "Not funny. Not appropriate."

Sylvia reached over and held Smitty's shoulder. "Are you okay?"

He nodded and straightened up. "Once my heart settles back into my chest."

Sylvia gestured toward the young man. "Meet Jason. He's my TA, and he's my number one source of trouble. Jason, this is Jonathan Smythe."

Jason reached in front of Joe and shook Smitty's hand. "Very nice to meet you, sir. Sylvia has said wonderful things about you. Sorry if I startled you."

Stepping closer to Joe in the crowded aisle between the stacks, he turned to face Joe, letting go of Smitty's hand.

"Who's this? And where have you been hiding him, Sylvia?"

"Behave yourself, Jason. He's taken."

"Too bad."

"In fact, Joe's wife just called. They need to head back to Stockton right away."

Jason touched Joe's forearm and said, "Well, if she ever lets you off that short leash, come see me some time."

Joe looked at Sylvia, who was still fighting not to laugh. "We need to leave, Dr. Williamson."

"Jason, please apologize to Mr. Joseph Conrad."

Acting the part of a scolded child, Jason held out his hand and pouted, saying, "I'm terribly sorry, Mr. Conrad, if I scared you." Then Jason looked over at Sylvia. "Did you call him *Joseph* Conrad?"

"That's his name."

Jason withdrew his hand.

"You aren't related to *the* Joseph Conrad, are you?"

Joe shot the slender man a cold look. "Not at all. Not even a fan."

"Well, my god. Who is anymore?"

"This isn't the time, Jason," Sylvia said, stepping between the two of them.

"But what better place? Surrounded by all these musty old books."

"Jason does his research on the Net," Sylvia explained. "He hardly ever touches an actual book."

"Too bad," said Smitty. "Sometimes one simply has to handle the page on which the ink is printed to learn the truth of the matter."

Jason tried to smile at the older professor but produced a look of sympathy, as if Smitty's words were the musings of a senile old fool.

The four walked briskly through the wide foyer of the library and pushed out through the front doors into a breezy summer day. Salty air blew in off the Bay as Joe and Jonathan rushed to Joe's car.

"Don't fret, lad," Smitty said as they drove back over the hills east of Livermore. "I'm sure your family's safe."

"This is the second time I've put Sara in danger."

"Are you sure she is in danger?"

"She thinks she is. I don't know. I'll check it out when I get home."

Joe glanced at the enormous surreal blades of the tall metal windmills as they rotated slowly above the dry, golden grass of the hillside. Seeing the blades slice through the air forced an image of a knife blade cutting through Sara's tanned flesh. Joe shook the unpleasant vision from his mind and concentrated on driving.

Back in Stockton, he walked Smitty to the front door and checked inside before bidding the older man farewell. The documents were still piled in neat stacks on the dining room table. Smitty walked down the hallway and Joe heard hushed voices from one of the bedrooms. Then Smitty reappeared.

"Alicia was taking a nap. She'd unplugged the phone in our bedroom and didn't hear it ringing out here."

"Is she okay?"

"Yes, yes. Just resting. At our age, we need more rest. Don't sleep well through the night, so we have to grab a nap during the day."

"Sounds like my two-year-old, Brian."

Smitty patted Joe on the shoulder and walked him out the front door. From the porch, he watched Joe jog back to the car.

"Call me later tonight, lad. Let me know you're okay."

Joe watched as Smitty opened the front door and stepped inside. As soon as the old man disappeared, Joe peeled out and raced through the neighborhood streets back to Interstate 5.

After thirty-five minutes of speeding north, hitting 90 miles per hour when it seemed safe, Joe shot by the enormous silver water tower, glancing at the sign that read, "Welcome to Sacramento City of Trees." He flipped open his phone and called Sara's cell.

"Where are you?" he asked.

"We're at Suzie's condo. Where are you?"

"I'm in the Pocket Area. Did you call the cops?"

"Yeah. They declined to investigate."

"What!"

"The operator said, 'The officer in charge says that, unless there's clear evidence of a crime, they must decline to investigate'."

Joe shook his head. "That doesn't make sense."

"They don't really know our history, Joe. They don't know you're a lightning rod for danger."

Unfair, thought Joe.

"Suzie called Bill Morgan, and Morgan called Detective Dunn."

"Good. It's time to get the law involved."

"Suzie convinced them to come to dinner tonight. They're meeting us here at seven."

Joe raced by traffic, cutting between cars and sliding into the slow lane when the fast lane was blocked.

"Sounds good. I'm going home first to check it out."

"Good," said Sara. "You can pick up a few things. We need a change of clothes and Brian needs more diapers."

"Will do," Joe said. "I'd better hang up and drive. See you soon."

"Be careful, Joe."

"Careful's my middle name."

"No it isn't. More like careless."

Joe closed his cell phone and dropped it into the cup holder. Then he put both hands on the steering wheel and drove expertly through traffic north on Interstate 5, merging into traffic on the bridge over the Sacramento River. The lights were on in the baseball stadium, so the River Cats were playing. *It'd be nice to take the kids to a game,* he thought, *when all of this is over.*

In Davis, after turning right off of B Street onto Tenth, Joe swerved too quickly into the narrow driveway, bouncing over the curb. He left the briefcase in the backseat, locked the car and sprinted to the back door, key in hand.

The house looked undisturbed. Joe walked through the rooms, opening drawers, inspecting bookshelves. Nothing looked different to him. He sniffed the air but couldn't detect a strange odor. Had Katie imagined it? Was Sara paranoid? She had every right to be—she'd almost been murdered, after all—but for the last year, their lives had gotten back to normal. Better than normal, with Joe's success at CLU.

He picked out a nice outfit for Katie, found a pair of cream-colored slacks for Sara and a silky, sleeveless red top, which he folded carefully into a little suitcase. He grabbed red panties and a red bra out of Sara's underwear drawer and tossed them into the suitcase, too. Then he retrieved six pull-up diapers from the kids' room, along with a pair of shorts, a clean shirt and pajamas for Brian.

Before closing the back door and walking to the car, he looked around again. The house seemed fine, but still, a feeling nagged at him and he rubbed the back of his neck. After tossing the suitcase into the back seat of the Mustang, next to the briefcase, Joe climbed in the driver's seat and started the engine. It purred to life and Joe pulled the stick shift into reverse. He backed out of the driveway carefully and pushed the stick into first gear, driving west on Tenth Street to the stop sign.

Joe didn't notice the plain sedan parked far down his street. The driver of the dark sedan also started his engine, after seeing Joe back out of the driveway. Once Joe had turned left onto B Street, Benedict put his car in drive and followed.

Part IV: Measure for Measure

CHAPTER 16

How oft the sight of means to do ill deeds
Make deeds ill done!
From *King John*

Not finding Joseph Conrad at the Berkeley campus made Benedict doubt his decision to waste time there. He needed to end this mission soon or take a new job. This one was jinxed. Back at his car, he debated. Drive from here to Stockton and search the offices on the CLU campus again, risk getting caught by the lame campus security wannabes or head back to Davis and sit on the Conrad home.

He knew he could use the wife and daughter as leverage and extract what he needed from Conrad. Benedict had done it before in Haiti. And again in Columbia. First work on the woman in front of husband, slicing here and there, defacing, dabbing blood on the husband's face until the woman was gone. Husbands often let the wives suffer. But afterward, bring in the daughter and show mommy to her in front of the father.

Usually, the child's cries of terror were sufficient. But if not, Benedict would begin to do to the girl what the father had seen done to his wife. Then he would talk. They always did.

Traffic heading east from Berkeley was surprisingly heavy, bumper to bumper until the tollbooth. But after he drove through Fairfield, traffic lightened and he was able to make good time.

Benedict drove through an In-and-Out Burger after taking the

Davis exit and took the hamburger and diet soda with him to eat while he waited on Tenth street near the Conrad home. No lights on and no cars in the driveway made him second guess his decision to come back to Davis. He'd just finished eating when he saw the Mustang take the corner too quickly and too wide, race half a block down and squeal into the driveway.

After wiping his mouth and hands with a napkin, Benedict opened his car door and climbed out, looking around to see if anyone was watching. The street was quiet. Dinner time in suburbia.

He strolled nonchalantly down the street, thinking about how he'd have to modify his plan since Conrad had returned without his wife and daughter. As he strolled down the street, he whistled a remembered tune, making up his mind that he would torture Conrad until one of two things happened. Either Conrad led him to the Shakespeare manuscripts or Conrad died.

Either way, that would be it. If he retrieved the papers, he'd meet with his client in the morning and collect the last payment. If Conrad died, from blood loss or shock, he'd still meet with the client, take the money if possible and then kill the client, or if the client was smart enough not to bring the final payment, he'd use the threat of blackmail to extract at least part of the funds he'd been promised. Either way, it was a win-win.

He'd just about reached the Conrad home when he saw the young man toss a suitcase into the back seat and climb into the car. Did that suitcase hold the papers?

The Mustang backed rapidly out of the driveway. Benedict spun around, not wanting to be seen, and walked briskly to the rental car. He climbed in and started the engine in time to see Conrad turn left onto B Street. *Now where the hell was he going?*

Conrad took the I-5 exit after the Bridge but headed north instead of south. Benedict followed at a safe distance as Conrad took an exit almost immediately and drove east through the congested streets of Sacramento.

The Mustang slipped into a parking spot in front of an apartment building too quickly for Benedict to park behind him, so Benedict drove around the corner as quickly as he could and found a space. By the time he'd walked back, he found the Mustang empty. Conrad was nowhere in sight.

The nearest building looked like condos. Benedict walked up the steps into the foyer of the twelve-story building, a place called the Phoenix Condominiums. He searched the directory, hoping to find a listing for "Conrad." Nothing. None of the other names looked familiar. *Who was Conrad seeing? Someone who might buy the manuscripts?*

Anger welled up inside him like hot lava. His chest tightened and his jaws clenched. He'd come this close to taking those manuscripts and now Conrad was giving them to someone. But who? He'd have to wait for Conrad to come out of the building and grab him. He'd have to force the information out of him. *That* part would be a pleasure, especially now that this amateur—this ridiculous civilian—was somehow managing to foil his every effort!

His only option, it seemed, was to keep his eye on the Mustang and wait.

Benedict walked outside into the warm summer evening air. A light breeze was blowing in from the west, bringing the temperature down from the 90s into the 80s. Traffic on the street was heavy but moving quickly enough that no one would notice him sliding his thin metal burglar's tool into the door. He walked around to the driver's door as if he were the owner and within seconds had slipped the lock and climbed inside.

The car, a semi-restored 1967 Mustang, was empty. Nothing under the front seats, nothing but the usual inside the glove box, nothing on the back seat. He climbed out the passenger's door and tilted the seat forward. Then he lifted the back seat up to check underneath it. Stray pieces of hard candy. A red and white candy still in its clear plastic wrapper tempted him. He grabbed it, pulled at the plastic, unwrapping the candy, and popped it into his mouth. Still sweet. It made him smile. It tasted of innocence.

The trunk proved more difficult. In new cars, a trunk release under the dash made entry easy. But older cars lacked this convenience. He'd have to jimmy the lock, which he knew from experience was not easy on these older models.

Picking the lock outside the car or ripping the seat from inside?

Either option made him vulnerable. People would notice. Someone might call the police.

Benedict put the back seat bench into place and closed the door, locking it first. He strolled around to the driver's side door and opened it just enough to lock it again. Then he walked to the back of the car and felt his jacket pocket for his lock-pick kit.

When he glanced up, Benedict noticed a tall man in a light-gray suit turn the corner, walking toward him. If this man wasn't a cop, Benedict would be surprised. Benedict turned around and walked to the car behind the Mustang, an SUV, and pretended to fit his key into the driver's side door, hoping the gas guzzler didn't have an alarm.

He glanced at the gray suit and the man glanced at him through his sunglasses. Benedict could almost read his mind. He calculated the time and effort it would take to reach behind his back with one hand and put his fingers around the grip of his Glock.

As the man walked closer, he imagined slipping the heavy black automatic pistol out of its holster on the back of his belt.

Someone behind him honked and Benedict jerked around, startled. Had the driver seen him bring the gun around? It didn't matter. That car was swept away in the steady stream of traffic, but Benedict decided to play it up, in case the cop in gray was watching. He smiled and waved at the car as it sped by, as if waving to a friend. When he turned around again, he grinned and made eye contact with the cop, who simply looked away and jogged up the steps into the condominium building.

Once the cop was safely housed inside the condo foyer, Benedict glanced at the front doors of the Phoenix Condominiums. Curious. Maybe the man in gray hadn't been a cop after all. Cops usually had a sixth sense when they saw someone they considered suspicious and would stop to check it out. Pretend to strike up a conversation. Or simply ask, "What the hell are you doing?" But this one seemed too weary. Maybe he just didn't care.

Now what?

He had an urge to hurt someone, anyone, just to purge himself of rage. *Fucking amateurs.*

He had only one real option, and he knew it. He'd go back to his car, drive around the block until a parking spot opened up close enough for him to keep an eye on the Mustang, and then he'd sit and wait.

As he strolled down the sidewalk and around the corner, he tried to whistle a happy tune, though he was seething. The only way he could rein in his growing rage was to imagine the throat of Joseph Conrad after he'd sliced it open.

That image brought a smile as he hummed the tune, "Whistle while you work."

CHAPTER 17

A valiant mind no deadly danger fears;
Who loves aloft and sets his heart on high
Deserves no pain, though he do pine and die.
From "Reason and Affection"

Suzie answered the door of her condo in downtown Sacramento and Joe stepped inside. She leaned forward and let Joe kiss her lightly on the cheek. With her hair pulled back tightly, Suzie was an older version of Sara, the Hollywood version, more put together, more professional. But years of smoking had aged her. She looked as if she were in her mid-forties instead of her mid-thirties, despite the heavy makeup.

"What've you gotten my sister into this time?"

"Not sure. A treasure hunt, maybe."

Suzie took the suitcase from his hand. "Like *Treasure Island*? Searching for buried treasure now, Joe?"

"Not exactly. Didn't have to dig it up. The treasure just sort of fell in my lap."

Suzie shot him a skeptical, sideways glance. "So what's the problem?"

"Someone else knows about it."

He followed her down the hall to the guest bedroom. When they walked in, they found Sara changing Brian and Katie reading in the padded rocking chair.

"Hi, daddy," Katie chimed.

"Hi, sweetie." Joe bent down and kissed the top of her head.

Sara looked over as she pulled up Brian's shorts. "I hope you remembered to grab a few pull-ups," she said. "This is his last one."

"I did." He stepped over as Suzie placed the suitcase on the bed and opened its latches. "There you are. Six new diapers."

"Six!" Sara giggled. "Jeez, Joe. He doesn't have diarrhea!"

"What'd ya expect, Sara," Suzie laughed. "Typical man."

"Daddy's only trying to be prepared for the worst," Katie scolded.

"Thank you, Katie," Joe said. He lifted her into his arms, hugging her and then tickling her sides.

"Daddy! Stop! No fair!"

Lying on his back, Brian looked up and smiled, pointing at his sister.

Joe and Katie set the table as Suzie and Sara prepared dinner. Brian played with toys on the plush carpet. At six-thirty, the doorbell rang and Suzie answered it. He watched as she gave Bill Morgan a friendly kiss on the cheek and ushered him in. Joe walked over to shake hands. He hadn't seen Morgan since a party at Suzie's condo just before Christmas. Bill looked the same, a fit, well-dressed middle-aged professional, clean-shaven with short, dark hair that was beginning to gray at the temples. His blue eyes looked alert and intelligent.

"How goes the law?"

"Still defending the innocent."

"Really?" Joe chuckled. Bill had defended him briefly, and *he* had certainly been innocent.

"All my clients are innocent until a jury and judge say otherwise," Bill said, grinning. "You know that better than most."

Bill took off his suit coat and laid it neatly over the back of an overstuffed chair, into which he sank.

"Would you like a drink?" Suzie asked.

"That would be loverly, Sooz."

"Scotch on the rocks coming up. Joe? You want something?"

Joe stood up. "Sure. I'll make drinks, Suzie."

"Thanks. I'll take Scotch on the rocks, too, then."

Sara leaned around the corner. "Hi, Bill." To Joe, she said, "I'll have a gin-tonic, if you're making one for yourself."

"You got it."

"I'll have a ginger ale *on the rocks*, daddy," Katie chimed.

The adults laughed. "On the rocks it is, Katie," Joe said.

They had just sat down when the doorbell rang again. Detective Ryan Dunn followed Suzie into the dining area.

Still tall and fit, Dunn looked older than Joe remembered. His hair had thinned a little and was not as well kept. His rugged face seemed kind to Joe—he could never forget that Dunn had saved his life.

"How are you, Sara?" he asked.

"I've been better. I'm worried about this thing Joe's gotten himself into."

"What's daddy gotten into?" Katie asked.

Suzie leaned toward her niece. "A treasure hunt, Katie. With pirates and secret treasure, and everything."

Joe glanced at Katie. She suddenly looked very frightened. He knew she still had memories of the events of the past, and those memories occasionally found their way into her nightmares. "Maybe we should discuss it after dinner," he suggested.

The adults nodded and everyone settled in to eat the salmon and seasoned vegetables that the two sisters had prepared. Joe poured cold white wine into his glass and topped off the other glasses on the table. The chilled Wente Brothers *Pinot Grigio* was perfect with the salmon.

After dinner, Joe and Sara put the kids to bed in the guestroom and then joined the others. Suzie poured coffee for everyone to sip with their slivers of cheesecake.

"Delicious, Suzie," said Bill after taking a bite. "Did you make it?"

Suzie chuckled. "You must be mistaking me for my sister. I don't bake."

"*I* bought the cheesecake," Sara said. "There's an Austrian bakery in Davis that I like."

Ryan Dunn sipped his coffee. "Okay, folks. Tell me what this is about."

Sara looked at Joe, then back at Dunn.

"I'm not sure, Ryan. Might be nothing."

"If it was nothing, I wouldn't be here. Start from the beginning."

Joe touched Sara's wrist. "I guess it started when I got a call from one of my old professors at LSU telling me about the death of Jack Claire, the Chairman of the English Department. They thought he committed suicide, but he might have been murdered."

"When did this happen?" Dunn asked. He'd grabbed a small notebook from his hip pocket and jotted something down. Claire's name, Joe guessed.

"About two weeks ago. Sara and I and the kids flew back for the funeral, and we learned that Jack Claire's wife had died suspiciously, only a week or so before."

"You got any names from Louisiana I can check with?"

Sara said, "Hayden Crawford, the Assistant Chair. He's the one who called Joe."

"But he's in France for a month and it's hard to reach him. You can call the English Department at LSU and speak to one of the secretaries. Missy is up on things."

"Anyone else?"

"Oh, yes," Sara said. "There's a detective who was looking into the burglaries."

Dunn looked up from his notepad. "Burglaries?"

"Yeah," Joe said. "Some of the offices in Allen Hall were ransacked and Dr. Claire's home, too, before he died."

"You have any idea what they were after?"

Joe nodded and stood. "Yeah," he said, stepping over to the coffee table where he had placed his briefcase earlier. "They were after these."

Joe lifted the lid.

The detective and the attorney leaned over the open case and stared inside. The gold lining cast yellow light up under the two men's faces.

"What are we looking at?" Morgan asked.

Suzie stood up and walked over, leaning against Bill's shoulder to get a better look. Sara stepped around the table and leaned against Detective Dunn to peer inside the case.

"Wow, Joe," whispered Sara. "So this is what all the fuss is about?"

"What's the book?" Dunn asked. "An old Bible?"

Joe sat back down in the armchair. "No, ladies and gentlemen. That's a bound collection of William Shakespeare's plays."

Bill glanced at Joe. "A copy of his *Folio*?"

Joe smiled. "Yes. A leather-bound copy of his *First Folio*."

"His *First* Folio?" Sara asked. "Were there others?"

"Oh, yes," Joe said. "A Second Folio and a Third, I think."

"Is it valuable?" Dunn asked.

Joe nodded. "My expert, Jonathan Smythe, Professor Emeritus at CLU, says only two-hundred or so remain. Smitty says this is in superb condition."

"What's it worth?" asked Bill Morgan.

"We're not sure. Maybe two-hundred grand. Maybe a million."

"How'd *you* get this?" asked Dunn.

"Jack Claire sent the manuscripts and *Folio* before he died."

"He sent them to *you*?" Dunn repeated. "Why?"

Joe shrugged and felt himself blush. "To be honest, I'm not sure. I mean, Jack was like a father to me, but he knew I'm no Shakespeare scholar."

"So, again, why you?"

Dunn's face was less than friendly. He looked the way he had two and a half years ago when he had interviewed Joe about the murders, back when he still thought Joe was guilty. The hard look made Joe squirm.

"I guess he wanted to get the papers as far away from Louisiana as he could, so whoever was trying to find them wouldn't know where to look. Maybe he figured since I wasn't a Shakespeare scholar, that, you know, whoever was after the papers wouldn't think I'd wind up with them."

"But you did," Dunn said. He sipped his coffee and looked suspiciously at Joe.

"A box was waiting for me when we got back from Louisiana."

"Waiting for you?" Dunn asked.

"Yeah. In my office. The secretary put it there. Along with a few other boxes of books. We get free books from publishers all the time, so…"

"So, what?" Dunn asked. "You just happened to wind up with this box after this professor friend of yours is murdered? And you don't call the police?"

Joe's face burned. "I know, I know. I probably should have called someone right away. But…"

"But what?" asked Dunn.

"Well, I didn't even open the box at first. I set it aside, thinking it was just another batch of textbooks. When I finally got around to opening it, I still wasn't quite sure what I had."

"What'd you do then?" Dunn asked.

"I called Smitty, the retired Shakespeare scholar from CLU. He was very excited about the documents."

"The documents?" asked Bill. "Not the *Folio*?"

"Oh, he was excited about the copy of the *First Folio*, sure. But he was thrilled about the papers."

Everyone looked back into the opened briefcase.

Dunn asked, "Can I pick up one of the papers?"

"Sure," Joe said. "Just be careful. They're surprisingly sturdy but very old."

The detective reached gingerly into the case and lifted one of the beige pages to his face. The others leaned in to get a better look.

"What is it?" Suzie asked. "A page from a play?"

Joe smiled. "A *handwritten* page from one of Shakespeare's plays."

Bill pointed to a word and read it aloud: "'Hamlet?"

Joe leaned over to see. "Yes, they're all there."

"What's all there?" Sara asked.

"All the plays of Shakespeare," answered Joe.

"Inside *that* briefcase?" Morgan asked skeptically.

"No, of course not. Those are just a few sample pages Smitty and I took to Berkeley."

"What's in Berkeley?" Dunn asked.

"We wanted the opinion of another expert, one who knows something about paper and handwriting, and the closest expert is at Berkeley. A woman by the name of Dr. Williamson."

Dunn handed the page to Morgan and wrote her name in his notepad.

Bill Morgan's hand began to shake. "Did she verify that these pages were written by Shakespeare?"

Everyone turned to look at Joe. He grinned before answering. "Well, that's the million-dollar question, isn't it."

"And what's the million-dollar answer?" Suzie asked.

"Dr. Williamson and Smitty agree that these *are* original manuscript pages of Shakespeare's plays, but there's a big problem."

"What?" Sara asked, exasperated.

"The handwriting isn't William Shakespeare's. Or I should say, Will Shakspur."

"Shack-spur?" Sara repeated.

Bill Morgan laughed. "Jesus. This is the whole authorship thing, isn't it?"

"What do you mean?" asked Dunn.

Morgan gently placed the manuscript page back inside the case. "It's quite well known among some lawyers. A few have actually published books on it. Even the Supreme Court Justices have weighed in on the matter. The *Wall Street Journal* had an article about doubts raised by Justice John Paul Stevens back in 2009, I think."

Suzie picked up her cup and took a sip. "Did William Shakespeare of Stratford-upon-Avon write the plays or did someone else?"

Dunn arched an eyebrow. "Like who?"

"Take your pick," Bill Morgan said sarcastically. "Christopher Marlowe, Francis Bacon, Sir Walter Raleigh."

Suzie added, "Some people think Queen Elizabeth herself wrote the plays. She was very bright, very learned. And she loved the theater."

"So who was William Shakespeare?" asked Sara.

"If you believe in the conspiracy theories," Morgan said, "nothing but a front."

Sara turned to Joe. "Why have you never talked about it before?"

Joe shrugged. "Doubts about the authorship get mentioned, but no one discusses it seriously in lit classes."

"If you're right about your old professor at LSU being killed over these papers," Dunn said, "then someone *will* have to take this seriously."

Joe nodded.

"What prompted your call to me today?" Dunn asked.

"Me, I guess," Sara said. "When the kids and I came home from the pool, we noticed an odor inside the house. Like a smoker had been inside."

"Your house smelled like smoke?" Dunn asked, lifting his eyebrow.

"Yes. It smelled like stale nicotine, like someone who's a heavy smoker had walked through the house."

"That's it?" Dunn put his notepad down on the coffee table. "Don't you smoke?"

Sara shook her head. "No, not anymore. Not since Brian was born."

Dunn frowned. "Pretty thin."

"It's hard to explain," Sara admitted. "Katie and I both felt like someone had been inside the house."

"Was anything missing? Any signs of a break in?"

"No," Sara said. "I know it sounds feeble, but..."

"But you had a feeling." Dunn used his fork to slice off a bite of cheesecake, which he pushed into his mouth. After chewing for a few seconds, he said, "Woman's intuition." He picked up the lukewarm coffee and slurped it.

"Ryan," Sara said. "You know us. You know we don't spook easily."

"If Sara thinks someone broke into her home," Suzie added, "then someone probably did."

"Do you know what this person looks like?" asked Detective Dunn.

Joe and Sara looked at each other. "No."

"I mean, are we looking for a black man, a white man, an Asian, a Latino? Old? Young? Middle-aged? Tall, short, medium build? He could be outside on the sidewalk right now, but we wouldn't know it."

"I suppose," said Sara.

Dunn took another bite. Chewing seemed to help him think.

"What do you think, Ryan?" Bill asked him.

Dunn swallowed. "I think Joe and Sara are a little paranoid after learning about the death of this professor in Louisiana. I also think it's unfortunate he sent Joe these papers." He lifted the last piece of cheesecake up to his mouth and chewed it as the others watched. Then Dunn shot Joe an unmistakable look of suspicion. "If, in fact, he did."

CHAPTER 18

Modest doubt is call'd
The beacon of the wise, the tent that searches
To the bottom of the worst.
From *Troilus and Cressidea*

Joe, taking a sip of his coffee, almost spit it out.

"What the hell do you mean by that?"

"You said it yourself, you're no Shakespeare scholar."

"So?"

"So, why send them to you? He didn't know any experts? Doesn't he have any children or other relatives?"

Joe dropped the cup into the saucer, splashing coffee on the table.

"I'm sure Jack knew lots of experts, but I'm also sure he figured whoever had found him would be able to find them. As far as relatives, Jack had a son who died quite a few years ago. His only living relatives are two granddaughters. One lives in Ohio and the other, somewhere in the Bay Area, I think."

Dunn raised his eyebrows and opened his notebook again. "San Francisco?"

Joe nodded.

"Why not turn the papers over to her?"

"I've tried," Joe explained. "Called her business and left a message, but she hasn't gotten back to me."

"What's the granddaughter's name?"

"Deirdre Claire. C-l-a-i-r-e. She owns an antique store in the City called French Quarter Antiques."

"French Quarter Antiques," Dunn repeated as he wrote the name in his notebook. "Where're the rest of the papers?"

"At Smitty's house in Stockton," Joe said.

"Think they're safe there?"

Joe nodded. "But you need to know something else."

Dunn looked annoyed. "What?"

"Some of the offices at my campus have been searched, too."

"Including yours?"

"Yes, including mine."

"Why didn't I know that?" asked Sara.

Joe faced her. "I didn't want to upset you."

Sara frowned. "Any other surprises?"

Joe nodded reluctantly. "Did I mention Janice Wilson?"

Dunn shook his head. "Who's Janice Wilson?"

"She was Dr. Claire's research assistant. She was murdered shortly after Jack's funeral."

Sara slapped Joe's shoulder. "Why didn't you tell me that your office had been searched? That's important."

Joe looked at her. "I told you, I didn't want to worry you."

"Jesus, Joe. You should have warned me." Sara stood up, trembling, and brushed by Joe's knees. She walked quickly into the kitchen.

"I thought I was protecting you," Joe called. "You and the kids."

Sara re-emerged with a bottle of water in her fist and glared at Joe as she twisted the cap off. "It's just like before."

"No, it isn't, Sara."

Taking a long pull from the water bottle, she nodded. "Yes, it is. You make a decision to do something without checking with me, and it backfires. Now *we're* in danger again."

The room fell silent. Sara stepped around Joe's knees again and plopped down into the chair.

Bill Morgan cleared his throat. "Where should we go from here, Ryan?"

They turned to Dunn.

"Did you report the break-ins at your campus, Joe?"

"The secretary did, yes. Well, to the campus police, I think."

"Check," he said curtly. "Make damn sure the local police know. I'll call your old pal Marino tomorrow and give him a heads-up."

Joe remembered Detective Manuel Marino, the heavy-set Latino officer from Stockton. Along with Ryan, he had investigated Joe for the I-5 murders.

"If you think it's necessary," Joe said.

Dunn looked at Joe, arching an eyebrow. "Don't you?"

"It's just..."

"For God's sakes, don't keep anything from me now."

"Well, Smitty and Sylvia—Dr. Williamson—think we should keep all of this quiet."

"Why?" asked Morgan.

Joe turned to look at him, saying, "They're worried about news of these manuscripts getting out to the public prematurely, before we've had a chance to authenticate them."

Morgan glanced at Dunn, then at Suzie, then back at Joe.

"The longer you delay going public," Morgan said, "the easier you make it for whoever's searching for the papers to work surreptitiously."

Joe nodded. "I'm just not sure. I trust Smitty and Sylvia."

"Sylvia?" said Sara. "Tell me about Sylvia, Joe."

Joe, feeling himself blush again, picked up his coffee cup as if to take a swig, hoping to hide his reddening cheeks. "She's an Elizabethan scholar at Berkeley. Smitty knows her. She's really interested in the papers."

"I'll bet she is," Sara said.

"What's she look like?" asked Suzie.

Joe turned toward her. "What difference does *that* make?"

"I think your wife would like to know, that's all," Suzie said, grinning.

"Tall, attractive, about thirty-five, I think. African-American."

Sara laughed. "Sounds like your officemate, Cass."

"Cass is *not* my officemate, Sara. You know that. She's in the office next to mine."

"Who's Cass?" Ryan asked.

"She teaches at CLU," Joe explained. "But she's gone for the summer. She lives in southern California, when she's not up here."

"Could she be interested in these papers?" Dunn asked.

Joe laughed. "No! Well, I mean, anyone would be interested in them. They'll be the find of the century, assuming they're real. But Cass Johnson isn't even around."

"No," said Sara. "Just another beautiful young woman who hangs out with Joe when *I'm* not in the picture."

Everyone went quiet.

Finally, Bill Morgan broke the chill. "I thought everything was fine between you two, after all that business two years ago."

"So did I!" blurted Joe.

"Everything *was* good," said Sara, standing again. "Until Joe got himself involved in another murder case." She picked up her empty cup and saucer in one hand and held the half-empty water bottle in the other.

Suzie stood, too, and picked up some of the empty cups and saucers. "You're a magnet for trouble," she said, looking at Joe and shaking her head.

Bill stood and stacked some of the plates. "I'll help you," he said to Suzie. "Let's leave these two to work things out with Ryan."

Detective Dunn chuckled. "I'm no marriage counselor."

Suzie turned her head to Bill as they walked into the kitchen. "I need a cigarette anyway. Care to join me on the balcony?"

"Sure," Bill Morgan said.

After taking her cup into the kitchen, Sara walked back to the couch and sat down. Bill opened the sliding glass door and Suzie stepped out onto the balcony.

Dunn looked Joe in the eyes. "Suppose you tell me why your pal Dr. Claire sent the manuscripts to you instead of to one of his granddaughters, if they're worth so much?"

"I've wondered that myself."

Dunn's bushy eyebrow arched as he lifted his gaze from his notepad to examine Joe's face. "Seems odd."

"Maybe Jack was worried the killer would harm his granddaughters, if he got them involved."

"Maybe," Dunn said.

"Do I need Bill Morgan back in here with me, Ryan?"

The detective put his pen down without smiling.

"You think you need a lawyer, Joe, by all means." Dunn gestured toward the balcony.

Joe shifted his weight in the chair. "I thought we were friends."

"We are, Joe. But this is a serious investigation now. If what you're telling me is true, it's a murder case, and the killer is here, moving back and forth between Stockton and Davis. You should've called me sooner."

"Sorry. I didn't put the pieces together at first."

"Maybe if your pal, Dr. Claire, had contacted the police sooner, he and his wife would still be alive, too."

Joe nodded.

"Now you've got others involved. How many people do you want to put in harm's way?"

"Look, Ryan. I'm not sure why Jack Claire sent the papers to me, but he did. All I know is, someone's looking for them and he's ruthless enough to kill. Jack must have had a reason to send the papers to me instead of his granddaughters. Maybe to protect them. Maybe he didn't think they'd know how to handle the manuscripts. I'm only just learning how complicated a discovery like this is, how much is at stake if you go public and it turns out to be a fraud. I mean, Jack's reputation as a scholar was on the line. Now I've got two other scholars involved. If we go public prematurely, their reputations could be ruined. Not to mention, my own."

Sara chuckled. "*Your* reputation, Joe? Forgive me, but what reputation? You said it yourself, you aren't a Shakespeare scholar."

Joe tried not to show his anger. "I know, Sara," he said. "But if these papers are real, I could be part of one of the most important discoveries in centuries. On the other hand, if they're fakes, I could lose my job."

Detective Dunn picked up his coffee cup, took a sip, and then added, "Still, going public now might be the best way to stop this guy from doing any more damage. Bring those papers to me, at the police station. Let Bill tag along, if you want. We'll tell the press that the documents are being examined by experts under police security. Then everything's out in the open, including your doubts about authenticity. Your asses will be covered."

Joe nodded. "Let me talk it over with the others. Maybe we can bring the papers in on Monday."

"What are you two going to do in the meantime?" asked Dunn.

"I don't know." Joe looked at Sara. "What do you think we should do?"

Sara shrugged. "I guess I agree with Ryan. Give him the papers and do your research, or whatever you need to do, with the police around. Go public, and the killer, whoever it is, will have to give up. Won't he?"

"I guess so," Joe admitted. Joe looked at Detective Dunn.

"Can you stay here?" Ryan suggested. "Whoever's after the papers probably doesn't know you're here."

Joe nodded.

"Okay," Sara said, "but then what?"

The three of them sat quietly, looking at Bill Morgan and Suzie standing outside the sliding glass doors on the balcony silhouetted by the violet sky over the Sacramento River. The sun had gone behind the coastal range. Suzie's cigarette glowed bright orange and they watched as she blew out a stream of smoke, laughing at something Bill said.

"Are they seeing each other?" Ryan asked.

"I don't think so," Sara answered. "Bill's still married. But they sure seem to get along, don't they."

Joe smiled, glad the attention was on someone else. "They do seem chummy."

Sara waved Suzie inside and they watched her crush out her cigarette. After opening the sliding door and stepping inside, Suzie smiled at Sara.

"What's up?"

"Can we stay here tonight, Suzie?" Sara asked. "Ryan thinks it would be safer."

"Of course," Suzie said. She sat next to Sara and put her arm around her. "Stay here as long as you want. Just like before."

Joe remembered before. Sara had taken Katie away from him and stayed here when Joe had been accused of the crimes. Suzie had been a little too protective for Joe's taste.

"Just tonight. We don't want to put you out," Joe chimed in.

"Stay as long as you like. That's why I have a guestroom. You know, for guests."

Sara nodded at Joe. "Joe's right," she said. "We don't want to impose. We'll stay tonight and head back to Davis in the morning, if that's okay."

"Sure," Suzie said, hugging her sister. "Whatever works."

Bill looked at Dunn. "You think they'll be okay going back to Davis tomorrow?"

"In the daylight? Probably. If they stay together."

"But then what?" asked the attorney. He turned his gaze toward Joe. "Any suggestions, Professor?"

Joe closed his eyes to think. "Well, Sara and the kids could fly back to Baton Rouge and stay with Sara's parents. But this whole thing started there, so that's probably not a good idea."

"I've got it!" Suzie announced. "You can go up to my cabin?"

"You've got a cabin?" Detective Dunn asked.

"On Highway 50, just south of Lake Tahoe, behind Strawberry Lodge."

"It's beautiful up there," Bill Morgan said.

"*You've* been there?" Sara asked.

Now it was Bill Morgan's turn to blush.

"Yes," Suzie said, standing. "Bill stopped by for lunch one time on his way to take a deposition at Tahoe. I happened to be up there and I invited him to see the place."

Sara smiled at her sister. "I see."

Suzie tried to hide her smile by feigning irritation. "Don't read too much into it."

"We get it," said Joe. "Just a couple of colleagues chatting about legal matters over lunch. *Corpus delicti*, and all that."

Ryan chuckled and asked, "Do you even know what *corpus delicti* means?"

Joe smiled. "Delicious body, right?"

"Not exactly," Bill Morgan responded.

"And did you two counselors have wine with lunch?" asked Sara.

Now Suzie blushed, saying, "I take the Fifth!"

CHAPTER 19

We that are true lovers run into strange capers; but as all is mortal in nature, so is all nature in love mortal in folly.
From *As You Like It*

Saturday morning, Suzie made French toast for the children and then showered and dressed for work. She stood in the foyer holding her keys and addressed Joe, who was helping Brian dress.

"I've got to go into the office for a few hours this morning," she said, "so you two let yourselves out."

Will do," Joe answered, tugging Brian's shirt over his head. "Thanks again."

Sara stepped out of the hallway wearing one of Suzy's robes and holding the cream-colored slacks and red panties Joe had picked out the day before.

"Suzy, look what my idiot husband grabbed."

Susan spun around, did a double take, and burst out laughing.

Joe glanced from one sister to the other, feeling his face turn red. "What?"

"Joe! If I wear these panties, they'll show right through my slacks!"

"What a moron," laughed Suzy. "Come with me. You can borrow a pair of mine—white ones. I have a new pair I've never worn." She led Sara back down the hall to her room.

Later, walking Sara and Katie out to his car, Joe didn't notice the stranger who started the engine of his sedan after watching Joe buckle his daughter into the passenger seat. The breeze that had blown in from the delta to cool the evening had died away, and now the morning sun was warming the streets of Sacramento.

With Katie in his car, Joe led Sara and Brian back to Davis.

Once at home, he showered and dressed while Sara packed suitcases full of clothes and toys for a week at Suzie's cabin.

Running behind schedule, Joe phoned Smitty.

"I'm just leaving Davis. Be there in an hour."

"Everything all right, lad?"

"Yes. How about with you?"

"Fine, fine," the older man said, sounding annoyed. "I'll call Sylvia and let her know we'll be there later. I have an idea, Joe."

"Another one?"

"How would you feel about spending the next couple of nights in Berkeley?"

"Spend the night? Where, at Sylvia's?"

Smitty chuckled. "No, though that would be lovely. I took the liberty of booking us two rooms at the Hotel Durant. It's across the street from the campus and it has a pretty good bar and restaurant."

"How much are the rooms, Smitty?"

"You don't have to worry, Joe, the rooms will be my treat. It'd be worth it, not having to be driven all over tarnation."

"I couldn't let you do that, Smitty."

"Nonsense. I get a senior discount."

Joe looked at Sara, who shot him a quizzical expression. "I guess that would be okay. Sara's taking the kids up to the mountains anyway, so they won't be home."

"Fine, fine. I'll call Sylvia and let her know. Maybe she'll join us for dinner."

Joe packed a bag for himself and helped Sara carry hers out to the car. He hugged the children tightly and gave Sara a long kiss.

"Don't go getting yourself in trouble," she warned.

Still holding Sara, Joe searched her eyes. "What do you mean?"

"Well, you're spending the night in Berkeley and you've already admitted this Sylvia woman is beautiful."

"Sara, you have nothing to worry about. Really."

"Just don't tempt fate, okay?"

"I won't, I swear. Now go enjoy yourself up at the Lake."

They kissed again and Sara climbed into her car and started the engine.

After locking up the house, with the children buckled safely in her car, Joe watched Sara back out of the driveway and waved as she drove away on the two-hour drive to the cabin near Lake Tahoe.

When he backed out of the driveway, Joe noticed a tall man climb into a sedan he hadn't noticed before on his street. The man looked out of place, like an attorney or an insurance salesman, or maybe an undercover police detective, Joe thought.

Joe watched the car in his rearview mirror. It stayed put as he turned left on B street. Joe checked his rearview mirror for the stranger's car but didn't see it as he drove south to Stockton. Once he picked up Smitty, he'd forgotten about it.

By 10:00 Saturday morning, Detective Ryan Dunn had learned little about both sisters, except that one lived near San Francisco part of the year. He managed to get her unlisted number and called her.

"Can I speak to you in person?" Dunn asked Deirdre.

"Sure, if you don't mind a trip to the City. My businesses keep me pretty busy."

"I can be there this afternoon or this evening," he assured her.

"You work on Saturday nights?"

"When it's important," Dunn said. "I set my own schedule."

"No wife to take out?"

"I'm separated, Ms. Claire," Dunn said matter-of-factly. "Like I said, I set my own schedule."

"Well, I have an estate sale in the Nob Hill area this afternoon, but I should be back in my store around three or four. Can you meet me then?"

"Like I said—"

"I know, I know. You set your own schedule."

After hanging up, the detective called other antique dealers in the Bay Area. Deirdre's reputation was solid. The other dealers described her as an ethical dealer who paid customers what their possessions were worth and charged reasonable prices when she put them on the market. All of them said that as far as they knew, she had never dealt with stolen property and had never cheated a client. Of course, the police were always suspicious of antique dealers because they often worked as fences for stolen property. And they covered for each other relentlessly, like doctors who rarely rat on one of their own. One bit of information Dunn gleaned made his ears perk up. Deirdre Claire sometimes dealt in old paintings and rare books.

That in itself was not suspicious. Dunn knew that the antique business in general had exploded ever since the television show *The Antique Roadshow* began airing on PBS. He knew from other investigations that the way antique dealers moved up was by shifting from large, bulky furniture to smaller, more expensive pieces—paintings, sculptures, books, jewelry.

He also knew this was often the step that led dealers into a life of crime. Some customers didn't care where the art or jewelry came from, they just wanted it. They didn't seem to understand that the more they bought stolen goods, the more they fueled the market for stolen property, and consequently the more they put themselves in danger of being robbed. On more than one occasion, Dunn had tracked a piece of stolen jewelry back to a couple who themselves had been the victim of a burglary only a year or two earlier.

Dunn left his home in Sacramento at 2:00 in the afternoon and found himself crawling through traffic on the new Oakland-Bay Bridge. Realizing he was going to be late, he called Deirdre's office.

"I'll be in Sausalito at five. Why don't we meet at the Wharf Café and get an early dinner?" asked Deirdre.

Dunn agreed. Once across the bridge, he drove along the Embarcadero through Fisherman's Wharf to the Golden Gate Bridge. As he drove across the Golden Gate, he looked left out to the Pacific and saw a fog bank hanging in the distance like a gray wall. To his right was Alcatraz. From the Bridge, he could see dozens of sailboats. The Bay was choppy. Whitecaps flared and disappeared on the water, but the sailboats cut through the waves easily.

Taking the Sausalito exit, he wound his way down the narrow, steep hills to the docks on the north side of the Bay. Within minutes he found the Wharf Café, its outdoor deck covered with tables and chairs and people reading the paper and talking. He had to park up the street on the edge of the road and walk back to the Café.

Inside, a tall, thin young man with a stud in his tongue and tattoos of thorns around his neck showed him to Deirdre Claire's table. She was sitting outside at the southeast corner of the deck already eating a salad. Dunn was struck by her stern good looks—her long, black hair pulled back and up on her head, her dark eyes with full but well-shaped eyebrows, her thin upper lip and full, sensuous lower lip, the slight cleft in her chin. She wore sunglasses but the lenses were not so dark that he couldn't see her eyes. In her stylish dark gray business suit, she looked out of place in Sausalito. The other customers were dressed like models from an L. L. Bean catalogue.

When Dunn reached out to shake Deirdre's hand, she stood up and leaned forward, and Dunn glanced down as Deirdre's white silk blouse fell open, showing a glimpse of her cleavage harnessed by a sheer pink bra. At the same instant, he caught a whiff of her perfume and recognized it immediately. Red, the same perfume he used to buy for his wife before their divorce. His wife's boyfriend seemed to like it, too. Still, the fragrance had the same immediate effect on him as it used to have when his wife would spray some on herself before coming to bed.

After Dunn ordered scallops, he took out his notepad and began questioning the woman, who sipped white wine as they spoke. He watched her lips press against the glass.

"Do you mind if we eat first, Detective?" she said, removing her sunglasses. "I'm starving."

"No, I don't mind," he said. He placed his notepad off to the side and opened his napkin, placing it on his lap.

"I love this place," said the woman, smiling. "The food's delicious."

"You come here often?" Dunn snorted. "Christ, that sounds lame, doesn't it."

The woman laughed, her eyes glistening. "No, Detective Dunn. It doesn't sound lame."

"I haven't been on a date since my wife and I separated, so I'm not very good at small talk."

"Is this a date?" Deirdre asked.

Dunn couldn't keep from blushing. "No."

She laughed again, leveling her eyes at Ryan. "I don't date much either. Too busy with my businesses, I guess." She sipped her wine again.

Dunn caught himself glancing at her cleavage and wondered if she found him attractive.

"Yes," she said, as if reading his mind.

"*What?*" he asked, startled.

"In answer to your question, yes, I come here often."

"Oh," said Dunn, chuckling at himself.

"It's perfect for me. Halfway from my downtown office to my house in Marin, and it's outside the city, so by the time I get here, I can unwind."

The waiter brought their entrees and placed the plates in front of them. The food was delicious—Dunn had to admit it. They ate quietly, comfortably, it seemed to Ryan, chatting about life in the northern Bay. When the check came, they each glanced at it and then took out a couple of twenty dollar bills and spilt the bill evenly.

Over coffee at the end of their meal, Detective Dunn opened his notepad and began to ask questions. "I've heard you *are* dealing in art work and rare books, first editions, now. At least, that's what some of your competitors tell me."

The woman smiled and leaned forward.

"You've done some detective work, I see," she whispered. Then she leaned back again, glancing out at the Bay as a breeze came up and lifted a few stray strands of hair off her forehead. "Yes, it's true. I have been dealing in fine oil paintings and some rare first editions." She turned to look Dunn straight in the eyes. "And if these papers you describe are as valuable as this English teacher thinks they are, then, yes, of course, I'd like to share the ownership. With my sister, of course."

"Well, that brings us to an awkward question, Ms. Claire."

"Please. I insist you call me Deirdre. Or Dee. Everyone calls me Dee."

Dunn held her gaze without smiling, and asked, "Why do you suppose your grandfather sent the papers to Mr. Conrad and not to you or your sister?"

The smile left the woman's face and she looked down at the table.

"My grandfather was becoming more senile in the last few years. Alzheimer's, probably. After grandmother's accident, I think he became paranoid. While we were there for her funeral, we found him with a gun one evening. We think he was contemplating suicide. Maybe he just wasn't thinking clearly. Maybe this English teacher, Conrad, tricked him into sending the papers to him instead of to us while he was there for grandmother's funeral."

"That's not likely, Ms. Claire."

"Oh?"

"Joe Conrad wasn't in Baton Rouge for your grandmother's funeral. He and his family only went back for your grandfather's service."

"I could have sworn I saw him at both services. They did happen within two weeks of one another, you know. What's the line from *Hamlet*? When Horatio refers to the marriage of Hamlet's mother immediately after the funeral for Hamlet's father? 'It fell hard upon.' Is that the line?"

Dunn grinned. "You know Shakespeare, then?"

"Of course, Detective. My grandfather was a Shakespeare scholar."

"You're avoiding the question. Why didn't your grandfather trust you or your sister with these manuscripts? Why send them to someone outside the family?"

The woman's face flamed red.

"Are you sure my grandfather really did send the papers to this English teacher? Maybe *he* stole them from my grandfather. Maybe this English teacher stole the papers while he was there. Maybe he's the one who killed my grandfather."

"Not possible. Mr. Conrad was in California on the morning your grandfather fell or jumped to his death."

"Huh." She took a sip of coffee. "Why doesn't this English teacher give the papers to me and my sister, and we'll just get everything out in the open. You know, diffuse the whole situation by calling the newspapers or something. Wouldn't that stop whoever's after the documents?"

"Working on it. But Mr. Conrad feels he should respect your grandfather's wishes and investigate the manuscripts himself. He thinks that's what your grandfather wanted."

"Forgive me for being blunt, but who in the hell does this English teacher think he is, anyway? I mean, shouldn't my grandfather's immediate surviving family be the ones who decide?"

"Perhaps. But Mr. Conrad is in possession of the papers, and as you probably know, possession is ninety percent—"

"But how can you be sure this English teacher acquired my grandfather's papers legally?"

"Do you have something against English teachers?"

Deirdre laughed. "Of course not! Why did you ask *that*?"

"The tone of your voice every time you refer to Mr. Conrad as 'this English teacher.'"

Deirdre laughed again, and then reached down for her napkin. She dabbed the corners of her mouth. Then she reached into her purse for lipstick and a compact. As she applied fresh dark red lipstick, she spoke. "I think this interrogation is over, Detective Dunn.." Closing the compact and putting it in her purse, she looked him in the eyes. "In the past few weeks, I've lost my grandmother and my grandfather. If what you're telling me is true, both of them may have been murdered. Over something my grandfather had in his possession, something of great value, possibly, which is now God knows where. I think it's time I spoke to my own attorney."

"I didn't mean to offend you, Dee. I have to ask tough questions."

Standing up and moving her chair back, Deirdre Claire let a tear slide down her cheek. "I suppose you do, Detective. But I'm not as tough as you are."

Dunn touched her hand as she pushed by and she paused, looking down. The scent of her perfume aroused him again. "I'm sorry," he told her. "I didn't want this interview to end badly."

He reached into the inside pocket of his jacket and fished out a business card.

"I don't need your card, Detective."

"Call me Ryan. If what Joe Conrad tells me is true, you and your sister could be in danger. Call me if something happens. If your home is ransacked or your store, that would mean the killer is still looking for the papers, and if he thinks you have them, you could be in danger."

Expressionless, she pinched the business card between her fingers and dropped it into her purse. Then she stepped around him. Dunn walked her out, drinking in the aroma of her perfume. In the parking lot, Dunn tried to open the car door for her, but she placed her hand on top of his.

"Really, Detective. I am capable."

"I can see that. It's just, I wanted to learn more about you and your grandfather. He meant a lot to Joe Conrad."

Deirdre chuckled. "I see what you're doing," she said.

Dunn blushed a little. "What am I doing?"

"Well, obviously you came here alone, so you don't have a partner. You're trying to play both roles." She opened the car door the rest of the way and climbed inside, setting her purse down on the passenger seat.

"Both roles?" Dunn asked, leaning in. He tried to smile.

"Really, Detective. You can't be both the good cop and the bad cop. It's just not as effective when one cop plays both parts."

"But I—"

She pulled the door closed, almost catching Dunn's cheek with the sharp corner, slamming it hard. Then she started the engine, flashed a caustic grin at Dunn and put the car into reverse.

As Dunn watched her drive away, perfume lingering, he smiled. "Don't do it, Ryan," he told himself. "You won't know whether to kiss her or kill her."

CHAPTER 20

Modest doubt is call'd
The beacon of the wise…
From Troilus and Cressida

Once again, Joe drove Smitty over the rolling coastal hills to Berkeley. Traffic on a Saturday was light, so they made good time. Smitty dozed during the first part of the drive, but by the time they had reached Oakland, he was just waking up. Joe glanced over at his passenger and smiled as the older man wiped his eyes and stretched like a child.

Joe negotiated changing freeways to head north on Interstate 80 to Berkeley. The blue sky over the Bay was clear, though a wall of fog hung farther west just beyond the Golden Gate Bridge. The Bay Bridge rose up to their left, and beyond it, the skyline of San Francisco disappeared into the lifting morning fog. Though the water was choppy, hundreds of sailboats cruised on the Bay. When it was safe, Joe glanced over to drink in the beauty, so different from the Gulf of Mexico off the coast of New Orleans.

"Your wife doesn't mind your staying the night?"

"No, she'll be gone anyway. Sara took the kids up to the mountains for a week."

"Oh?" Smitty asked, sounding surprised. "What prompted that?"

Joe glanced over at Smitty, noticing the large black-glassed building beyond him. They were passing Emeryville. "We thought it might be wise to get her and the kids out of harm's way. Sara's sister has a cabin on Highway 50, just south of Lake Tahoe."

Joe noticed a beige sedan several cars back. It looked like the one that had been parked on his street earlier. He took the University Avenue exit and watched in his rearview mirror. The sedan did not exit, so Joe felt safe as he drove toward the campus. Rising up on the hillside in front of them stood the majestic clock tower at the center of the Berkeley campus.

At the Hotel they checked in at the front desk and were handed two room keys. Joe noted that the keys were actual, old-fashioned metal keys, not the plastic cards he was accustomed to. Then they walked across the street and found Sylvia in her office looking through several large books.

"You left your office door unlocked?" asked Joe.

Sylvia looked up from the book she was reading. "Sure. I knew you two were coming."

Smitty strode toward the work table, leaving Joe at the door. "Smells wonderful in here," he said. "You made coffee?"

"Yes, of course, Breakfast Blend from Starbucks. One of my few indulgences."

"You're a saint, Sylvia," said Smitty, pouring himself a cup. "In fact, I christen you St. Sylvia, patron saint of aging Anglo-Saxons!"

"You'll find a few croissants there, too."

"Should I lock the door?" asked Joe.

Looking back at him, Sylvia shrugged. "If you think you should."

Joe reached for the door handle, but Smitty's voice interrupted him.

"What kind of croissant do you want, Joe? There's one strawberry and two almond-filled."

"I like the ones with almonds," he said. He walked over and placed the briefcase down on the table next to Sylvia. "How's it going?"

"I've collected lots of handwriting samples," she said. "We can do a preliminary comparison using these books and narrow the field considerably."

Smitty stepped over to the table, a cup of steaming coffee in one fist and a flaky croissant in the other. Joe opened the briefcase. All three of them simply stared at the contents for a few seconds, anticipating the joy of the research they were about to conduct.

A few hours later, Smitty straightened up and removed his glasses, rubbing the bridge of his nose.

"Wasn't an Earl of Pembroke also a likely candidate?" Smitty asked.

After hours of reading various texts, Joe was just beginning to realize how little he really knew about British literature and the aristocracy.

"Yes," Sylvia answered, "but I've definitely ruled him out. Here. Check this."

She slid an opened book across the table for Smitty and he slipped his glasses back on to compare one of the manuscript pages to a document copied in the book.

"Even if he were ambidextrous? Some writers wrote with both hands, using one hand for one identity and the other for their alter ego," Smitty explained.

"And some writers could write backwards. Leonardo Da Vinci, for example," said Sylvia.

Closing the book he was reading and picking up one of the handwritten pages again, Joe tried to put what they were doing into perspective. "Wait. First things first. Are the documents authentic?" he asked.

Sylvia nodded. "The preliminary report from the lab says yes, in terms of their age, the ink and probably the penmanship."

A bit frustrated, Joe asked, "Do they prove that Shakespeare wasn't the author?"

"Not necessarily," replied Sylvia, the strain in her own voice evident. "Even if the paper *is* from the 16th century, as well as the ink, the writing could have been done within the last twenty years or so."

"What do you mean?"

Smitty piped up. "Forgers often get their hands on old materials from the time period of the work they're trying to forge. If a forger is trying to reproduce a Rembrant, for example, he would buy an inexpensive painting of the same time period, from the same region, of approximately the same size or larger and then wash the canvas to remove the old painting. Then, using paint made from old ingredients, the forger paints a copy."

"Remember William Henry Ireland?" Sylvia asked Smitty.

"Oh, vaguely."

"Who was he?" asked Joe.

Sylvia stretched her arms and arched her back, and then looked at Joe. "The man responsible for one of the biggest Shakespeare hoaxes in history. His father was a fan of the Bard, so to please his father, William Henry pretended he had found a large cache of Shakespearean papers—deeds bearing Shakespeare's signature and even an undiscovered play. Remember the title, Smitty?"

Smitty knitted his brow and shut his eyes. "*Rowena and somebody.*"

"*Vortigern and Rowena*!" Sylvia remembered. "That's right. Anyway, William Henry Ireland forged promissory notes signed by Shakespeare, love letters to Anne Hathaway, even a few pages of supposedly unused text from several plays."

"When did all this happen?" asked Joe.

Smitty looked at Sylvia. "Late seventeen hundreds?"

"Between 1794 and 1796, I think," Sylvia answered. "Ireland's father actually published a book titled *Miscellaneous Papers and Legal Instruments under the Hand and Seal of William Shakespeare.* It was well received by all the best scholars at that time, by the way."

"Who later had egg on their faces," scoffed Smitty. "We don't want to end up like those fine fellows!"

"I have a copy of that damn book somewhere," said Sylvia, glancing over her shoulder at her wall of shelves.

"What happened?" asked Joe. "How did they find out the papers were fakes?"

Smitty deferred to Sylvia.

"Well," she began, "a respected authority named Edmund Malone discredited the Ireland papers just days before the new play was scheduled to open."

"You're kidding," laughed Joe.

"Do you recall the name of Edmund's work?" asked Smitty, pressing his finger against his temple.

"*An Inquiry into the Authenticity of Certain Miscellaneous Papers.* I've got a copy of *that* book around here, too. Hundreds of copies of it were printed just before the premiere of the play."

"Did the play open anyway?" Joe asked. He was beginning to see how truly embarrassing it would be to go public before they were absolutely certain.

"To a packed house!" said Smitty.

"But it was terrible. People lost interest in it and began leaving straight away," Sylvia explained. A trace of her Cambridge years came into her voice. "At first, people assumed Henry's father had produced the forgeries. The scandal was going to ruin him. But seeing how the whole affair had injured his father, William Henry Ireland eventually did the right thing."

"Confessed in one of the first 'tell-all' books!" noted Smitty.

"Yes," Sylvia added. "*The Confession of William Henry Ireland*, published in 1805. *That* I do not have a copy of, but I wish I did."

"So, you see, we might be regarded as forgers and meet the same fate as William Henry Ireland and his father."

"What happened?" asked Joe. "Prison?"

Smitty laughed. "Worse. Disgrace."

"Ireland left England for almost ten years."

"Where'd he go?" asked Joe, laughing. "Ireland?"

Smitty chuckled. "No, lad. Some place far better. France!"

"I love Ireland!" said Sylvia.

"As do I, my good woman. Just teasing."

They fell silent again and went back to their studies. Joe, uncertain if he would know what he was looking for, pulled out a copy of *The Mysterious William Shakespeare* by Charlton Ogburn and sat down in an easy chair in a corner of Sylvia's office to read.

"Wow," announced Joe, startling the others. "Listen to this. Ogburn is quoting Henry James: 'I am sort of haunted by the conviction that the divine William is the biggest and most successful fraud ever practiced on a patient world.' Ogburn lists a number of people who doubted the authorship."

"Mark Twain, of course," said Smitty.

"Yes, he's listed, along with Freud, John Galsworthy, Charlie

Chaplin, Orson Welles. Plus a bunch of scholars I'm not familiar with."

"I haven't scanned that book in years," admitted Sylvia.

"Well," Joe said, smiling. "He makes a lot of use of the book you showed us in the library, the one in the purple cover."

"Looney's book, *Shakespeare Identified*?" Sylvia asked.

"Yeah," answered Joe. "Some of the reviews of Looney's book, at least according to Ogburn, said it was as impressive a work of scholarship as Darwin's *Origin of the Species*."

"Impressive indeed," said Smitty. "Keep reading. I'm going to spend some time rummaging around in Looney's books, now that you've piqued my interest again."

"Well," Sylvia added. "Based on the samples of Edward de Vere's handwriting in Looney's, the handwriting on most of the pages we have here looks identical."

"We're closing in," Smitty said. "I can feel it."

Joe settled back into the easy chair and began reading Chapter 11 of Ogburn's book. Much of the writing seemed to record the various petty battles between the Stratfordians and the anti-Stratfordians, as well as personal battles the author had fought. He found it slow-going, jotting down notes when he read something useful and putting Post-it notes on pages that held a piece of solid evidence.

But as he worked, the stress of the past few days caught up with him, and he drifted into a dream world where scholars and playwrights swirled in his imagination, as if he were floating down a slow-moving stream, odd faces of both scholars and aristocrats appearing briefly from the shadows of trees and shrubs along the bank of the waterway—a dark, slow-moving waterway that, even in his dream, he knew was something like the place known as Lost Slough where he and his wife had nearly died.

CHAPTER 21

How oft when men are at the point of death
Have they been merry!
From *Romeo and Juliet*

Driving behind Joe Conrad at a safe distance, Benedict had taken the next exit north of University Avenue and circled back, assuming they were headed to Sylvia Williamson's office on the Berkeley campus, the place he'd visited before.

He parked in a garage just south of the campus and walked uphill to a building called Wheeler Hall that was all but deserted, save for one large office where the name Dr. Sylvia Williamson was engraved in a plastic nameplate on the door. Benedict glanced through the narrow window on the side of the door and saw three people inside sitting at a large table covered by books and papers.

He grinned. They were so absorbed in their work, they didn't notice him peering through the window. His heart beat faster. He'd found the documents at last. He could see the young one—Joseph Conrad—holding an obviously aged piece of paper and examining it as he listened to one of the others speak. It would be nice to hear what they were discussing.

Benedict pulled back from the door and glanced up and down the hallway. No one was around. A Saturday in the middle of summer. Should he risk entering the office now and taking the papers, knowing he'd have to kill all three people? Or should he risk waiting until they left the office and then return and break in. Assuming they left the papers inside when they left, perhaps for lunch or dinner, he could easily take them and meet his contact before they even discovered that their treasure was missing.

But what if they took the documents with them?

So close. Benedict fought the urge to barge into the office. He didn't mind killing them, but it would be sloppy. Someone might scream and be heard. Campus police might come before he'd gathered all the documents.

Knowing the smart course of action was to wait until later, Benedict nevertheless decided he would test the door handle and allow it to make the decision for him. If it was unlocked, he'd go in now and finish the job. If the door was locked, then he'd wait until they left.

He unzipped his windbreaker, pulled on a pair of leather gloves, took his pistol—a 10 mm. Heckler & Koch—from its holster and screwed on the silencer that came with it. With the silenced weapon in his right hand, hidden inside the windbreaker again, Benedict placed the fingertips of his left hand on the doorknob and closed his grip. A smile on his face, he glanced up and down the hallway once again, glanced through the window of the door to confirm that the two men had their backs to him, and then he tried the handle.

It yielded a little as he turned it clockwise. But then it met resistance. He turned it counter clockwise. Again, it yielded at first but stopped. *Locked?*

Benedict tightened his grip on the handle and turned it again, quietly, to make sure. Yes. Locked.

Fate had decided for him. The lucky bastards would live—at least a little while longer.

Benedict stepped aside so he wouldn't be seen through the window and held his gun as he unscrewed the silencer. He tucked the silencer back into its holder and holstered his pistol. He zipped up the windbreaker, tugged the driving gloves off his hands and crammed them into his jacket pocket.

He would wait and listen. He had seen, across the room, the high windows on the other side of the office. Perfect. He'd place a bug on the window. He could go somewhere and listen all afternoon, as long as he stayed within a thousand yards of the bug.

Yes. Maybe he'd learn something useful he could use with his client, to jack up the price.

He smiled, confident about his decision. Then he turned toward the door at the end of the hall and walked quietly toward the sunlight.

Suddenly, he was very hungry.

CHAPTER 22

Oft expectation fails, and most oft there
Where most it promises…
From *All's Well That Ends Well*

Two hours later, a noise awoke him. Then Sylvia's voice pulled him from a dreamy slumber. He stretched and focused on his haggard colleagues.

Joe stood. "What was that noise?"

Smitty smiled. "Welcome to the living!"

Joe grinned, embarrassed. "Sorry. Guess the last few days have taken a toll." He looked around the room and noticed the door handle. "Is the door unlocked?"

Smitty nodded. "I stepped out to use the restroom. May have forgotten to lock it."

Joe stepped over and locked the handle again. Then he joined his colleagues at the worktable. "Thought I heard a noise. Was I dreaming?"

Sylvia shot him a preoccupied look. "Just a bird hitting the window. Happens once in awhile, especially at sunset. The glare, I guess."

Joe rubbed the back of his neck. "I'm feeling a bit paranoid. Sylvia, might be a good idea to call your campus police and asked them to look around."

She leveled her eyes. "You're not serious."

"Yes, I am. I've learned to trust my instincts."

Smitty studied Joe's face. "Couldn't hurt, Sylvia. Joe's had some experience dealing with...darker forces, let us say."

Trying not to look exasperated, Sylvia put down Looney's book and walked to her desk. She picked up the phone and dialed a number while Joe and Smitty watched.

"How long have I been asleep?"

Smitty patted his shoulder. "Not long, Lad. But we've made some progress."

"Oh?" Joe looked at the documents and books spread out before them. "Have you figured out who the author is?"

"Yes," chimed Smitty.

Sylvia spoke to someone, then hung up and stepped back over to the table. "We've put together the time line and drawn a few inferences from the evidence."

"Good." Joe looked up at Sylvia. "So what's the answer to this riddle?"

"The answer is in the handwriting and the dedication," she replied. "The early plays must have been written by Edward de Vere, but the later plays, after de Vere's death, were either revised by, or written by, Mary Sidney, the Countess of Pembroke. The *First Folio was* dedicated to her sons, Pembroke and Montgomery, after all."

Smitty nodded excitedly, his voice going up. "It also explains why Ben Jonson refers to the author as the 'sweet swan of Avon.' Mary Sidney's personal symbol was the swan!"

"Ben Jonson had to know," Sylvia added, beaming.

Smitty agreed. "He was giving readers all the clues they needed to figure it out for themselves."

"And the Countess of Pembroke was highly educated," said Sylvia, a smile of pride gracing her lips. "Perhaps not as well traveled as Edward de Vere, but Mary Sidney encircled herself with the best writers of her time."

"So Shakespeare was really two people, one male, one female?" asked Joe.

"Not exactly," Sylvia explained. "Will Shakspeare was his own man, but he was a front, a poser. His *dramatic works*—and probably all of his poems—were the products of at least three people who, because of their high station in society could not be associated with works deemed vulgar by the Mayor of London or perhaps treasonous by the Queen herself. People lost their heads for less."

"Yes, but many of the plays were in support of the Queen," said Smitty. "She'd have no reason to take the playwright's head."

"But that's even more reason to hide the fact that the plays were written by a nobleman, someone close to the monarchy," added Sylvia.

"Didn't any aristocrats publish under their own names?" asked Joe.

"Oh, yes, yes, lad, of course. But they had to be careful."

"We have to go public," Sylvia said, as if trying to convince herself.

"We'll face a lot of resistance," Smitty said. "It's not easy to topple a titan."

"But you have the proof, now, don't you?" asked Joe. He put the book down and stood up. "With these manuscripts as evidence and the scientific data—the dating of the paper and ink, the handwriting analysis—nobody can deny your findings."

Sylvia smiled. "Proof never convinces anyone of something they'd rather not believe. Consider Galileo. Or Darwin."

"But now you're talking about science versus religious faith," quipped Joe, stepping over to the worktable.

"Belief in the Stratford man *is* a kind of religious faith," Sylvia replied, "and we who question his authorship are considered heretics. No proof needed."

"I'm afraid Sylvia's correct, lad. We will present this evidence to the world, but I'm afraid this is only the opening salvo in a long, long struggle."

"People have tried to expose the truth about Shakespeare before," said Sylvia. "Many careers have been ruined."

Joe stared at the handwriting samples on the table in front of his colleagues. "One thing still troubles me."

Sylvia and Smitty looked at him.

"What is it, Joe?" Smitty asked.

"Well, where have these papers been all this time? And how in the world did Jack Claire get his hands on them?"

Sylvia shrugged. "Good questions, Joe, but I'm not sure they need to be answered, not to start the ball rolling on the revelations we're about to share with the world."

"Maybe," Joe admitted, "but I think we ought to tie up as many loose ends as possible before we go public."

Smitty nodded. "The lad has a point. The more unanswered questions we have, the less credible we'll seem."

"Yeah," agreed Joe. "Think about it. Reporters are bound to ask where these papers came from. It won't be enough to say, well, before he died, Dr. Jack Claire sent them to Joseph Conrad."

"What do you suggest, Joe?" asked Smitty. "We can't very well ask Jack Claire now that he's dead."

Joe grunted. "Mary Sidney and Edward de Vere are dead, too, but that didn't stop us."

Sylvia laughed. "He's got a point."

"We investigate further?" asked Smitty.

"We investigate further," said Joe.

Sylvia smiled at Joe, asking, "Do you have a suggestion as to where we begin?"

Joe closed his eyes and tried to think. Something Hayden Crawford had said two weeks ago was coming back into his mind, something about Jack's travels just before his change, his reinvigoration.

"I'm not sure," admitted Joe, "but I think we need to speak to Hayden Crawford, the man who took over after Jack died."

"Why?" asked Smitty. He placed a hand on Joe's shoulder. "Do you think he might be behind the burglaries and...?"

"And the murders?" Joe shook his head. "No, at least, I hope not, but when I was there for Jack's funeral, he said something about a trip Jack took to England a few years ago. Hayden knew Jack had found something."

Sylvia took a step toward her desk, reaching for the telephone. "Call him right now and ask him what he knows," she said. "What time is it in Baton Rouge?"

"He's not in Baton Rouge," said Joe. "He's in Europe. He's almost impossible to reach. I've tried."

Smitty shook his head, trying to understand. "Wait a minute. Hayden Crawford is outside the country right now, while all of this is going on?"

Joe looked at him. "Yes."

"Doesn't that seem odd?"

"He and his wife go to Europe for a month every summer. They do some sort of house swapping."

"Oh," said Smitty. "I see. But still…"

"Yes," said Sylvia. "With everything that's going on—losing your colleague and the chair of the department, having to step into his shoes, getting the department ready for a new academic year—yes, it does seem rather strange that he would be outside the country."

"I agree," said Smitty. "I think we may have found the culprit, the man behind the search for these papers."

Joe thought about it for a minute. As ambitious as Hayden Crawford was, Joe didn't think he was capable of murder, or of sanctioning it.

"No, I don't think he's behind it."

"Why not?" asked Sylvia. "I mean, I don't know the man, but it seems to me he could have delayed his trip for at least a few days to get things in order."

Joe shrugged, unable to defend his hunch.

"Well, lad, what's our next move?"

He looked at Smitty and then back at Sylvia. "Me? Why is it up to me?"

"Because Dr. Claire sent the papers to you," Sylvia said gently. "He obviously trusted your judgment."

Joe turned to Smitty, who nodded.

"*You* must decide, lad."

Joe shook his head, but then scanned the beige manuscripts that were spread out over the large table in front of him. A shaft of orange light from the setting sun streamed into the room through a high window, casting a warm glow over the documents.

"I don't know, I don't know. I'm tempted to ask, What would Smitty do?"

"Sorry, lad. This decision you make alone."

What would Jack do? he wondered. The fading orange light moved slowly across the piles of papers. The warmth of the light reminded Joe of staying late at the swimming pool with Sara and the kids. He wished all of it were out in the open so he didn't have to fear exposure. He knew now why Jack Claire had been so reluctant to go public with the documents. Even if Sylvia and her experts were right, the three of them were bound to face tremendous skepticism, even ridicule. For Smitty, it didn't much matter—he'd done his work and finished his career with honor.

For Sylvia? Well, she'd be stirring up the pot, creating controversy in her own field, doing precisely what was expected of her. And defending the claim that a seventeenth century female writer was one of the geniuses behind Shakespeare's works wouldn't hurt her career.

But for him? If these papers were proven to be fraudulent, he'd be the fall guy, the scapegoat. After all, he was the one who'd brought the papers to the two experts. *He'd* be blamed for trying to perpetrate a deception.

Suddenly, he had a sense of the anxiety Will Shakspeare must have felt, as the front for the real authors. No wonder he left London and returned to Stratford and lived out the rest of his days in relative anonymity. Joe wanted to return to Davis-upon- Interstate 80 and live out his days quietly, too.

On the other hand, if the papers were authentic, and obviously someone believed they were—believed it enough to murder at least three people—if the papers really were what Sylvia believed they were, then Joe's future seemed assured. Who knows how much money the three of them could make!

The shaft of light was gone. Now only the simple lamp on Sylvia's desk illuminated the room, the walls of bookshelves hidden in half shadow.

He looked Smitty and Sylvia in the eyes to see their reaction. "If we go public, will that stop the guy who's searching for these papers?"

"Presumably," said Smitty.

"If exposing this will stop the killer, then I think we must."

"Yes," said Sylvia. "Going public might stop the person who's after them, but it might not."

"Why not?" asked Joe. "A collector will look pretty suspicious if he shows up with these papers after we've announced that they're in our possession and that we think the person looking for them is responsible for murdering three people or more."

Smitty patted Joe on the shoulder. "True, but that's never stopped ruthless collectors in the past."

"Great works of art are stolen from museums all the time, Joe. Not because the thieves want them. The thieves are usually commissioned by someone who's willing to pay a fortune to get his hands on something rare and priceless."

"And the perverse thing is, lad, the very act of stealing a great work actually increases its value."

Joe shook his head in frustration. "We have to go public, and the sooner, the better. For one thing, we'll be able to get the police involved and that should help protect my wife and yours, Smitty."

CHAPTER 23

Fortune reigns in gifts of the world.
From *As You Like It*

Benedict shot an electronic dart from the air pistol and hit the window easily. Then he placed an earpiece in his right ear and adjusted the dial on the tiny receiver. The voice of the younger man, Conrad, crackled to life. "*What's the answer to the riddle?*"

Benedict listened, intrigued. He, too, wanted to know what all the fuss was about. Maybe the information could help him jack up the price for recovering the documents.

He glanced around as he walked in a stand of trees, finding a good spot where he could sit unnoticed. The last glimmers of sunlight faded against the tops of the hills in the distance. He'd be well hidden in the copse of trees in the dark.

Finding a bench, Benedict sat and glanced around to check the parameter. He took out a small notebook and a penlight. As the subjects of his surveillance mentioned names and dates, Benedict jotted them down. *De Vere. Mary Sidney. Pembroke.* He was unsure what it all meant, but the more he knew, the stronger his hand when it came time to re-negotiate with the client.

Holding the penlight in his mouth, Benedict sat contentedly, filling page after page with unfamiliar words and names, confident they would yield more profit later. He failed to see the two campus policeman strolling between the building and the trees where he sat.

But their voices alerted him.

He grabbed the light from his teeth and switched it off, watching the uniformed men as one of them swept the beam of a flashlight back and forth over the ground in front of them.

Quietly, Benedict allowed the penlight, pencil and notepad to drop into his lap. He tugged his pistol out of its holster, grabbed the silencer and screwed it onto the barrel efficiently, keeping his eyes trained on the other men.

Their voices grew indistinct as they walked farther away and Benedict allowed the air to leave his mouth silently as he exhaled. The figures disappeared into the darkness at the far end of the building.

He sat stone still, his pistol in one hand, the index finger of his other hand turning down the dial of the receiver he'd been listening to. He waited.

As he'd expected, the men turned back and approached from the far end of the trees, the beam of light now sweeping back and forth over the slanted ground under the branches.

Benedict stood slowly, allowing the penlight, notepad and pencil to drop to the debris at his feet. He kicked dried leaves and twigs over his items, and then stepped behind a wide redwood. With his back to the tree, he might be missed by the men as they walked by.

The voices grew closer. If they missed him, he'd let them live.

Suddenly, a woman's laugh could be heard through his earpiece, even though he had turned down the volume.

He heard a guard say, "*What was that?*"

The man with the flashlight stepped around to his left, a foot from Benedict's face, shining the light into his unblinking eyes. Benedict leveled the gun at the cop's forehead, but then his head exploded with pain.

The other cop had stepped around the tree on Benedict's right and cracked him on the back of the head with his own flashlight.

Benedict swung his arms around to defend himself, but the first cop kicked him in the side of the leg at the knee, buckling his legs. He rolled as he fell to shoot the cop who'd hit him, but the other man knocked the pistol from his hand with the flashlight.

Dazed, Benedict clenched his teeth and let the two men handle him.

"Stand up," one cop barked.

The other man grabbed his arm and pulled him to his feet.

"Hands against the tree."

Benedict complied. He knew the procedures.

As one cop frisked him, the other reached down and picked up his gun.

"Would you look at this! A damn silencer!"

"You're kidding." The cop patted down Benedict's sides. "Yeah. He's wearing a holster. It's empty."

"What the hell are you up to, Mister?"

Benedict remained silent, waiting.

"I'm calling Dispatch."

When the cop's hands were on Benedict's calves, he made his move. He kicked backward at the squatting cop and pushed off the tree, spinning to swing at the other cop who held his pistol. The cop reacted by shooting Benedict with his own gun, which infuriated him. The bullet passed through Benedict's side as the assassin gripped the cop's chin in one hand and the back of his head in the other, twisting the head sharply, breaking his neck and killing him instantly.

Then Benedict kicked the other cop in the face as he struggled to his feet and fumbled for his gun. The cop rolled down the hill and Benedict, in a karate stance, kicked him again.

On all fours, the police officer crawled on the ground to flee his attacker. But Benedict, composing himself, stepped relentlessly closer. He landed another hard kick against the cop's side, breaking several ribs, which pierced the man's lungs and made him roll onto his back, unable to catch his breath.

Benedict stood over the man, looked down into his fearful eyes, raised his leg and planted his foot into the soft portion of the man's throat, crushing his windpipe. The cop's eyes—even as he lay dying—widened with the sickening reality of his own mortality.

Benedict grinned. Then winced with pain. He felt his side. Sticky.

He took a long, deep breath, then exhaled slowly. The wound was not bad, through and through in muscle only. No arteries or organs had been hit. He'd had worse.

He couldn't treat the wound now, though. He had to hide the bodies. The trees would have to do. Then he could find a restroom and bind his side.

Benedict bent down, grabbed the expired cop by the wrists and tugged him up the hill into the deep, deep shadows of the trees. This had gone on long enough. It was time.

CHAPTER 24

Foul deeds will rise,
Though all the earth ov'erwhelm them, to
men's eyes.
from Hamlet

They decided to call local television stations in the morning. Meanwhile, Joe and Smitty would take the documents back to the Durant, in case someone broke into Sylvia's offices.

As they left Wheeler Hall, walking through Sproul Plaza, they heard the bells of the Campanile chime. It was eleven o'clock.

"Ever want to teach at a large university like this?" Joe asked Smitty as they strolled to the hotel.

"I *went* to a large university like this. I felt lost. No, I enjoyed my years at CLU. I could really reach students in my small classes. And I had time for research."

"Still," said Joe. "Wouldn't you love to have an office like that, a large workroom?"

"I do," Smitty said. "In my house."

"True, true," admitted Joe. He shifted the briefcase from one hand to the other as they walked. "But wouldn't it be nice to have the financial resources to buy the old books and papers you'd like to own? To travel the way she has?"

He turned to see the smile on Smitty's face, that Buddha grin. He waited for an admonition against worldly possessions when he heard footsteps race up behind them.

At first, Joe thought a bat had flown over Smitty's head. But then he heard the crack of the blackjack coming down and saw the stunned expression on Smitty's face.

"Smitty!" screamed Joe.

The older man crumpled to the pavement.

Joe swung around in time to glimpse the blackjack descending. He ducked, and the blow glanced off the side of his head, sending searing pain through his skull and causing him to stagger backward.

A tall figure, silhouetted by the campus lights, stepped toward him. An arm went up again and Joe knew he was about to be hit.

Get him away from Smitty! thought Joe.

He ran down the hill, carrying the briefcase of papers, blinding pain blurring his vision.

To his left was Telegraph Avenue, filled with people, but traffic was too thick to run through.

"Help!" Joe yelled. "Help me!"

No one turned to look, the crowd noise too great. Like Bourbon Street in New Orleans during Mardi Gras, the avenue was filled with people oblivious to the outside world.

But Joe could hear the footsteps rushing up behind him, so he turned right and ran back into campus. Cutting through a slight opening in a thick hedge, he stumbled onto a dirt path that dropped down onto pavement again. He heard the swish of the person behind him breaking through the bushes.

If he could find the library, there would be people. Joe ran as hard as he could, carrying the papers.

Poor Smitty. Joe had caught a glimpse of him writhing in pain on the pavement, so he knew Smitty was still alive.

Glancing back, Joe saw the tall figure catching up, though he was limping. *He's injured.* Maybe he could get away after all.

He cut between two buildings and ran as fast as he could. Turning a corner, he raced back up the hill toward the clock tower. If his pursuer were injured, maybe running up hill would be too hard for him.

Coming out of the shadows of the buildings, Joe glanced back. The dark figure was having trouble keeping up, jogging more slowly, his limp more pronounced.

Joe looked left and right to find somebody, anybody, he could yell to for help. The campus was empty. Saturday night in the middle of the summer. Hell, what student in his right mind would be on campus?

The top of the clock tower was lit up brightly. Its light shone like a beacon. *People.* He headed for the tower, ducking to the left behind another building. The dark pursuer was losing ground.

Joe looked for a safe hiding place for the case. Without it, he could run faster, but leaving it behind, he risked losing it. Still, if he could disappear from the other man's line of sight long enough to stash it, then...

Joe didn't know the campus layout, but at the next left he turned and ran the length of the building. When he looked back, he saw the man stop at the far end of the building. In shadows, the man was hard to see, but Joe suddenly recognized his stance. Turned sideways, his arm outstretched, he was aiming at Joe.

The instant Joe saw the flash, he jerked right as the bullet ricocheted off the side of the building next to his head. Shards of stone struck his temple, barely missing his eye. Why hadn't he heard the shot? *A silencer.*

Bleeding, Joe turned the corner as another shot hit the edge of the building behind him.

A loading dock. Two Dempsey Dumpsters overflowed with garbage. Stacks of cardboard boxes stood on either side of the dumpsters. As he ran toward a stack of boxes, Joe scanned them to find one that was about the same size as the case. All the boxes on the south side of the dumpsters were larger, but he side-stepped when he reached the boxes on the north side.

There in the middle of a stack was a box the same size and shape as the briefcase he was carrying. Joe tucked the briefcase behind the stack, then pulled the thin box—the decoy—out from the middle, which caused the stack to tumble over, covering the case of papers he'd been carrying.

The decoy box was much lighter. He held it in one hand as if it were a briefcase. From the squeaking noise it made as he ran, Joe figured it must have Styrofoam inside.

Ahead was a line of trees and beyond, the opening of lawn that would lead him to Sather Tower. He ran for the protection of the trees' shadows just as bark exploded beside him.

Another gunshot!

Can I make it across the lawn before he has a clear shot?

Running as hard as he could, Joe broke through the trees and raced across the lawn, up a flight of stairs and toward the glass door of Sather Tower. Pushing the box under his left arm, Joe raced for the tower, hoping there would be people, but when reached the glass door, he found the door locked and the lobby, empty.

Glass shattered in front of him.

The killer, just running up the hill behind him, had unwittingly shot the door.

Joe climbed through the broken glass and ran to the elevator. He pushed the button and the door opened immediately. Half falling into the elevator, he pushed the button for the top floor and waited. The doors did not close. Joe panicked. *I'm going to die inside a damned elevator!*

He found the button with two arrows pointing to each other and pushed it repeatedly until, with exasperating slowness, the doors started to close. Just before they closed, Joe heard footsteps crunch on broken glass.

The old elevator began its slow ascent to the top of Sather Tower. As the elevator car clambered to the top, Joe panted, bent over, trying to catch his breath. He felt his temple, sticky with blood, and wiped blood out of his eye.

"Okay, smart guy," he queried as he panted. "What the hell do I do when I get to the top?"

Before he had fully caught his breath, the elevator stopped and the doors struggled to open. Joe stepped into a dim hallway. Before he realized what was happening, the elevator doors closed behind him and the indicator showed that the elevator was headed back down to the ground floor.

Joe wasn't sure what to do. He looked around. To his left, a narrow stairway led to the upper level, and he ran up the steps, taking two at a time, turning and turning again to a small room. Up another short flight of stairs and he stood on the observation deck.

Still holding the decoy box, Joe raced to the half wall and looked down. The campus seemed deserted. He walked around to look at another section. From where he was standing, he could see the campus below him, the brightly lit streets of Berkeley to his left, and beyond it all was San Francisco Bay and the City shrouded in layers of fog. Between the top of the wall and the ceiling were iron bars, like prison bars, to stop jumpers, Smitty had told him. He didn't think he could squeeze between the tops of the bars and the ceiling that overhung the observation deck.

Like a caged animal, Joe paced the deck, looking up and down, from side to side, trying to think of what to do.

Joe dropped the box and hopped up on the wall, grabbing the bars with both hands like a Chimpanzee. He pulled himself up and tried to squeeze through the bars, but it was impossible. The space between was too narrow. The strain started the flow of blood again from his temple.

No. He couldn't pull himself through. Too winded from running.

He heard footsteps on the stairs below.

Joe dropped down, grabbed the decoy box again and quickly stepped around the corner out of sight.

Now he was facing the lights of San Francisco. While *he* was too thick to squeeze through the bars, the box he was holding wasn't. He turned the box sideways and pushed it through the bars without letting it fall. He held it just outside the bars below the wall as the tall pursuer stepped around the corner and pointed a black pistol toward Joe's face.

"Give me that case," the man said in a deep voice.

Joe wiped blood out of his eye and shook his head. "Drop the gun over the side and I'll give you the briefcase."

The man's expression did not change.

"Why don't I just shoot you?"

Joe laughed. "And risk having these fragile documents drop to the ground? They'll blow all over campus. You'll have a helluva time rounding them up before the police get here."

The man's cold stare caused Joe to shudder. But he had looked evil in the eyes before. He knew that showing weakness simply increased its power.

"Look," Joe said to the killer. "I don't want to die for these damned documents. Drop the gun over the side, and I'll pull this case back through the bars and let you have it. Of course, I want your guarantee that you'll let me get on the elevator first."

The man smiled. "I think I'll just shoot you and let the papers fall."

"Have it your way," said Joe. He extended his arm, as if to drop the box, keeping it just out of the man's line of sight.

"No! Okay. Bring it inside the bars."

"First, drop the gun over the edge."

Joe's pursuer stood there for a few seconds, his right arm outstretched, the gun still pointed at Joe's face. Then he turned and walked over to the bars a few feet away. He put his hand through the bars and opened it. The gun disappeared into the darkness.

Joe smiled. He slowly turned his hand over and the box slipped off. It too disappeared into the darkness as the man drew in his arm.

"No!" he screamed, but as he lurched toward Joe, his outstretched arm caught on the bar, giving Joe just enough opportunity to kick him in the side.

He screamed in pain and doubled over as Joe raced passed him to the stairs.

But the other man beat him to the doorway, blocking Joe's escape.

Joe stepped back as the man—his face twisted with pain—lurched toward him,

"I've been looking forward to this," he said, his teeth clenched.

Joe tried to kick him, but he easily blocked it and punched Joe in the chest, knocking the wind out of him, sending him back against the low wall and high bars. Joe tried to catch his breath.

Straightening up, Joe saw the many bells, large and small, hanging above his head. Underneath was the little glass-encased room with a keyboard used to play the bells. The roof was low and with the window frames providing something to grip, he knew he could climb higher. The question was, could his pursuer.

Like a football lineman, Joe leaped forward, driving his head into the other man's gut, hearing a gush of air escape from the man's lungs.

The other man fell backward and groaned. Joe could see the other man's wound through his torn shirt—it was bleeding badly. Drops of blood splattered on the floor.

Joe hoisted himself up to the roof of the carillon room. From there, he climbed up between the structures holding the many bells until he reached the ceiling.

A gunshot exploded below him and one of the bells rang out, piercing the air with its shrill ring. *The killer had a second gun!* Another gunshot and the small bell next to his ear rang, nearly breaking his eardrum. Joe covered his left ear and searched the ceiling. There had to be a way into the attic space and the upper level.

A third gunshot and two bells clanged. He knew it was only a matter of seconds before the killer found the right angle through the many hanging bells to find his target.

He climbed from one beam to another, feeling the ceiling for some means of escape.

Finally, the outline of a square trap door became visible to him in the dim light. He pushed on it, but it was locked and wouldn't budge.

Joe glanced down. He could see the killer looking up at him, a sadistic grin on his face. The killer pointed his gun at Joe.

This was it.

Instinctively, Joe jerked out of sight just as another shot rang out. The bullet struck the door above him, and Joe heard it bounce.

The killer's missed shot had unlocked the trapdoor!

Joe scrambled through the door, which fell backward and clanged noisily as it dropped. Joe flipped the trap door closed again, crawling on top of it to prevent the man from climbing up after him. His eyes adjusted to the darkness and he looked for some kind of opening.

Feeling his way up the wall, cobwebs brushing his face, Joe found another edge and pulled himself up.

Another shot rang out and more light poured through the two holes.

Enough light to illuminate the crawl space. Joe looked around and found the other door. He crawled toward it through cobwebs. Once he reached it, he found that it was locked.

Would he have an advantage on the roof? Maybe. Someone must have heard the gunshots, his yelling. Somebody must be on the way.

Another gunshot exploded below him, shattering roof tile beside his head.

Too close!

Joe turned around to see the man struggling to climb up through the bells. Now Joe had to move. The gunshot cracking the roof tiles gave him an idea. Starting with the cracked and shattered tiles around the bullet hole, Joe tried to use his fist to knock away enough of the tiles to climb out onto the roof.

But the tiles were rough on the inside and his knuckles were taking a beating, beginning to bleed. He reached down and removed a shoe, putting his fist inside it and then using it to knock away the tiles. First one, then another, and then several came free. Cool night air rushed in and washed over his face.

He pulled his shoe back on and grabbed the rough edge of the hole he'd created. Suddenly, the bells clanged underneath him. Joe hoisted himself through the hole just as the assassin struggled once again to climb through the opening.

Joe managed to climb up and sit on the sharp, broken edge of the hole in the tiled roof. He jerked his legs up out of the darkness, fearing the assassin would grab his foot, like a shark biting down.

The roof was impossibly steep, but Joe grabbed at the corner and found edges he could grip. *Just like the Rocknasium!* He clambered up the roof, but as he climbed toward the steep apex, he started to slide.

Carefully, Joe caught himself, his finger tips gripping the edges of the tiles, and he climbed slowly to the peak. At the top was a metal decoration—a lightning rod perhaps—that he held onto. He wiped blood out of his eye again and looked around.

What are my options? If the killer made it to the roof, Joe was dead.

There was nowhere to hide. His choices were to drop to his death over the side or wait to be shot.

A cool breeze chilled his neck. He'd broken a sweat.

The image of Smitty crumpling to the ground like a limp piece of cloth flashed into Joe's mind. Was Smitty all right? Maybe he was telling the police everything right now.

Or maybe he was dead. The crack to the back of his head had been loud.

What would Joe tell Alicia?

Joe heard a scraping sound. He dared not look. He heard the other man grunt, and Joe knew the killer, too, had climbed up onto the roof.

The killer tilted his head to look up at Joe.

"Why don't you go for the papers?" yelled Joe. "They're blowing all over campus. Go after them."

The man pointed the gun, but Joe scurried around to the other side of the roof, holding the metal object at the apex. The killer fired anyway, and Joe could have sworn the bullet blew by his cheek.

"No rush," the man said. "I have a new goal now. I'm a very task-oriented person, Professor Conrad."

"Did you kill Jack Claire?" Joe asked the man. "Was it you?"

Even in the dim, bluish light, Joe could see the smile stretch across the killer's mouth and expose his white teeth.

"Oh, yes," he said softly. "That was quite a morning."

Picturing Jack Claire's dead body smashed on the pavement and Smitty crumpled like a rag doll, he was overwhelmed by rage. "God damn you!" Joe yelled. He swung back around and slid down the roof straight at the man, hitting him in the side where he had kicked him before. The pursuer howled in pain, and they both slid down to a small landing edged by a two-foot wall.

Joe tried to stand but fell back against the roof, facing the assassin who struggled to balance on the narrow landing.

Clutching the edge of the roof, Joe kicked him hard in the stomach, feeling the rush of stale breath as the wind rushed out of the man's lungs.

The man let out a guttural groan, and Joe kicked him again. Now

Joe's attacker staggered backward, his legs catching on the wall, and he lost his balance. But somehow, cat-like, he pirouetted and fell face first on the narrow stone guardrail. Clinging precariously to the edge, his feet slipping over, the man looked up at Joe and grinned.

Sirens screamed in the distance.

"The police are on their way," Joe said.

The man shook his head. "They won't make it in time for you, Professor." Holding the wall, the killer tried to draw himself up.

As hard as he could, Joe planted the bottom of his right shoe in the killer's face. Stunned, the man tried to grab Joe's leg, but failed. Arms flailing, hands trying in vain to clutch anything, the man leered at Joe—a grimace of disgust twisting his face. Then he disappeared over the side.

He did not scream.

Part V:
The Taming of the Shrew

CHAPTER 25

To mourn a mischief that is past and gone
Is the next way to draw new mischief on.
From *Much Ado about Nothing*

Joe Conrad stood over the killer's broken body. The man had evidently landed on his head—it looked like a crushed melon. The paramedic kneeling at the body checked for a pulse but shook his head. Three campus police officers stood with Joe over the corpse, looking down at it and then over at Joe.

"How'd this happen again?" a stocky, middle-aged officer near Joe asked.

"I told you. He chased me up to the top of the clock tower. I managed to climb onto the roof. He followed me up there and lost his balance."

The stocky cop eyed him with suspicion. "Lost his balance?"

"Yes, as he was trying to stand up to shoot me."

The other two cops—one young African-American, the other tall and white—glanced at each other skeptically.

"You didn't push him?"

"*Okay!*" Joe screamed. "I admit it—I kicked the hell out of him. He was trying to kill me, for God's sakes!"

"Calm down, Mr. Conrad."

Joe closed his eyes and felt his knees go weak. It was happening again, just as Sara had feared. Here he was, next to a corpse, the police suspecting him of murder. How the hell had he wound up like this again.

Just then, he heard a woman's voice calling his name. At first, he thought it was Sara. But how could it be? She was at Suzie's cabin in the mountains with the children. Wasn't she?

"Joe! Joe! Are you all right?"

He looked around in the darkness. The woman running up the hill toward him was too tall to be Sara. As she ran into the light, Joe recognized her. Sylvia Williamson rushed up and threw her arms around Joe.

"Are you all right?" she asked again, her mouth next to his ear.

She embraced him, and he didn't care. It felt so good to be held by someone he knew. His body, as taut as a bow string, relaxed finally in her arms.

"I'm all right."

He drew away just enough to look Sylvia in the eyes. She was as tall as he was. She glanced down at the smashed skull of the bloody corpse.

"Oh, *God!*" She buried her face in Joe's shoulder.

"How about Smitty?" Joe asked. "Is *he* okay?"

Sylvia nodded. "I just left him. Paramedics took him to the hospital. He might have a mild concussion, but he's alert and talking. He told the police everything. Says you led the man who assaulted him away and saved his life."

"I don't know about that," Joe said, his eyes welling up. "I wasn't sure what to do. I figured the guy wanted the manuscripts more than he wanted to hurt Smitty."

"Well," Sylvia said, forcing a sympathetic smile, "you're a hero again. If you hadn't fled with the papers, he"—she jerked her head toward the dead man—"he might have killed you both."

"Excuse me," said the stocky officer. "You know this gentleman?"

Sylvia stepped beside Joe, keeping her arm around his waist.

"This is Joseph Conrad. He's a Professor at Central Lutheran University. He and a colleague were here working with me on a research project."

The cop gave her a skeptical look. "And who are you, ma'am?"

"Who am *I*?" Sylvia smiled. "My name is Sylvia Williamson—*Doctor* Sylvia Williamson. I'm a professor here."

Joe smiled. She reminded him of Sidney Poitier saying, "They call me *Mister* Tibbs."

"Do you have some ID?"

"No, not on me. My purse is back in my office."

Joe started to tense up again and Sylvia, feeling it, rubbed his back.

"Can anyone vouch for you?" asked the officer. At least his tone was respectful.

"I can," said a voice from behind Joe.

The tall, white officer spoke up again. "I've known Dr. Williamson for years. She's one of our most distinguished professors."

"All right, Lieutenant. But can you vouch for *this* gentleman?"

The lieutenant looked Joe up and down. "No. Never saw him before in my life."

Joe looked at Sylvia, who looked at the cops.

The tall Lieutenant said, "But if Dr. Williamson vouches for him, then he's righteous."

Sylvia smiled.

Righteous? Joe thought about the word. It seemed an odd choice.

The stocky officer nodded. "Good enough. But we'll still need a written statement at the station, don't we, Lieutenant?"

"Absolutely," the tall cop said.

"Tonight?" asked Joe.

"Yes, sir. I'm afraid so." The Lieutenant looked at Joe. "If you're up for it, it would be better to get your statement down while the details are still fresh."

Still fresh. The words made Joe glance at the bloody head of the killer. The paramedics were just covering the body with a sheet.

"Do you know someone who can go with you?" the stocky cop asked.

Joe glanced at Sylvia.

"I mean, like a lawyer."

Joe closed his eyes—but in his mind, he saw the man slip off the edge of the roof again. He opened his eyes and looked squarely at the cop.

"Yeah. I've got a defense attorney in Sacramento."

"A defense attorney?" asked the Lieutenant. "Have you been arrested before?"

Joe's heart sank. "Yes," he admitted.

"Recently?"

"No, not recently." He wasn't going to say more than he had to.

"How long ago?"

"About three years ago."

"For what?"

Now Joe was watching a game of ping pong, looking from one cop to the other.

"I'd rather not say."

"Hold on, hold on," Sylvia said. "You remember the case, I'm sure. Joe Conrad is the one who caught the I-5 Strangler, remember?"

The Lieutenant nodded and the black officer stepped closer to Joe. "Yeah, I remember. *You're* that college professor who was accused of raping and murdering his students? Dumping their bodies in the delta."

"I remember that case," the stocky cop said. "Seems to me, it was a Detective out of Sacramento who caught the killer."

"Detective Ryan Dunn," Joe said. "Detective Dunn saved my life. We're friends now. I just had dinner with him last night."

The three cops looked at one another.

The stocky one nodded. "I think we'd better take you in anyway." He reached back and removed his handcuffs.

"That'd be a good idea after all," the lieutenant admitted. "Sorry, Dr. Williamson. We're already on alert. Two campus cops who responded to your call earlier haven't checked in. Maybe your colleague here knows something about that."

"Two cops are missing? I had nothing to do with it," said Joe. He pointed to the ambulance. "*He* probably killed them."

"You think the missing officers are deceased?" asked the Lieutenant. "Why would you think that?"

"Because that guy was a cold-blooded killer," Joe said, trying not to sound angry.

"This is ridiculous," Sylvia said. "This man saved a colleague's life. He thwarted the killer." Sylvia pointed to the corpse now resting crookedly under the white sheet, a crimson stain blooming at its head. "He deserves a medal, not those handcuffs."

The cop held out the handcuffs, saying, "That may be true, Ma'am, but we'll have to determine that for ourselves."

Joe pulled away from Sylvia. "It's all right. Been through this before. You stay with Smitty. I'll get there when I can."

"No, Joe," Sylvia said, reaching for his hand. "This isn't right."

"Like I said, been here, done this." Joe reached for his wallet, and all three cops reached for their guns. "Relax, officers. I'm just getting the business card for my lawyer so Dr. Williamson can call him."

Joe gingerly removed his wallet, showed it to the cops, and then opened it enough to extract Bill Morgan's card, which he handed to Sylvia. "Give him a call. Ask him to drive down as soon as he can. Tell him I won't say a word until he shows up."

The cop started to put the cuffs on Joe, but Joe reached into his wallet and pulled out another card, handing it to the cop. "Here's Detective Dunn's card, too. Why don't you give him a call and ask him to join us?"

"I will," the cop said. He took the card from Joe, glanced at it, and tucked it into his breast pocket. Then he slapped the steel handcuffs onto Joe's wrists and they clicked closed.

Riding in the backseat of the police car, being escorted to a holding cell, hearing the angry voices echoing in empty hallways, smelling the urine and bleach odors—it all brought back Joe's earlier experiences. He sat on the cold metal bench with his head in his hands, eyes closed, and tried to think about being at the pool with Sara and Katie and Brian, or floating in the Gulf on a breezy day—anything but where he was.

Finally he heard a friendly voice and looked up to see Ryan Dunn's haggard face smiling at him from the other side of the bars.

"What did your sister-in-law call you?"

Joe shook his head. "She's called me plenty of things over the years."

"A magnet for trouble, I think she said."

Joe forced a chuckle as he got to his feet.

The tired Detective reached through the bars and shook Joe's hand. "More like a lightening rod, I'd say."

After getting Joe released, Dunn took him to the hospital, but the nurses wouldn't allow them to visit Smitty. They went to the Durrant and crashed. Dunn slept in Smitty's adjoining room.

Sunday morning, after a quick breakfast, they went to the hospital and visited Smitty. Awake and alert, he was furious the doctor hadn't released him yet.

"Officer Dunn, be a good lad and spring me from this hell-hole, please!"

"Sorry, Dr. Smythe. Can't do it. Doctors outrank detectives."

"Joe," pleaded Smitty. "Can't you appeal to the Detective's native sanguinity?"

Joe smiled, pleased to hear the older professor sounding normal, healthy.

"Better stay until the doctors are sure you're okay. I'd hate to lose another friend over those stupid manuscripts."

"Damn," said Smitty. "I was so looking forward to spending the day with you and Sylvia. We're so close."

"Oh my GOD!" yelled Joe.

Smitty clutched his chest. "You damn near gave me a heart attack. What's wrong?"

"I just remembered the papers."

"The papers? What about the papers? You have them, don't you?"

Joe felt the blood drain from his face.

"The manuscripts you showed me night before last?" asked Dunn. "You don't have them, after all you've been through?"

Joe looked at Dunn and then back at Smitty.

"I hid the briefcase behind a dumpster."

"*When?*" demanded Smitty.

"Last night, Smitty. You know, when I led the killer away from *you*."

"Relax, Joe," Dunn said. "They're probably right where you left them."

"Well, go to it, lad. Get those documents."

Joe turned to rush from the hospital room but stopped, asking, "You'll be all right?"

"Not if you don't get those papers!"

Joe looked at Smitty, whose face had turned bright red.

"They don't pick up garbage on Sundays, do they?" he asked.

"Good God, lad. Get those papers before some garbage man recycles them!"

The hospital wasn't far from campus, and in fifteen minutes Joe and Dunn were standing at the dumpster.

"I think this is it," said Joe. "It all looks so different in the daylight. When you're not running for your life."

Joe reached down and pushed away some of the boxes leaning against the over-flowing dumpster. A rat jumped away from Joe's hand—Joe jumped back as Dunn laughed. The slick brown rodent disappeared under the dumpster.

"*Rats?* I hate rats," Joe said.

"Want me to shoot it?" Dunn asked dryly.

"Yeah, please."

"No can do. Animal rights people would go ape."

Joe groaned. "Go *ape*?"

Dunn laughed, saying, "No pun intended."

"Are you sure?"

"No, really. Said it without thinking."

Joe reached down cautiously and felt around. "Got it!" He pulled the briefcase out of the stacks of discarded boxes triumphantly.

"See?" Dunn said. "Told you it'd be where you left it."

"I'm glad *you* weren't worried. I sure as hell was."

"You've got this dumb luck thing going for you."

"Dumb luck? Is *that* what you call it?"

"Yeah," laughed Dunn. They walked down the alley together.

"It's when you think about things too much, you get yourself into trouble."

"Now you're making me sound like Hamlet."

Dunn chuckled. "Hamlet, huh. You're a prince, Joe. A real prince."

Joe groaned again. "Leave the puns to us English teachers."

"Why should you guys have all the fun?"

"It's one of the perks, Ryan. You know, like you guys getting to shoot people."

"Don't tempt me," the detective said.

CHAPTER 26

With patient mind each passion to endure,
In one desire to settle to the end?
Love then thy choice wherein such choice thou bind,
As nought but death may ever change thy mind.
From the sonnet "Love Thy Choice"

After lunch, Smitty was released. Joe, Ryan, Sylvia and Smitty stood outside the hospital in the warming sunlight breaking through the dissipating coastal fog.

"We're safe now," Smitty said. "With the killer out of the picture, we can take our time and do our research more methodically."

Sylvia nodded. "Thanks to Joe, we don't have to worry about someone stealing the papers. And we can keep all this under wraps for a while."

"Well, the police and reporters want some answers," Dunn added. "They've already been told about the Shakespeare papers, so there're bound to be more questions."

"Yeah," Joe added. "But now we have a perfect excuse to clam up."

The others looked at him.

"We say we can't discuss any of it because it's part of a police investigation. Gives us the perfect out."

Dunn laughed. "Your brushes with the law are turning you into quite the politician, Joe. You'll be running for office next."

Joe shook his head. "Me? Are you kidding? No way. Give me a classroom of eager young students. That's my constituency."

"Well said, lad," Smitty chimed in, patting Joe on the shoulder.

Sylvia smiled at Joe and glanced at Dunn. "So, what's next, Detective? What should *we* do?"

"Go back to your regular schedules, would be my suggestion. Give the local police time to sort things out. Joe's family is up at Tahoe, right?" He glanced at Joe.

"Yeah. No TV or cell phone service up there and I haven't bothered to call the cabin phone, so Sara probably doesn't even know what's happened. Otherwise, my cell phone would be ringing. I'll call her from home later."

"I know Licia's worried, though," said Smitty. "I'd like to get home as soon as we can, Joe."

"Of course."

Sylvia put her arms around Smitty and gave him a gentle hug. "Are you sure you're all right? No blurry vision?"

"I'm fine, dear woman. Slight headache, bruised shoulder where I hit the pavement, but otherwise good as new."

Then she hugged Joe, and with tears in her eyes said, "Thanks for taking care of this gentle man. Drive him home safely."

"I promise," Joe whispered in her ear. She was almost as tall as he was. Embracing her was very different from embracing Sara. "Thanks for vouching for me last night."

"Take care of yourself, too, while you're at it." She released Joe and stepped back. Then she reached her hand out to Ryan Dunn. "Nice meeting you, Detective."

They shook hands and smiled.

"The pleasure's all mine," Dunn said.

"What's your next step, Ryan?" Joe asked him.

Dunn let go of Sylvia's hand and looked at Joe and Smitty. "We need to find out who hired that guy. It's not over until we know who he was working for. I'll make a few calls. Have to be careful, though. This isn't my jurisdiction."

"What about you, Joe?" Sylvia asked.

Dunn's cell phone rang and he stepped away from the others to answer the call.

Joe turned back to Sylvia, saying, "I have to teach tomorrow, but I think I'll drive up to the cabin after class and spend the night with Sara and the kids."

"Sounds like a good idea," Smitty said. "Let's get back together on Friday, since Joe has the day off. We can resume our research then."

"Meanwhile," said Sylvia, "we'll do what we can on our own."

"Good," Joe said. He waved at Dunn and walked Smitty to the car.

After getting an update from his contact inside the Berkeley Police Department, Detective Dunn called Deirdre Claire and asked if she could meet him to discuss the latest turn of events.

"Ghastly," she said. "The man fell from the Campanile? I'm just reading about it in the *Chronicle*." Her voice sounded drowsy on the phone. "To be honest, I'm still in bed. Sunday's my only day to sleep in."

"If you don't mind, I'd like to talk about this with you as soon as possible. I've already informed the Berkeley PD that I have an interest in the case, so they gave the green light for me to interview you. I'm sure someone from their department will contact you Monday. You better be prepared."

"Prepared? Prepared for what?"

"Well, to free up some of your day to discuss the case. This guy who was after Joe—Professor Conrad—is probably the same guy who killed your grandparents."

"Well, then, I'm glad he's dead."

Dunn tried to visualize her, sitting up straighter in bed, more alert, concerned now. He imagined her in a white silk nightgown, a strap falling off her shoulder, a breast revealed. He tried to block the image from his mind.

"Look, Deirdre, I don't want to upset you. But the police are going to show you a photo of this guy to see if you recognize him. He was using the name Edward Lowe, but he also had fake IDs in the names of Edward Teach and Robert Surcouf. Any of those names ring a bell?"

"Edward Low?" Deirdre repeated. "I'd have to check my phone records. That name does sound familiar, but I can't place it right off the top of my head. What were the other two names?"

Dunn repeated them.

"Edward Teach. *That's* an odd name."

"If it sounds familiar, that might be because all three of these names are names of famous pirates."

"*Pirates?*" Deirdre asked. "Are you kidding?"

"No," Dunn said. "I Googled them earlier. Edward Teach? Better known as Blackbeard."

Deirdre's laughter surprised Dunn. "I guess it is kinda funny," he admitted.

"I know I shouldn't be laughing, if this man killed my grandparents, but really. *Pirates?*" Her voice rose and fell as each new wave of laughter swept over her.

Dunn tried to stop himself, but soon he too was laughing.

When their shared fit of laughter finally subsided, Deirdre emitted a loud sigh and Dunn saw her again in his mind's eye, leaning back against her pillows, the newspaper pages spread across her bed, a cup of coffee on the nightstand next to her. Would she have flowers in a vase nearby? Of course she would.

"Maybe we'd better talk after all," she said. "Would you mind coming here, though? I mean, to my house in Marin?"

Dunn's heart skipped a beat, but he tried to sound calm. "What time?"

"Give me an hour or so to shower and dress. We can have a late lunch on my deck."

"How about 3:30?"

"Perfect. That gives me two hours to dress and prepare a little food."

"Don't go to any trouble. I just ate lunch, so I'm not all that hungry."

"Oh, but I will be. I just had toast and coffee for breakfast, so I'll be ravished when you get here."

"You mean famished, don't you?"

"Yes." She laughed lightly. "Did I say *ravished*?"

"Yes, you did."

"I must still be thinking about those pirates."

Dunn smiled and tried to think of something clever to say.

"What's your address?" he asked instead.

"You mean, you don't already have it? What kind of detective are you?"

Promptly at 3:30, Dunn rang the doorbell of Deirdre Claire's house, an impressive craftsmen style on a hillside north of San Francisco.

Deirdre opened the door. When Ryan Dunn saw her, he tried to control the expression on his face. She stood in front of him wearing a revealing dark-green, string bikini top and a sheer white wrap over a matching green bikini bottom. Her high-heeled sandals revealed toenails painted deep red, matching her lipstick.

"I hope you don't mind," she said, smiling. "It was so warm, I had to take a dip in the pool."

Dunn shook his head. "It's your day off. You should, um, be comfortable."

"Come inside," she said, stepping back. "I was just making a Cobb salad."

After she shut the door and locked it, she walked through the sunken living room and into a spacious, modern kitchen with rich gray and black granite countertops. A large salad bowl was already half filled with vegetables and on the cutting board was a block of Swiss cheese and a chicken breast, which she had begun dicing up. A few pieces of bacon lay on a paper towel next to the cutting board.

Dunn took a seat on a barstool and faced her as she finished dicing the chicken and adding ingredients to the salad. A bottle of Riesling was open and a glass of the white wine stood next to it. When Deirdre saw Dunn glance at the wineglass, she picked it up and offered it to him.

"Would you like a sip? Or I can get you a glass, if you like."

"No, thanks."

She took a sip of the wine herself and went back to work.

"That's right. You're here in an official capacity."

"Well, technically, I'm not on duty. This isn't exactly an official visit. That will come tomorrow when the Berkeley detectives question you."

"Oh," she said. She glanced up and held his gaze. "Then why not loosen up a little and have a glass of wine. I promise not to get you drunk."

"No thanks," Dunn said, trying to keep a neutral expression plastered on his face.

Deirdre stopped cutting up the chicken and scraped the pieces into the bowl. Then she started slicing the Swiss cheese. Mid-cut, she stopped. Pointing the knife at Dunn, she said, "I'm sorry. I mean, I didn't think about it. You might be an alcoholic. A lot of cops are, I know. And here I am, tempting you."

Dunn laughed. "No," he said, shaking his head. "I'm not an alcoholic. Could be soon, I guess. I have been drinking more than I used to. Helps me sleep, now that my wife—I mean, my ex-wife—is out of the picture."

"Yes. I know what you mean. Living on your own can make you lonely sometimes. How long have you been separated?"

"It's been awhile." Dunn glanced around the room. He'd imagined that she would have a house filled with antiques, but the furniture was modern. And large. And expensive looking.

"You don't want to talk about it, I take it."

"Rather not."

"Still painful?"

He turned and held her gaze. "I'm not here to talk about myself. I'm here to interview you about our pirate friend."

"That reminds me," Deirdre said. She brushed the cubes of Swiss cheese into the bowl and began breaking the crisp bacon into small pieces. "I checked my phone logs and client lists. I don't have any of those names in my records. I do have a Ron Low, but he's an Asian client from a few years ago. An older gentleman. I don't think he's your pirate. At least, based on the description of the dead man in the newspaper."

"No," Dunn chuckled. "Our pirate or mercenary, I should say, definitely wasn't Asian."

"The *Chronicle* said well-built, ex-military, about thirty or thirty-five. Short, dark hair. About 6'2" or 6'3". Is that right?"

"Pretty close."

"Do you have a picture?"

"No. I mean, I do, but I'm not going to show it to you. I don't want to taint the official investigation, if I can help it."

Deirdre sipped her wine. "Won't our meeting like this taint their investigation?"

Dunn watched her lips as she sipped the wine, watched as she rolled the liquid around in her mouth.

"Not if I don't cross certain lines."

The woman swallowed her wine. "Certain lines?"

"Yeah. Like showing you the dead guy's picture."

"Oh," she said, grinning.

"Look, maybe I will have a glass of wine."

"Sure." Deirdre reached up and opened the cabinet above her head.

Dunn watched her right breast lift as her arm extended upward, the outline of her nipple showing through the shimmering green fabric of her suit. She brought a wine glass down and placed it next to hers. Then she poured him a generous portion of wine and refilled her own glass.

Handing the glass to Dunn, she picked up her own, holding it by the stem.

"What should we drink to?" she asked, leaning toward him.

"I don't know, Ms. Claire. You decide."

She smiled. "*Mz.* Claire? So formal again. And here, I thought we were getting to be friends."

"Okay. To new friends, then."

They clinked glasses again and then both took long sips of the wine, holding one another's gaze.

"Hmmm. How could your wife leave a handsome guy like you?"

Dunn set his glass down. "Let's be careful not to cross those lines, okay?"

"Just wondering."

Dunn lifted his glass and took a long drink.

"If you must know, she left this handsome middle-aged man for another handsome, younger man. Who makes more money, if I'm spilling my guts here."

Deirdre shook her head and sipped more wine. "Help me take the napkins and place mats out to the table. You don't mind eating outside, do you?"

"Of course not." Dunn picked up the place mats, napkins and silverware that were on the end of the counter, while Deirdre pulled two large plates from the freezer and grabbed a pepper mill with her free hand.

Dunn followed her as she walked to the sliding glass door, watching her hips move under the sheer white wrap, seeing her calf muscles, lean and taut, flex and relax as she stepped, looking at the thin gold chain around her right ankle, smelling her perfume.

She managed to push the door open with the hand that held the pepper mill and she walked briskly around the shallow end of the long pool, between two large redwood lounge chairs, both with plush cushions, toward a white iron patio table. The umbrella above the table was open wide, providing good cool shade.

Dunn studied the yard beyond the pool. Manicured bushes and trees provided cover from the neighboring houses on both sides, but the yard opened at the long end, affording a magnificent view of the northern-most part of San Francisco Bay. A dozen sailboats were coming in to berth for the evening. A slight breeze rustled the branches of the bottlebrush and palm fronds above them. Otherwise, the yard was private, concealed from view, professionally groomed, lush and green with colorful flowers around the borders.

"Nice lawn," Dunn said, putting the place mats and napkins down on the table.

"Thank you." Deirdre placed the plates on the place mats and straightened the napkins, placing the forks next to the plates. "My little patch of paradise. Very private. My own Garden of Eden. I can sunbathe in the…in privacy."

She looked him in the eyes and smiled.

He returned the smile, trying not to let his feelings show.

She laughed. "C'mon," she said, reaching for his hand. "Let's get the salad and the wine glasses."

She led him back toward the house but slowed as she walked between the lounge chairs. Then she stopped, turned around and looked up at his lips, her perfume stronger than ever.

Suddenly he grabbed her, pulled her close, crushed her body into his own and placed his mouth over her lips. She opened her lips and their tongues played feverishly as she stroked his temples with her fingers and moved her pelvis against his.

Then she undid his tie, throwing it on one of the lounge chairs. She unbuttoned the top button of his shirt, and then the next, and then the third until finally he reached down and pulled his shirt out of his pants and tore it off.

She leaned back to look at the hair on his chest. She kissed his chest and sucked his nipples, running her hands over his shoulders and down his back.

Then she unfastened his belt buckle, unsnapped the button at the top of his pants, unzipping his pants as quickly as she could. With his trousers loose, she reached in and found that he was already fully aroused.

She stepped away and untied her top, letting it fall onto the pavement, letting her firm, round breasts sway invitingly, her nipples erect. Then she untied her wrap and pushed her bikini bottom down her legs until they fell to her ankles.

She stepped out of her bikini and climbed onto the cushion of the flat lounge chair, lying back, opening her legs, her eyes and lips beckoning.

Ryan Dunn dropped his trousers and boxers, pushed off his shoes and socks, and stepped out of his clothes. Fully erect, he climbed on top of Deirdre Claire, placing his mouth over hers, pushing his tongue into her open mouth as he pushed himself into the wetness between her legs.

She pulled her mouth from his and let out a moan of pleasure, her hot breath on his earlobe.

Her body felt like heaven. He slipped in and out of her fiercely as she writhed with pleasure. Before he could stop himself, he exploded in blinding ecstasy and collapsed on the sweat-drenched body of the woman beneath him.

"Oh my god, I needed that!" he cried.

She laughed. "I could tell." She nibbled his earlobe. "You felt amazing, amazing," she whispered.

He rested on top of her, supporting his weight with his elbows, lifting his face to meet hers, kissing her gently on the lips. They smiled and gazed into each other.

"Do you want me to get off?" he asked.

"Never," she said. Her fingers stroked his back, his buttocks, and she squeezed each buttock with her strong hands.

He rested on top of her, enjoying the play of her fingers on his back and shoulders, drinking in her perfume, letting his lips caress her check. They rolled onto their sides, facing each other. Her eyes closed, a smile on her lips, she seemed to fit next to his body comfortably.

He dozed, falling quickly into a deep sleep, dreaming of what had just happened, until he felt her breath on his face.

Dunn opened his eyes and kissed her closed eyelids and cheeks.

She smiled. Then her lips parted and she shivered with dreamy arousal.

He felt himself hardening again and kissed her deeply, closing his eyes and rocking back and forth.

"Oh, God!" she moaned.

They made love again, this time more slowly, and when he felt she was ready, he quickened his strokes until she writhed and squirmed and tried to escape his thrusts, but then every muscle of her body tensed and suddenly released as she screamed with pleasure. Her cries and panting and the perfume aroused him more fiercely, and finally he let go and found a deep pleasure he'd never known before, collapsing on top of her, even as she clung to him and shivered.

This time he rolled off without asking and stood over her, helping to pull her to her feet. Without saying a word, they embraced, kissed and stepped toward the pool. They walked into the water together, stepping down the steps, then floated away from the side, swimming, kissing, cooling off, brushing each other's bodies. He stood on the bottom, the cool, clean water up to his chest, and she swam over to him and wrapped her arms around his neck. He hugged her and kissed her, the water restoring them.

Resting their arms on the edge of the pool, they turned to face the sky in the east. In the distance, sunlight glowed against the Berkeley hills. Occasionally, a breeze swirled across the lawn and lifted their hair.

"This *is* paradise," Dunn whispered.

"Yes it is," Deirdre replied, looking at Dunn. She reached over and stroked hair off his forehead. "I guess that makes us Adam and Eve."

Dunn smiled. It had been years since he and his wife had enjoyed this kind of intimacy, and he couldn't help but think of her, though he tried to push the image of her out of his mind. Finally, with this woman, he'd lost himself for a little while. It felt good. Too good.

"What are you thinking about?" she asked him.

Dunn turned to look at her. Her clear eyes glistened, her lips invited, the skin of her neck and shoulder beckoned.

"How damn nice this is, that's what I was thinking."

"I think so, too," she whispered. Then she parted her lips expectantly.

He kissed her, and she responded with equal passion. They pushed away from the edge and floated on their backs side by side.

"We'd better get out," said Deirdre, "before I turn into a prune."

They swam to the shallow end, and she turned around and sat at the edge of the pool looking at him. He stood before her, smiling, looking into her eyes. She reached over to the lounge and pulled a towel off, drying her hair and face as he watched. He stepped up on the first step and she looked down at him.

"Oh my God," she said, smiling. "You can't be ready again, not this soon."

"Lie back," he said. He took the towel from her, folded it, and laid it on the pavement behind her.

She leaned back, first on her elbows and then opened her legs. He knelt on the step and buried his face, his tongue playing as it had played inside her mouth earlier.

In minutes, she shuddered, then tensed, then shuddered again.

And then she cried out and rocked back and forth, holding his face and writhing with pleasure until she could take it no more. She reached down and gently pulled his face up toward hers.

They lay on the warm concrete side by side under the low evening sun, staring at each other's bodies. She had no tan lines at all, just a beautiful, firm, bronze body, while he was slightly tan, except where his swimsuit had blocked the sun. Though he was tall and lean and muscular, he had started to allow the rolls of flesh to form on his sides. Now, lying next to her naked, he was slightly embarrassed that his love handles were exposed.

She seemed to take no notice, as she allowed her fingers to play in the thick dark hair on his chest.

"So, Detective," she whispered, smiling. "Have you tainted the evidence?"

"Yeah. Guess I did."

She smiled and stroked his hair.

"I didn't know tainting evidence could feel so wonderful."

He held her gaze and smiled. "Well, not every cop taints the way I do."

She laughed.

"You're good at it."

He stroked the wet hair hanging over her ear. "That's our mission statement, ma'am. *To serve and protect.*"

"You need to revise it. *To serve and pleasure.*"

Dunn sat up, staring at the tanned flesh of her stomach, smiling at the firm, tanned mounds of her breasts, examining the sharp curve of her chin.

"You must be starving," he said.

"I am. Now I can honestly say I'm both."

"Both?" he asked.

"Ravished and famished!" she laughed. "Let's eat."

CHAPTER 27

In sight of sea, and at my back an ancient hoary wood,
I saw a fair young lady come, her secret fears to wail…
From" Echo Verses"

Deirdre made coffee, which they sipped as they watched darkness spread across the northern part of the Bay. The sun set quickly behind them, beyond the coastal hills west of the house. Lights surrounding the grounds came to life, casting warm yellow light under the manicured shrubs and across the well-groomed lawn. Blue and white web-like reflections of pool light played upon Deirdre's sensuous face and body as Dunn savored the view.

"Tell me about your parents," Dunn asked. "I know something about your grandparents from Joe. He thought very highly of them, especially your grandfather. But I haven't heard anything about your mother or father."

Deirdre sipped her coffee, but set the cup down as her expression changed. "My mother? Let me tell you about my mother, Detective." She had brought out a package of cigarettes and a lighter, and now she reached down, picked up the cigarettes and shook one out. She placed it between her lips and leaned forward as Dunn held the lighter up for her. After inhaling deeply and blowing the smoke above her head, she looked back in Dunn's direction.

"I'm not sure how my father met her, but her name was Virginia

Delacroix. Everyone called her Ginger, you know, like the bombshell on Gilligan's Island. They say I got her looks, and Mel, bless her heart, looks more like our daddy."

Deirdre put the cigarette to her lips, closed her eyes, as if considering whether or not to go on, held the smoke deep in her lungs for a few seconds, and then exhaled a stream of gray smoke toward her feet.

"When Mel and I were little, my mother used to bring our 'uncles' to the house while dad was at work. She told us they were her brothers or half-brothers or step-brothers. Mel and I would come home from school—Melinda's a year younger than I am—and we'd find one of mom's so-called brothers locked up in the bedroom with her, drinking and doing drugs."

Ryan studied Deirdre's face—contempt filled her eyes as she took another long drag from her cigarette.

"I think I was eight or nine when I realized what was going on."

"Was she turning tricks?"

Deirdre chuckled as she blew out another stream of smoke. "Turning tricks? What a lovely expression. Sounds like something a magician would do. She certainly knew how to cast a spell over men. Turning tricks?" Deirdre repeated. "Probably. Or just trading sex for drugs. I'm not sure. She told us not to tell our father, that he was jealous of her brothers. 'Don't tell your father that Uncle So & So stopped by, okay, girls? Your father doesn't like my brothers, so I have to meet them when he's not around. We wouldn't want to hurt daddy's feelings, would we?'"

"And your father? Did he suspect?"

"I'm sure he did. Turned a blind eye, though. Pretended all was well, for our sakes, I'm sure. But he knew. The more uncles mom brought around, the more dad worked. He built that business up from a simple used furniture store to a first-class antique business. But it cost him."

"Cost him?" Ryan asked. "What do you mean?"

Deirdre looked at her cigarette before taking a last drag and crushing it out in the ashtray. "He was a chain smoker. You could smell him before you'd see him. I don't recall ever seeing him without a cigarette. Died of lung cancer."

"I'm surprised *you* smoke, knowing that about your father."

Deirdre looked out at the Bay. "I don't very often. A few times a week. On special occasions."

Ryan set his empty coffee cup down on the little table between the lounge chairs and touched Deirdre's wrist. "Is *this* a special occasion?"

She looked over and smiled. "Yeah, I think so. It *feels* special. At least, to me."

"Me, too," Ryan said.

He leaned over and kissed her cheek. She smiled and pulled her knees up to her chin.

"I don't make time to date," she said. "I guess I haven't found someone I'm interested in."

Dunn laughed. "I asked a gal out a few months after my divorce. 'Not interested in a rebound romance,' she said. *That* was a boost to the old ego."

Deirdre rested her cheek on her knees and stared into Dunn's eyes.

"She doesn't know what she was missing."

Dunn smiled. "Thanks," he said. Returning her gaze made him squirm.

"So, what happened to your mother? After your father died, I mean?"

Deirdre turned away and stared into the darkness.

"Oh, she left us long before daddy died. Just before Melinda's tenth birthday. I remember trying not to cry while I helped dad plan Mel's party. We invited her entire class from St. Jude's Elementary and tried to make it festive. Decorated the house, blew up balloons, had a cake—the whole works. Mel tried to enjoy it, but you could tell..."

Dunn reached over and rubbed her shoulder. "Tell what?"

Deirdre looked at him, smiling sadly. "She kept looking for our mother, kept expecting her to show up with a bunch of presents, I guess. But she never did. Melinda cried her eyes out that night."

Dunn pulled his hand away. "Musta been disappointing."

"Disappointing? Yeah, real damn disappointing," she said, her voice dripping with sarcasm. "Maybe a blessing in disguise. Eventually, dad hired a woman to care for us during the day, a very loving black woman named Sharlene. She treated us much better than our mother ever did."

"When did you last see your mother?" Ryan asked. "Maybe *she's* behind all this?"

Deirdre looked over at Dunn, surprise on her face. "Are you interrogating me?"

Ryan grinned and blushed. "Sorry. I don't mean to, but I am a detective, after all."

Deirdre nodded. "I don't know. That seems kind of far-fetched, but it's possible, I guess. I used to see her sometimes, after dad died and I took over the business. Mother used to stagger into the store drunk, barely able to walk. She demanded money, claiming *she* should have inherited the store. But they'd been divorced for years, so she had no legal claim to the business. Besides, Dad knew she'd sell it, if she ever got her hands on it, and use the money to buy drugs."

"Sounds bad, Deirdre."

She glanced over, rested her cheek on her knees again and smiled.

"Call me Dee. Yeah, it was pretty awful. At first, I used to give her ten or twenty bucks, just to get her to leave the store. But a few days later, she'd turn up again, hang around, her hand out, acting like she owned the place. She was practically living on the street by then, dirty, smelly. She drove customers out of the store. Broke things a few times—a fairly expensive porcelain vase, a teapot, a mirror.

"I finally stopped giving her money and started calling the police. After she was arrested a few times, she stopped coming around. But I know she tried to break in at night a few times."

"Oh?" Ryan said, sitting up. "How do you know?"

"I installed security cameras, both outside and in. The cameras caught her and one or two of her friends trying to force the bars off the windows and the backdoor in the alley behind the store. The burglar alarms sounded and she'd scurry away like a cockroach when you turn on the lights."

"Hmm. Sounds like the kind of person who might be behind these crimes, the burglaries at LSU and at your grandfather's house. If she had the means."

Deirdre nodded. "Yes, detective. If she had the means."

"You don't buy it."

"I think she's dead, Ryan. She stopped coming around after Hurricane Katrina."

Dunn watched her face, intrigued but trying not to seem obvious. "You haven't seen her or heard from her since Katrina?"

"No. When the levees broke, a lot of good people drowned. A lot of good people and some not-so-good people. I suspect dear old mom got washed away like the street rodent she was."

Dunn, without his notepad, made a mental note instead. *Had she gotten money from the government after the hurricane?*

Trying to lighten the mood, Dunn asked, "Tell me more about your father. What kind of a man was he?"

"An insecure business man whose wife cheated on him. Too weak to do anything about it. He had a real talent for spotting a bargain, though. Knew when to buy up an estate. Really built up the business."

"You admired him?"

Deirdre laughed. "I admired his ability to create a good business, despite his inferiority complex."

"Why so insecure?"

Deirdre reached for another cigarette but stopped herself and glanced at Dunn.

"I don't know for sure. I have my theories, but I'm not sure."

"What's your theory?"

"First of all, my grandparents expected him to follow in their footsteps. Go to college, become a professor, or a professional. A doctor, a lawyer. He just didn't have the aptitude. Or the interest in books. I know he disappointed my grandparents. They tried to hide it, but we could tell. Dad joked about it sometimes. 'I have a Ph.D. in Antique-ology, Dad.' There were other problems, too."

"Oh?" asked Dunn. "Like what?"

"You can't really find this interesting?"

"Sure I do, Dee. I find *you* interesting."

She turned and looked out across the water. "It's probably hard for you to understand, living out here in California, but life was very different in Louisiana back then. I mean, segregation was outlawed but it still existed. Most middle class and upper class white kids went to private schools. Public schools were integrated but there was a lot of tension and they were dangerous. Daddy was forced to go to public school in Baton Rouge. Integration and busing were being enforced, and there was just a lot of hostility. But Grandpap taught at a public university and Grandma taught at a public high school, so how would it look to have *their* son in a private school? Daddy told us he used to get beat up about once a week. That's why he sent us to private schools."

"Beat up? For being white?" Dunn asked incredulously.

Deirdre laughed. "No, not just for being one of the few white kids in school. Imagine a boy whose last name is 'Claire'. He got teased mercilessly. Called a girl, 'Fair Haired Claire', all sorts of things. You know how cruel kids can be."

Dunn nodded.

"Did you resent your grandparents for that?"

Deirdre blinked. "My grandparents didn't beat up my father."

"Still..." Dunn didn't finish his thought, but he made another mental note.

Deirdre reached over and took Dunn's hand.

"Can you stay tonight?"

He smiled and studied her face. He could just picture how it would look in the morning if the S.F. police showed up and he answered the door wearing one of Dee's bathrobes. No, not a good idea.

"I shouldn't," he said. "Technically, I'm still investigating these crimes."

"Will I see you again?" she asked. Her voice sounded tender.

"I'm sure of it, if you want to."

Deirdre Claire nodded and squeezed his hand.

A breeze picked up and both of them shivered.

"Time to go inside," she said, standing.

Dunn climbed out of the chair and stood in front of her, and they kissed again deeply. Then they turned and walked toward the house.

"What about your sister? Where does she live?"

She pulled her hand out of Dunn's and opened the sliding glass door.

"Mel? Why do you want to know about her?"

Dunn followed her into the kitchen. Trying not to sound so

damn official, he said, "I'd like to speak to her, see if she's had any burglaries."

"Oh, I see." Deirdre went over to the counter by the phone and pulled out a piece of paper. "Here's her number," she said, writing it down. "Call her if you like, but I'm sure I would have heard something."

Ryan took the paper. "What about you?" he asked. "Have *you* had any break-ins, Dee? Here or at one of your stores?"

"No," she said, shaking her head.

"You still have a shop in New Orleans, though, right?"

"Yeah," Deirdre said.

"And that store wasn't burglarized recently?"

Deirdre shook her head. "No. I told you. We have a pretty good alarm system and surveillance cameras."

Dunn looked into her face. "And when you were back for your grandfather's funeral, no sign of attempted burglaries at your New Orleans store?"

Deirdre shook her head. "No, not that I was told about. I'm sure my manager would have mentioned it. He's very reliable. Raymond reminds me of you, in fact."

"Oh yeah?" Ryan asked, smiling. "How so?"

"Ex-military. Fit and all business. Very resourceful."

"Sounds like I have some competition."

Deirdre leaned forward and stretched up to kiss him.

"You don't have to worry," she whispered, kissing him lightly on the lips. "He can't compete with you. Not with—well, you know."

Dunn returned her kiss and they held each other for a moment. Finally, he gathered up his things and walked out to the car. Deirdre lingered in the doorway and waved. Then she closed the door, blocking out the light that had shone behind her.

In his car, before he started the engine, Dunn found his notepad and pen. He turned on the overhead light and wrote a few notes. *Check whereabouts of missing mother. Katrina money? Had the store in New Orleans been searched? Why not?*

As he looked at his last note, a troubled expression infiltrated his face. Then he wrote—

The dog that didn't bark.

CHAPTER 28

Love whets the dullest wits…
From the sonnet "Love is a Discord"

Returning to his condominium in Sacramento well after midnight, Dunn showered and went to bed. But sleep eluded him. He rolled over and faced the clock, counting the hours, trying to dispel his growing feeling of dread. Falling asleep finally a little before 4:00, he awoke groggy when the alarm sounded at 7:00. Daylight and coffee did not allay his concerns.

In his office later that morning, he put his other cases on hold and called Melinda Sloan, Deirdre's sister, in Ohio.

"I'm investigating some burglaries out here in California. They might be related to the ransacking of your grandfather's home and office."

"Oh?" Melinda responded. "Why do you think they're connected?"

Dunn explained that a former student of Jack's had received a package from her grandfather and now suspected that his offices had been searched.

"A package? What kind of package?" she asked him.

"Can't get into much detail, but old manuscripts that might be pretty valuable."

"Manuscripts?" she repeated. "Have you spoken to my sister, Deirdre? She lives out there in California."

"Yes," Dunn admitted. "She gave me your number."

"Is *she* all right?"

"Yes," Dunn said. "Why do you ask?"

"Maybe it's just a coincidence."

Dunn could hear music from a cartoon on the TV and children giggling in the background. "What do you mean?" he asked.

"It's just, Dee asked me about old manuscripts, too. She wondered if Grandpap had told me about them."

Dunn's heart sank, but he made a note. "When was this?"

"Oh, gosh. About four or five months ago, I think."

"Are you sure?"

"Yes. It was shortly after Christmas. Just a casual conversation on the phone. Had I talked to the folks lately? That's how we referred to our grandparents. But I recall those same words."

"What words?" Dunn asked.

"She said something like, 'I heard Grandpap got his hands on some valuable old manuscripts. Has he told you anything about it?' I said no and that was the end of it."

Dunn wrote down every word. "And this was back in January?"

"Yes. January or February. Anyway, after the New Year. We'd all gotten together for Christmas in Baton Rouge. That was the last time I saw Grandma alive."

"And you never discussed these manuscripts with your grandparents or your sister again?"

"No," Melinda said. She remained silent for a moment. "Oh, my god. Does this have something to do with Grandpap's death?"

Dunn waited to answer. "It's possible."

"Oh, god. *Please* warn Deirdre. I don't want anything to happen to *her*."

"Yeah, we've…conversed. I think she's on the lookout."

"Maybe you should give her protective custody or something."

"No need to get too worked up about this yet. It might be nothing."

"Are you sure? I'm starting to think there might be something going on after all."

"What do you mean?" Dunn asked.

"It's sort of silly, but a few days ago, when we got back from our place at the lake, we suspected we might have had an intruder in *our* house."

"Why'd you think that?"

"It's hard to explain. Our dog went crazy and my daughter thought someone had moved one of her stuffed animals. We thought we heard noises in the attic, but when my husband checked, he didn't find anyone."

"Was anything missing?"

"No, not that we've been able to discover. It could have been nothing, though. I mean, there weren't any broken windows or unlocked doors. You know, any of the usual signs of a burglary."

Dunn frowned. He didn't want to tell her how easy it was for someone to break in without leaving a trace. People preferred the illusion of safety.

"So you really can't be sure someone searched your premises?" Dunn asked, hoping to get a more definite response.

"Not really. Just…"

"What, Mrs. Sloan? Anything could be important."

"You'll find it silly."

Dunn shook his head but tried to keep the exasperation out of his voice. "Any detail could be useful."

"Well, *I* didn't notice anything, but my daughter insisted that the house smelled like cigarettes. You know, like someone had smoked a cigarette inside our home recently."

Dunn made a note—*house smelled of cigarette*—and nodded. "Sometimes kids have a better sense of smell than we do."

"Of course, it could have been our neighbor. She was bringing our mail in while we were gone, so maybe she smoked while she—I don't know—while she went through our things. That's possible, isn't it?"

"Yep," Dunn admitted. "A definite possibility."

She remained quiet again. Finally, she asked, "So you don't think I should worry?"

"No," Dunn said. "If there was a reason to worry, I think it's moved on now." He didn't want to explain about the death of the man who'd almost killed Joe.

"And what about my sister? Will *she* be all right?"

"Yeah, I think the threat has passed."

"I certainly hope so," she said.

"I know your father passed away quite some time ago, but have you heard from your mother recently?"

"My *mother*! God, no. We assume she died in the hurricane."

"What about before Katrina? Did you see or hear from her regularly?"

"No, Detective. Mother was a drunk and drug addict. I was glad she didn't know where to find me. I wouldn't have allowed her near my kids."

"One more thing, Mrs. Sloan. Can you give me the number for your sister's shop in New Orleans?"

"Daddy's old store? Sure. It's French Quarter Antiques on Bourbon. Here it is."

She read the number over the phone as Dunn jotted it down.

After hanging up, Dunn looked over his notes and sipped his coffee. It had soured. Nothing tasted very good now.

Next he called the antique store in New Orleans.

A man with a deep voice answered.

Dunn asked to speak to the manager and the man said, "Speaking."

"This is Detective Ryan Dunn from the Sacramento Sheriff's Office. I'm investigating some burglaries in this area that might be related to similar crimes in Louisiana."

"What can I do for you, Detective?"

"What's your name, sir?"

"*My* name? Why do you need *my* name?"

That was the first red flag. Dunn made a note. Innocent people were quick to give their name, even if a note of reluctance sounded in their voice, because they wanted to show they were innocent.

"I'd like to know who I'm talking to."

"*I'm* not suspected of anything, am I?"

"Not at this time, no."

"Not at any time, buddy. Look, I'm a Marine. I don't *do* crime. Understand?"

"Got it, pal. Read you loud and clear. Now get this, " Dunn said. "I'm a police detective investigating a crime. Okay?"

The other man stayed silent and Dunn knew he was debating hanging up.

"*Semper Fi*, so am I, asshole," Dunn said. "I'm a Marine, too."

"Okay, okay. Why didn't you say so?"

"One more time. What's your name?"

"Raymond. My name's Raymond Crew. People call me Ray or R. C."

"Ray Crew?" Dunn repeated as he wrote down the aliases. "Sounds like a fashion designer."

"I get that a lot."

"Okay, let's begin again. Ray Crew? Ryan Dunn. Glad to meet you."

"The pleasure's all mine, Detective. What can I do for you?"

"First, has the store had any break-ins or burglaries in the last month?"

"No. Which is surprising."

"Surprising?"

"Yeah. I mean, for months after Katrina someone tried to break in almost every night, seemed like."

"Tried? But failed?"

"Yeah. We've got heavy bars on the windows and doors, and a first class alarm system, thanks to me. I used to run a security guard business. That's one of the reasons Ms. Claire hired me."

"What was the name of your business?"

"R. C. Security."

"Catchy," Dunn said. "What happened?"

"What happened?" The man laughed. "Katrina happened! After the levee broke, my little office was under ten foot of water. Time I got into her, even my guns was rusty. Computers no good, files ruined, everything water logged like it had all sat in a fuckin' latrine for a month!"

"You had insurance, though, right?"

Ray Crew laughed again. "You don't want to hear about my insurance company, man. First of all, my agent? My agent drowned.

His office? Wiped out, just like mine. *He* had no records, *I* had no records. The main office in New Jersey claimed *they* had no record, which was bullshit."

"What're you gonna do."

"Fuckin' people in New Jersey. Talk about assholes."

"So Deirdre Claire hired you."

"Yes, she did, God bless her."

"Did you know much about antiques before you went to work for her?"

"Hell, no. But I studied up before my interview."

"You were able to bullshit Ms. Claire?"

"Hell, no. Saw right through me, but said she was impressed I went to the trouble. Said I was a quick enough learner and as long as I treated customers properly, I could have the 'position.' That's how she referred to it—the 'position'. I loved that. Made it sound sexy."

Dunn tried not to gag.

"How did Ms. Claire want you to treat the customers, in your newfound 'position'?"

Crew chuckled. "Well, first of all. They aren't customers, Detective. They're our 'clientele'."

Dunn let himself chuckle. "Yeah, I've called a few of my own civilians that."

"And I was supposed to be genteel. 'Genteel and soft spoken.' That's what she wanted. And that's what I do for her. That and protect the place."

"Tell me about Ms. Claire. She a good boss? Honest? Treat you right?"

"She's great. Pays well, lets me run the place, more or less. I have a couple of clerks who know a helluva lot more about antiques than I do. They know how to deal with our clientele, but I know bookkeeping and security, so I keep the scum out and keep an eye on the occasional tourist who wanders in."

Dunn waited for more, but Ray wasn't giving up anything else. "Honest?" he prodded.

"Honest? Sure, of course. Honest as the day is long. Why do you ask?"

"Need to make sure, that's all. What about you?"

Ray laughed. "Of course I'm honest, officer."

Dunn could have done without the sarcasm, but he was trying to think of what to ask next. He wished he could watch Ray Crew's face as he asked these questions, but he'd just have to read his voice.

"You know Deirdre Claire's grandparents died recently, right?"

"Of course. Deirdre was here for both funerals—I mean, up in the Red Stick—but she came down after the funerals to check on things and take care of business. She's here about once a month for a week. Spends a week in New York. But she lives out there in California, so you know her SF store is her favorite."

"How'd she seem after the funerals?" Dunn asked.

"How'd she seem? Jesus, that's a weird fuckin' question."

Dunn waited for an answer, looking up from his notepad.

"What you'd expect. Sad. Depressed. Pre-occupied. But she coped."

"Pre-occupied? How?"

"I don't know. Had to clean her grandparents' house after her grandmother died, so she was exhausted after that trip."

"She cleaned their house?"

"Yeah. You could see she was concerned about her grandfather living alone in Baton Rouge, but she couldn't do anything about it, so..."

Ray went quiet again. Dunn knew he was worried about saying something wrong about his employer. "Go on. What else?"

"What else? Christ, a week later, she had to come back for her grandfather's funeral. I mean, barely gets back to California and boom! Has to turn right around and come back."

"How'd she seem then?"

"Tired, I guess. I mean, she had to sell all the shit in the Baton Rouge house that she and her sister didn't want. Told me her grandparents didn't have many nice things, so she donated most of it. Her sister took the china, I think, and Deirdre brought the silver down here to the store to be sold."

"Much silver?" Dunn asked.

"Not really. Incomplete settings for eight, missing a few salad forks. Couple of silver trays. Maybe a thousand bucks worth of stuff."

Dunn knew there had to be more, but he was running out of questions.

"Look, I've got to get back out on the floor," Ray Crew said. "I've been shut up here in my office for twenty minutes. You need anything else?"

"Yeah, some recon. Give me the lay of the land. Is there something you know you need to tell me, but you're holding it back?"

Ray chuckled, but it wasn't joyful. "I have no idea what you mean, officer."

"No bullshit," Dunn barked. "Has something odd happened within the past few weeks? Other than the deaths of Deirdre Claire's grandparents, something out of the ordinary?"

"You're fishing with a pretty long damn pole, aren't you?"

"Yeah, Ray. But make no mistake. This pole can reach all the way down to the Big Easy."

Now Ray laughed as if he had the upper hand. "Sure, sure, tough guy."

"You thought Katrina hurt? I got friends in the NOPD, make your life hell."

"I know a few guys here myself."

"Yeah, I'm sure you do. We may even know some of the same guys, Ray. But who are they gonna dance for? You? Some ex-wanna-be cop? Or a brother in blue?"

"Okay, okay. Don't go all ape-shit on me. Really, there's nothing."

"Nothing? You're sure?"

"I'm sure. Deirdre's a decent woman. I mean, sure, she's interested in the bottom line. Wants to make sure her stores are turning a profit."

"Greedy?"

Ray laughed. "Aren't we all?"

"More than most?"

"Yeah, I guess. But, I mean, she owns these businesses. She *owns* them, right? So she has a right to make money."

"Back to her grandfather's death. Did it shake her up, depress her?"

"Sure. I guess. I mean, as much as anyone would for a grandparent."

Dunn listened to the familiar silence of someone trying to decide whether or not to say more.

"Honestly?"

"Yeah, Ray. Be honest."

"I mean, she held it together pretty well, for someone who'd just had one blow after another. I tried to comfort her. You know."

"Go on," Dunn said. He clenched his teeth.

"Well, when she first hired me, we dated a few times. Got close a couple of times. I mean, intimate. You know."

"Yeah," Dunn said. "I know." He glanced up again from his notepad, closing his eyes, remembering, regretting.

"Anyway, since those first couple of times, never again. It's like..."

Dunn waited patiently, tapping the tip of his pen on the paper, knowing what was coming.

"I mean, it's like she slept with me to gain my loyalty, and then when she knew she had me, she didn't feel the need to keep giving out. Not to be crude about it. You know the type?"

"Yeah," Dunn chuckled, though he wanted to vomit. "I was married to the type." Even as he was saying it, he knew it wasn't true. Not about his ex-wife. But it was true, he was now realizing, about Deirdre Claire.

"Oh, she still flirts. Gives you that come-on grin. Brushes up against you. A little kiss on the chin once in awhile. But there's always an excuse when you want to see her later."

"Okay," Dunn said. "Now you've given me some insight into her character. That's great. But let me ask you again, has anything out of the ordinary happened?"

"No, not really."

"Might seem trivial, unrelated, the kind of thing you're telling yourself can't possibly be connected to anything. What's that little voice telling you not to tell me?"

"Nothing. Honestly."

Dunn just listened for a few seconds, letting the little voice work.

"I mean, the only thing I can think of, and I don't really think it's connected—"

"Try me."

"You ever read *Soldier of Fortune*?"

"Yeah, sometimes. You?"

"Yeah. *Car and Driver, Penthouse, Soldier of Fortune*—all that intellectual crap."

"Keep it coming. You're almost back to your bunk."

"All right. So months ago, I mean, around New Year's when Deirdre was down here after visiting her grandparents, I showed her an ad in *Soldier of Fortune* for a guy I used to know, another Marine. We were in the Gulf together. You know, the first war, when we still knew when to quit."

Dunn chuckled—he knew it'd help Ray continue.

"Anyway, there was this ad for a guy I knew. The ad said something like, 'Will do what it takes.' I saw the name and the photo and recognized him right away. That guy wasn't right."

"What do you mean?"

"Too gung-ho"

"Like how? Overly patriotic? Love of country?"

"No. Love of killing, is more like it. It disappointed him that the war ended so quickly. Hell, he hardly got to fire his gun! Loved the weapons, loved the precision. Thought he was King Bad-Ass. You know the type?"

"Oh, yeah. We got 'em on the force, too."

"Deirdre seemed to be interested. She pretended she was interested in the entire magazine—'I've never read anything like *this* before', she said—but I could tell she zeroed in on this guy."

"What'd you make of that?"

"I mean, at the time, I figured she was just looking for a good lay. You know, some excitement. Someone who'd play a little rough."

"You still have that magazine?"

"Hell, no. Lost it a long time ago."

"What's the guy's name?"

"Benedict Anderson. Liked being called Benedict, not Ben. We called him Benedict Arnold behind his back. Never to his face. He heard that, he'd go off on you. Broke a dude's nose once. We also called him B. A., you know, for Bad Ass."

"Is his ad still in *Soldier*? Have you seen it lately?"

"Yeah, I think so. I mean, I haven't really looked for it in the most recent issue, but I guess it's still there."

Dunn jotted down a few more notes. Now against his wishes, he'd found the link he suspected was there.

"Does that help you, Detective."

"Yeah, it does. I think you just helped the Berkeley PD identify a body, too."

"No shit?"

"No shit."

"Whose body?" Ray Crew asked.

"Your Bad Ass pal, Benedict Arnold."

"Well, I'll be damned," the Marine said.

CHAPTER 29

O hateful hands, to tear such loving words;
Injurious wasps, to feed on such sweet honey,
And kill the bees that yield it, with your stings!
From *The Two Gentlemen of Verona*

Dunn took his notes with him to lunch and studied them as he ate alone by the window at P. F. Chang's. He didn't like the way the pieces were fitting together, but they were. No denying it. Deirdre Claire was a viable suspect. He needed to search her home.

As he sipped his coffee, he weighed the options. He could call her for another "date" and search unofficially. But whatever he found would be thrown out. Besides, a second date with a suspect would ruin any case he could build.

His other option was to ask for a warrant and make the search official. But there were a few problems. He didn't have enough evidence yet. That meant finding a sympathetic judge who owed someone a favor and who didn't mind stretching the ever-elastic bounds of the law. Next, since Marin County was outside his jurisdiction, he'd have to work with someone in the Bay Area. He had an old friend, Detective Mike Wang, he'd been thinking about all morning, which had probably led to his choice of lunch spots.

No. P. F. Chang's was a favorite. He and his wife had come here often, and he still tried to eat here once or twice a week. Part of him hoped to run into her, even if it meant seeing her with that new asshole of a boyfriend.

After he finished his coffee and paid the bill, Dunn stepped out into the hot afternoon sun and flipped open his cell phone. He called Detective Wang and explained the situation, finishing with, "I know this isn't exactly kosher, Mike, but I need your help."

"I'll see what I can do. Give me the rest of the day."

Mike didn't sound pleased, but Dunn knew if Mike Wang said he'd try, then he definitely would.

They agreed to meet in the City the next morning, unless Wang couldn't pull any strings. In the afternoon, Dunn worked on his other cases.

Monday night he tried to sleep. But flashes of Deirdre Claire's nude body and the pleasurably pained expressions on her sensual face disrupted his dreams.

Dunn met Detective Wang Tuesday morning at a packed Starbucks on Lombard. Wang had a small table by the window and flagged Dunn over as he walked in.

"It's freezing out there!" Dunn said, squeezing into his chair. "When I left Sacramento at 9:00 o'clock, it was already 80. Come over here to nothing but fog."

"You know what Mark Twain said, don't you?" Wang asked, handing him a cup. "The coldest winter I ever spent was the summer I spent in San Francisco."

Dunn, dressed in a light-weight gray suit, sipped the warm espresso. He wanted regular coffee, hot as hell, to wrap his hands around. "You got the warrant?"

Wang patted the breast pocket of his tweed jacket. Dunn noticed his V-neck sweater under the coat. Wang was dressed for the chill. "Used a major favor to get this. A judge who got caught cheating on his boyfriend. With a woman, if you can believe. Only in San Francisco would accusations of being straight get you in hot water with your constituents."

Dunn chuckled and shook his head. He sipped the espresso and looked at Wang. "We've got nothing, you know," Mike said.

"We do now. We got a dead mercenary whose cell phone shows three calls to Deirdre Claire. That's not nothing."

"When did you hear *that*?" asked Wang, annoyed.

"My contact at Berkeley PD called me this morning while I was driving over."

"Jeez. I wish I'd had that information for the judge last night when he issued the warrant." Wang sipped his steaming tea. "You interviewed her. She seem like the kind of woman who could've had her grandparents killed?"

Dunn drained his cup and shook his head. "I don't know. Nothing surprises me anymore. But she does give off a vibe."

"A vibe," Wang repeated. "Pretty thin."

"Pretty thin, I admit. But there's something hinky about her."

Dunn looked at the line of people. "Man, I'd love a cup of regular coffee to go."

Wang stepped over to the counter where a young Asian woman was busily making drinks. Speaking Mandarin, he handed the girl a five. She grabbed a large paper cup, filled it with coffee and handed it back.

Dunn heard the officer say something to the clerk, and then Wang handed him the cup of burning hot coffee.

"*Shay, shay, knee*?" Dunn repeated.

"It means thank you in Chinese."

"We'll, then, *shay, shay, knee* to you, Detective."

"You're welcome. Want me to drive?"

Dunn didn't want Wang to know that he'd already been to her house. Not yet. "I did the MapQuest thing, but if you know the area, then…"

"Went to college up there, but rarely went into neighborhoods like hers."

"It's gated, isn't it?"

"Yeah. Why?"

Dunn put a lid on his coffee cup and they pushed out through the crowd onto the sidewalk. The air was still damp with heavy fog that smelled of the ocean, salt, dead fish, and something else.

"Had a case once at a gated community in Rancho Murrieta. The security guard, a retired cop, called the homeowner after letting us in. Gave the guy a heads up. The suspect flushed evidence and fled before we got to the house."

"Why the hell the cop do that?"

"Liked the Christmas bonuses from the perp, I guess."

"Shit," Wang said. "You find the guy?"

"Oh, yeah. We had another car at the back gate, grabbed him as he was leaving. Plus, the guy's fingerprints were all over the baggies, and there was enough trace of heroin. We were able to make the case."

Wang pulled his keys out of his pants pocket and punched the button, unlocking his black Mustang Cobra.

"Are you shittin' me?" Dunn said, staring at the car. "You drive a Cobra?"

Wang grinned and opened his door. "What'd you expect? A Prius?"

"This isn't government issue, is it?"

"Hell, no," laughed Wang. "It's a 2007 GT 500 with a 5.4 liter V8. If I went with the City issue, I'd be stuck in some damn Chevy."

Dunn cringed, trying not to glance at his own Chevy parked across the street as he climbed into the passenger's side and buckled up.

"Nice. Still smells new."

"So what'd this guy do, besides the heroin possession?"

"Oh, he was a real humanitarian. Ran a good sized drug ring and killed two of his distributors when they cheated him."

"Give that man a medal."

"Next best thing. A San Quentin jumpsuit." Dunn sipped his coffee. "Anyway, we better lean on the guy at the gate so he can't warn Ms. Claire. I don't think she's home, though."

"Oh? Why not?"

"I called her house on my drive over and got the answering machine. Called her office, too. The store clerk said she expected Ms. Claire in thirty minutes or so. That was almost an hour ago."

"Good. We'll have the place to ourselves. But we should watch the security guard anyway."

"Let's make him ride up to her house with us so he can't get out of our sight."

"I like that idea," Wang said. He started the engine and smiled at Dunn as the engine roared to life powerfully. Then he revved it, setting off the car alarms of nearby cars.

Dunn smiled and nodded. Wang let the engine settle into a low, throbbing rumble.

The Mustang launched into the lane and Wang snaked through traffic. The fog blew across the lanes on the Golden Gate Bridge. Traffic thinned enough for Wang to gun it up the hill into the tunnel. On the other side, the fog lifted as they drove north. By the time they reached their exit, nothing but low, broken clouds filled the sky.

Wang drove through the residential streets expertly, heading into the hills west of Highway 101. The houses became larger as the roads grew narrower. When they arrived at the gate, the security guard, a Pillsbury Doughboy in his thirties, looked frightened when Wang showed his badge.

"Can I help you?"

"Did you let a locksmith through here in the last hour?" Wang demanded.

"Yes, sir. He had a work order."

Wang shook his head with disgust while Dunn tried not to laugh.

"He had a work order and you just let him breeze on through?

"Yes, sir. I took down his driver's license number."

Wang shot Dunn a mocking look. "Hear that? He took down his license number."

"That's standard procedure," the young guard said, his voice cracking. "We got to let service people in if they seem legit."

Wang turned back to the guard, saying, "We need you to take us to a residence right away. Lock up your booth and get in the back seat."

The chubby pale face stared down at the detective blankly.

"I can't leave my—"

"Do it!" Wang shouted.

Dunn leaned over, showing his badge. "It'll take five minutes, son. We need your help."

"But I'll lose my—"

"Lock up and get in this damn car right now," Wang ordered.

"Better do it, son," Dunn said sympathetically. "I don't want him to go Jet Li on your ass."

The Doughboy blinked.

"You want me to arrest you?" Wang growled.

The young man closed the window and locked the door. He walked around the car as Dunn climbed out and pushed the back of his seat forward so the overweight guard could climb in the back. The Doughboy looked at the opening and then at Dunn.

"You're kidding, right?"

Dunn looked at the opening, then at the young man, then shook his head with a disgust while Mike Wang laughed.

Riding in the back seat, his knees pressed up to his chin, Detective Ryan Dunn wished they had taken his four-door Chevy. When the Doughboy turned around, Dunn spotted the grin on his face. Mike Wang couldn't help it—he glanced in the rearview mirror and burst out laughing. Then the Security Guard started laughing, too.

"Yuk it up, chubby," Dunn said. "After you show us Ms. Claire's house, you're hoofing it back to your caddy shack."

The Doughboy stopped laughing and Detective Wang bit his lip.

The locksmith Wang had called was waiting in his van parked in front of Deirdre's house.

"That's him," said the guard. He climbed out of the Cobra and tried to shoot a hard stare at the locksmith who was smoking a cigarette.

"Okay," said Wang, patting the guard on his chubby shoulder. "We'll take it from here."

Dunn unfurled himself and climbed out of the car, stretching as he stood.

"Take a hike, pal. The walk'll do you good."

"You really gonna make me walk?"

Dunn tilted his head and scowled. The doughboy got the message and started down the street.

"How you doin', Perry?" Wang asked.

The locksmith crushed out his cigarette and ambled over. They shook hands.

"Meet an old friend, Ryan Dunn. He's a detective over in Sacramento."

Perry reached over and shook Dunn's hand reluctantly.

"Perry was one of my first collars, Ryan. Part of burglary ring I broke up about ten years ago. Did a nickel in Chino and stayed out of trouble ever since. Isn't that right, Perry."

The tattooed excon nodded. "You know it."

Dunn recognized the tone of voice. Perry was probably clean, but just barely, and he did favors for cops to stay out of trouble. Probably informed on his pals when he had something to sell. All detectives needed people like Perry.

After doing his work, the locksmith drove away and the two detectives began their search.

They started in the den, searching the woman's desk. The papers on top of the desk concerned her businesses and bills of lading for shipping furniture to various cities—nothing useful. A drawer on the bottom right side of the desk was locked. Wang took out his picks and had the drawer open in a few seconds. Nothing.

Wang looked at the drawer and then at the side of the desk and scratched his head.

"These drawers look short to you?" he asked Dunn.

Dunn glanced at the file drawer Wang had pulled almost all the way out and then at the side of the desk.

"Yep."

Wang felt the side panels, knocked on the wood, and then opened all the drawers. He removed the top right drawer and reached inside the opening.

"Here's something." He'd just finished saying it when they heard a click and a side panel opened. The space behind the drawers was roomy enough to hide long, wide ledgers. The Detective reached inside and tugged out a fat, accordion folder.

It held the mother lode.

A file folder revealed a receipt for a cashier's check made payable to Benedict Anderson for $20,000, and another actual cashier's check for the same amount. Dunn held it up to Wang.

"The second installment, obviously. To be paid when she had the Shakespeare papers."

Wang nodded. "Guess Mr. Anderson's fall from grace cancels all debts."

"I'm surprised she didn't get rid of this. Burn it in the fireplace."

"Jeez, Ryan," said Wang. "You sound like you're sad about it."

"No. I mean, she's a smart woman."

"Maybe she's too smart. Maybe she thinks she's smarter than us dumb cops."

"Yeah." Ryan looked through the papers. "Or maybe there wasn't time. I mean, it was late Saturday night when the guy fell to his death, so she didn't learn about it until Sunday."

"And Monday the cops came and interviewed her," Wang offered. "But still, that leaves all day Sunday. What kept her so busy on Sunday, she couldn't burn the evidence?"

Dunn tried not to gulp, but he was feeling queasy.

Underneath the checks in the folder was a handwritten letter from someone named Marcus, a name Dunn didn't recognize. Dunn read it out loud as Wang looking over his arm.

> *Dearest Dee,*
>
> *It was wonderful seeing you again. I wish you could find excuses to visit more than once a month, but I'll take what I can get. It's so very different from my life with Gillian. It's not that I don't love her—I do want to be honest about that. It's just wonderfully different with you.*
>
> *I was so surprised to see your grandfather again. He's looking old. I was thinking about your questions. Yes, you're probably right. If the manuscripts are authentic, then they belong in a museum. But really, I wasn't shown enough to know and I really think your grandfather is getting a bit senile. Otherwise, he would have been more forthcoming with me.*

As I mentioned, my rare-books man in the Village sent him more books, so I know Jack thinks he has something. I'll be happy to follow up with him and offer my services , if he wishes. But honestly, I think it's a lot of sound and fury signifying nothing, as the Bard would say. And you're right. We should keep this our little secret. One of many little secrets we share...

Half my heart and all my soul,

Marcus

After finishing the letter, Dunn felt nauseated.

"Sounds like she was playing him," Wang offered.

Dunn nodded. "Yeah. He was being played, all right."

"The letter lets him off the hook. Whoever he is, he seems innocent enough."

"If you ignore the fact he was cheating on his wife."

Dunn placed the letter back in the file folder and put the file down on the top of the desk. He took a deep breath and blew it out, forcing himself to pull it together.

Wang thumbed through the documents in the folder while Dunn bent down and looked inside the cubby hole again. Then he turned his head and looked up at Wang, a smile spreading across his lips.

"What is it?" Mike Wang asked.

Dunn grabbed the magazine and held it up. "December issue of *Soldier of Fortune*." He thumbed through it and found a dog-eared page. The magazine opened to a page of ads. In the lower left corner was the face of the man who had fallen off the clock tower on the Berkeley campus just a few nights before.

"Merry Christmas," Wang said, smiling. "Is this enough to arrest her?"

Dunn nodded. "I'll call the store to make sure she's there." He paced the den as he spoke on the phone. Mike Wang continued to look through papers in other drawers of the desk, but nothing else seemed to indicate guilt. "Shit!" Dunn said, closing his phone.

"What is it?"

"The clerk said Deirdre is headed out of town today to do an appraisal on an estate."

"Okay," Detective Wang replied. "What's the problem? We wait till she gets back and grab her."

"That's the problem," Dunn answered. "I'm afraid to wait. She's headed up to Lake Tahoe, the clerk says."

"All right, so she'll be gone all day. What's the big deal?"

Wang didn't know what Dunn knew. How could he?

"My friend Joe Conrad? His family's up there."

"Up where?" Wang asked. "Lake Tahoe?"

Dunn nodded, opening his phone again. "I'm calling Joe right now, but he's probably in class. He teaches at CLU in Stockton."

"Oh," said Wang. "*That* Joe Conrad? The guy you cleared last year?"

"Couple years ago, yes." Dunn listened as the phone rang and went quickly to voice mail. "Joe. It's Ryan Dunn. Listen. I'm worried about Sara and the kids. The person behind the killings is headed to Tahoe. Call Sara and tell her to leave Suzie's cabin. Go to the Lake. Spend the day at the beach. Somewhere public with lots of people. Call me as soon as you get this message. It's urgent."

"Try calling the campus," Mike suggested.

Dunn nodded. He called information and got the number for the English Department at CLU. When the secretary answered, Dunn quickly explained who he was and asked to speak to Joe.

"You're the second person to call for Professor Conrad today," Molly said. "But as I told the woman who called this morning, Professor Conrad isn't here. He cancelled his class and drove up to Lake Tahoe last night to spend the day with his family. Some sort of emergency, he claims."

Something—maybe the coffee—was eating a hole in Dunn's stomach.

"The woman who called this morning, did you tell her exactly where Joe's family was staying?"

"Well, yeah," Molly said. "I didn't think it was a secret. I mean, Professor Conrad gave me the telephone number and the address. There's no cell phone service up there, he said."

"What's the address?" Dunn demanded.

"It's no secret," Molly repeated. "His sister-in-law's cabin, Number 17 Strawberry Lane, off Highway 50."

After Dunn ended that call, he punched in another number. Holding the phone to his ear, he said to the other detective, "I'm calling the sister-in-law. She's an attorney in Sac. It's her cabin Joe's family went to." Dunn laughed at the irony and added, "To stay out of harm's way."

CHAPTER 30

I charge thee, fling away ambition:
By that sin fell the angels.
From *Henry VIII*

The danger behind him and heartened by a call from his publisher telling him that orders for his book had increased since his name had been in the news, Joe drove his '68 Ford Mustang up to the cabin Monday evening to be with his family. Tuesday morning, he called a much-annoyed Molly and told her to post a notice that Tuesday's class was cancelled. Then he drove his family over Echo Summit on Highway 50 to Lake Tahoe.

The beach at the Marina was crowded with families, but they found a spot for their blanket and towels, and spent the day watching the children splash in the shallow water near shore as farther out, teenagers on jet skis raced in circles, spraying geysers of water in their wake. After midday sandwiches and salads, Joe dozed next to Sara as she read and watched Katie build sandcastles, while Brian napped in the shade.

Late Tuesday afternoon, when Joe and Sara returned from the lake with the children, they saw a strange car parked in the driveway of Suzie's cabin. When he opened his car door and saw the woman on the deck, the sight of her was so incongruous, it tickled the hairs on the back of Joe's neck.

Under the boughs of enormous redwoods, the scent of pine in

the air, Deirdre Claire sat in a lounge chair on the deck, smoking a cigarette. She smiled and stood as Joe climbed out of the car.

"I thought we should talk," she called.

There was nothing to do but usher the weary children inside the cabin and invite the well-dressed woman inside. When Joe glanced at Sara, she didn't seem pleased. They were all dressed in damp swimming suits under t-shirts and shorts. Sara made a face Joe couldn't read—maybe she felt outclassed by the sophisticated, older woman.

After getting the children settled, Sara made coffee and handed Deirdre a cup and sat down next to Joe.

"Thank you. As I was saying, I understand why you want to donate the Shakespeare papers to various libraries and universities, but out of respect for my grandfather, I'd like to urge you to give them to me instead. And my sister, of course. I'm willing to pay you a handsome reward."

Joe glanced at Sara who turned toward the other woman.

"My sister's an attorney, Ms. Claire," explained Sara. "After consulting with colleagues, her advice is to follow your grandfather's instructions."

Deirdre strained to smile. "Don't you think he would have wanted his own granddaughters to have the papers?"

Joe felt torn. "I've thought about it a hundred times," he said. "I'm not sure why Jack chose to send the papers to me. Maybe he was afraid that the killer would track them to you."

"Yes," Deirdre said. "I think that must be the reason. He knew you'd be able to flush out the killer and deal with him, just as you did before."

"Yeah," said Joe. "Or maybe Jack wanted me to have the papers because he was still trying to help my career."

"From what I've seen on TV, your career *has* been helped." Deirdre put her cup down. "But don't you think he'd want to help his granddaughters, too?"

Joe looked at Sara, and then turned back to Deirdre. "Our attorney says we can discuss sharing ownership of the documents with you once the police investigation is finished."

Deirdre closed her eyes and nodded. Her expression was hard to read. It seemed to Joe that she was deciding something. Finally, she said, "That seems reasonable." She turned toward Brian, who was playing on the floor with Katie. "What's your son's name?"

"Brian," said Joe.

"Brian," repeated Deirdre.

Hearing his name, Brian looked up, first at Joe and Sara, but then he turned to look at Deirdre, who beamed a smile back at him.

"You're a very handsome little boy, Brian. Handsome like your father," said the woman. "Would you like to come over and give your aunt Deirdre a hug?"

Smiling, Brian stood up and waddled over in the woman's direction.

Sara reached out, but he was too fast. "I don't think—"

"Don't think that's a good idea," Joe finished, springing to his feet, but Brian had already climbed into Deirdre's lap.

The face of Jack Claire's granddaughter darkened.

The expression made Joe freeze.

"Your son must be very precious to you," she said. She pulled a small silver and black pistol from her purse and held it to the back of Brian's head, just as Brian hugged her neck. "You must love him very much. My own father was always too busy to spend time with us. He felt inadequate, with the great Jack Claire's reputation to live up to. Not a scholar. But a damn good businessman. He died so young, so young."

Joe stood in front of the woman, a sickening feeling rising in his throat.

"I took over daddy's business and made it something he'd be proud of. But it was still not good enough. Too commercial for *Doctor* Claire! My grandfather despised me."

"I doubt that," Joe said, trying to calm her.

Deirdre shook her head at Joe. "He disapproved of my—how did he put it?—my blind ambition."

"Joe," whimpered Sara behind him.

"I was never good enough. Never quite smart enough, not quite as well read as Melinda. Oh, I tried. I pretended to be interested in the arts, to please him."

"I'll give you the papers," Joe said firmly.

Katie looked up and saw the woman holding the gun to her brother's head.

"Daddy?"

Katie stood and ran into Sara's arms.

Brian turned around in Deirdre's lap as she shifted the gun so it pointed at Joe.

"I'll give you the papers," he said again.

"Where are they? They aren't here, are they?"

Joe tried to think. Had she thought through what she was doing?

"How do you plan to get away with this?" he asked. "You'll have to kill us to keep us quiet, won't you?"

Deirdre wrinkled her brow, feigning a quizzical look. "Not necessarily. Your deaths would make me look terribly guilty, wouldn't they?"

"Not if you can stage it to look like a professional job, as if a second mercenary had been hired."

Sara pulled Katie's face into her shoulder. Then she said, "There's no way you can get away with it. The police must already be investigating you."

"The police? You mean Detective Dunn?" Deirdre asked. "He won't be a problem."

"Don't be so sure," Joe said. "He figured things out pretty well the last time."

"Did he?" Deirdre shot back. "My impression is, many people still think *you're* the I-5 Strangler, Joe."

"So?"

"So, maybe the young Professor Conrad has a little cabin fever. You know, Jack Nicholson in *The Shining*? 'All work and no play makes Joe a dull boy.' I see a murder-suicide in your future. Poor man. The strain of being accused of those rapes and murders, maybe thinking he got away with it, but then killing again in pursuit of those valuable manuscripts. Who knows? Maybe your wife finally discovered the truth, and you killed her to keep her quiet."

"Mommy," whispered Katie.

Joe stepped in front of Sara and Katie, putting himself between them and the woman who held his son on her lap. "If you come with me now, I'll take you to the manuscripts. Just leave my family alone."

Brian looked up at the pistol in the woman's hand and squirmed, trying to grab it, as if it were a toy. As Brian strained to touch the shiny object, Deirdre instinctively jerked the gun away.

Joe saw his chance. He lurched across the floor and grabbed at the gun.

Deirdre swung her arm back to point the barrel at Joe, but Brian reached up and clutched the woman's wrist, pulling the gun downward as it fired.

The explosion was deafening in the small cabin, but the first round went into the carpet beside Joe's foot. Deirdre jerked Brian off her lap—he fell to the floor, smashing his face on the carpet.

"Brian!" yelled Sara.

The toddler burst into tears, but Joe ignored his screams as he grabbed the woman's arm and struggled to control the direction of the gun's barrel.

Another shot rang out and the large window over the sliding glass doors shattered, shards of glass raining down on the deck outside.

But Joe now had the woman's wrist, even as she strained to twist and point the gun in his direction.

"Joe, watch out!" Sara screamed.

A third explosion and Joe had to look back at Sara and Katie. The bullet had pierced the chair just inches from Sara's left shoulder.

With her free hand, Deirdre reached around and dug her sharp fingernails into Joe's left eyebrow and cheek. Joe pushed the woman's arm up so the gun pointed to the ceiling. Then he pushed his weight into the woman's body, and down both of them fell.

Joe could feel the air gush out of Deirdre when she hit the floor and he landed on top of her, desperately holding the gun away from Sara and the children.

"Get the kids out!" he yelled.

From the corner of his bloodied eye, he saw Sara grab Brian and Katie and run out the front door.

The pistol fired again—the deafening explosion rang out next to Joe's ear. Now the room smelled of gunpowder.

"Get off me, you bastard!"

"Let go of the fucking gun and I will!" Joe yelled.

"I'm going to kill you," screamed the woman.

She scratched at his face again with her free hand as they rolled back and forth on the carpet. Joe tried to slide his hands closer to the gun while still controlling the woman's wrist. She twisted her hand toward his face and fired again, the bullet grazing Joe's left cheek. Blood gushed from the wound.

"You're dead now, you bastard."

She strained again to point the gun at Joe's face, but instead of pushing the gun away, Joe suddenly jerked it in the other direction, pulling Deirdre's arm across her face as she fired another round. The bullet struck a flowerpot, shattering it. Dirt and flowers flew across the tabletop.

Joe rolled the woman onto her stomach and sprawled across her, using his weight to hold her down. Her arm outstretched, the gun exploded again, a hole appearing in the wall just above the floor. Joe pressed down upon her like a wrestler pinning his opponent, pushing the gun down to the floor.

Exhausted, she seemed to give up.

"Okay, okay," she gasped. "You win. Get off me."

"Let go and I will."

She relaxed her grip on the pistol and it dropped to the floor. Still holding the woman's wrist tightly, Joe rolled away from the gun and pulled her over on top of him. Now he rested on his back, clutching the woman in his arms, her back on his chest.

His left eye smeared with blood and his cheek throbbing, he tried to roll again, away from the gun on the floor a few feet away, but as he rolled onto his right side, the woman squirmed and slithered free of his grip just enough to reach for the pistol.

"Damn, you're stubborn," he said. He grabbed the woman's hair and jerked her head back. Then climbing quickly to his feet, he dragged her by the hair farther from the gun.

"Let go of me, you prick!" she screamed, her arms flailing. She slapped his forearms as he dragged her. Then Joe reached down, grabbed her under the arms and lifted her into a chair, dumping her into it like a sack of rubbish. She lurched forward, but Joe shoved her back down. Looking up angrily, she lurched forward again. Joe shoved her back down more forcefully.

"I've never hit a woman in my life, but by God, lady, if you don't sit still, I'm going to knock you out."

"Fuck you," she hissed, and then she tried to jump up again.

Joe swung hard and caught the woman's chin, her head rocking back. She went limp, out cold. Joe breathed a deep sigh of relief before stepping across the room. He picked up the pistol and examined it carefully. Silver with a black handle, a Beretta .32caliber Tomcat.

Tomcat? Joe looked at the woman slumped in the chair. *More like a Hellcat.* The gun wouldn't do anymore damage.

"I can see why Jack didn't care for you, lady." He wiped blood out of his left eye and assessed the damage to the cabin. A broken window, a hole in the ceiling, a hole in the back of a chair, a busted flower pot, and a hole in the wall by the front door.

"Daddy!" He heard the terror in Katie's voice. "Daddy, come quick."

Joe glanced again at the hole low in the cabin wall, and suddenly he knew.

"Oh, God," he yelled, running out the front door.

Sara sat on the dirt, Brian in her lap, Katie standing in front of her. Sara looked pale. Her eyes met Joe's. Katie turned and looked at her father.

"Hurry, daddy. She's bleeding."

Joe dropped the pistol and ran from the porch.

"It doesn't hurt much," Sara said, looking down.

Joe saw the wound in Sara's thigh. The hole looked like a thimble with blood oozing from it.

"Do something, Daddy," Katie screamed.

"Did it go through, Sara?"

"What?"

"The bullet. Did it go all the way through your leg?"

Sara looked at Katie and then back at Joe. "I'm not sure. I just sort of collapsed when it hit me and I couldn't get up to run with the kids."

Joe tugged Brian out of Sara's arms and handed him to Katie.

"Let me see the back of your leg. Roll over."

She leaned onto her side. Joe felt the back of her leg up under her shorts.

"I can't feel an exit wound. The bullet must still be inside."

"Oh, Daddy," Katie whimpered.

Joe tugged his white tee-shirt off and wrapped it around Sara's leg, tying the arms around the wound as tightly as he could.

"Can you stand?" he asked her.

"I don't know."

She struggled with Joe's help and finally stood on her good leg.

"I'm going to be sick."

Sara doubled over and vomited.

"We've got to get you to the hospital."

Joe helped her limp toward the car and opened the passenger door.

"Katie, get Brian buckled into his car seat, okay?"

"Okay, daddy," Katie said. But she started to cry, even as she climbed into the backseat and helped Brian.

Joe helped Sara onto the front passenger seat and looked at the children in the back seat as he buckled Sara's seatbelt. Brian's face turned from bewilderment to fear, and he, too, began to cry.

"Damn it!" Joe said.

"What's wrong?" asked Sara.

"The keys. I left the damn car keys in the cabin."

After buckling the seatbelt around Sara, Joe slammed her door shut and turned to jog back to the cabin.

What he saw stopped him dead.

Standing on the porch, her swollen jaw the color of a ripe peach, Deirdre held the pistol in both hands, pointing it at Joe.

"Why didn't you just give me those papers? You could have saved everyone so much trouble. Just like my grandfather. I asked him, you know. When I learned about those manuscripts, I asked about them. He pretended he didn't know what I was talking about. Didn't think I knew what they were worth."

Joe stared at the woman, unable to believe she was related to the man he'd loved so much.

"But *you* know how valuable the Shakespeare papers are, don't you?" Joe said.

She strained to smile, though the pain made her wince. "I have a collector who's willing to pay forty million dollars for them."

"Forty million?" Joe repeated. "That's about ten million for each life you've taken."

Deirdre shrugged. "Time to say good night, sweet prince."

CHAPTER 31

You do advance your cunning more and more
When truth kills truth, O devilish-holy fray!
From *A Midsummer Night's Dream*

"Do you have enough bullets for all four of us, Deirdre?"

"What?" the woman asked.

"You fired four or five inside the cabin. How many bullets does that Beretta hold? Maybe six or seven in the clip? So you shoot me, maybe it takes only one shot, but maybe two. How do you do my wife? How do you kill my daughter and son? Are you capable of strangling children? Or bashing their heads in with a rock?"

Joe bent down and picked up a stone the size of a baseball.

"Put the rock down," the woman commanded.

Joe stepped toward her and held the rock up as if to throw it.

Deirdre smiled, then winced with pain and placed one hand against her jaw while holding the gun in the other and pointing it squarely at Joe's head.

"To answer your question, *Professor* Conrad, yes, I do have the will power to strangle those brats, if I have to."

"Well, get on with it, then," yelled Joe defiantly.

Deirdre gazed at him in disbelief. Then she grinned and squeezed the trigger. Nothing happened. She turned the gun on its side, checking the safety as Joe stepped closer. She flipped the small safety level back and forth, and then pointed the gun at Joe again, squeezing the trigger. Again, nothing.

Joe reached into the pocket of his shorts and pulled out the clip, along with the loose round he'd jacked out of the chamber.

"I should bash your head in," he told the woman. But he reached over, twisted the pistol from her hand and tossed it into the dirt. Then he tugged the woman by her wrist to his car. Pushing the button under the dash, he opened the trunk.

"I'm not getting in there!" she screamed, fighting him.

"The hell you aren't!"

Joe lifted the lid with one hand and reached in for a roll of silver duct tape. He taped the woman's hands behind her back, fighting to control her as she wriggled to free herself. Then Joe wrapped her waist to make sure her hands stayed behind her. The woman still squirming, he lifted her in his arms like a bride and dumped her into the trunk like a sack of cement.

Looking up with hate-filled eyes, Deirdre yelled, "Fuck you! Fuck your whole family! Why'd he send those papers to *you*?"

Joe tore off a strip of tape and covered the woman's mouth. "The lady doth protest too much," he said. Then he slammed the trunk lid and jogged into the cabin for the car keys.

Looking pale, Sara forced a smile at Joe when he started the car.

"Two and a half years ago, *you* were the one headed to the hospital with a gun-shot wound, remember?"

"I remember."

"And you lived to tell about it, right?"

Joe looked at the blood-soaked shirt wrapped around Sara's leg. He stomped on the gas and peeled out of the driveway.

"Yep, I lived to tell about it," he said. "And so will you."

He drove the car much too fast down the narrow street and the tires squealed when he turned the corner. He merged quickly into the heavy traffic on Highway 50, ignoring honks from angry drivers, weaving in and out between cars up to Echo Summit.

The narrow, winding road down the mountain was a frightening drive even when he drove the speed limit. Every mile included sharp turns and the road clung to the side of the mountain precariously. On the passenger's side was a sheer drop.

Joe glanced at Sara's leg. A ribbon of blood snaked down her thigh and calf. He gunned the engine and tore around slower cars, swerving back into the right lane just in time to miss on-coming cars.

"Don't kill us!" Sara screamed as Joe jerked the car in and out of traffic.

"Hold on, Sara."

He dared not take his eyes off the road or his hands off the steering wheel, but he knew Sara's eyes were pinched closed—she hated the highway even at normal speeds.

Joe saw another opening and raced into the left lane, almost losing control when the rear tires hit gravel next to the mountain.

"Daddy!" screamed Katie.

Rounding a bend, he saw the truck coming straight at them.

Joe honked the horn and swerved back into his own lane behind a slow SUV, nearly smashing into its rear bumper under the distinctive BMW symbol.

The truck with three cars behind it lumbered up the road. As soon as the last car passed, Joe turned back into the other lane and roared around the SUV as another car approached.

The driver of the BMW sped up, as if trying to force Joe to have a head-on collision.

"Asshole!" Joe yelled.

He stomped the gas pedal down and merged toward the SUV, but it held its ground.

The on-coming car slowed and moved closer to the mountain.

Is there room for three cars? he wondered.

Joe's car was barely ahead of the SUV as the other car still approached. He jerked toward the BMW's front left fender and finally the other driver backed off.

Joe swerved into the right lane and sped forward while the drivers of both cars laid on their horns.

Finally the road flattened and straightened out, and Joe easily passed other cars as he raced into the Tahoe valley. In five minutes, he had the car at the Emergency bay of the hospital.

But Sara had passed out sometime during the drive.

Joe ran around the front of the car, yelling for someone, anyone, to help, as he threw open the passenger door and lifted Sara's limp body out—Katie crying, Brian screaming, and the woman in the trunk kicking.

Several people dressed in green scrubs rushed outside with a gurney and Joe gently lowered Sara's body down, reluctantly giving her over to the others.

He could only watch as they wheeled his wife away, Katie rushing into his arms, burying her face in his stomach.

Then a security guard ambled over and asked Joe about the noise coming from the trunk.

Dunn arrived at the cabin shortly after Joe left for the hospital. Seeing the door open, the broken glass, the discarded pistol and the blood on the dirt, he quickly pieced together what must have happened and drove toward the Lake, trying to reach Joe on his cell phone.

Near the Lake, Joe's cell phone worked again, and after being told to wait outside the operating room, he finally returned Dunn's calls. Dunn made it to the hospital just as the local Sheriff arrived, and the two of them listened to Joe's story. Then they said they'd have to talk to Deirdre Claire. They disappeared for an hour. Joe tried to calm the kids and waited for news about Sara.

When the doctor returned, his face wasn't as promising as Joe had hoped. Joe held Brian and Katie as they listened to the doctor. Joe couldn't take his eyes off the blood on the front of the surgeon's white gown.

"She's lost a lot of blood, but if she responds well to treatment, she should be okay. We need to let her rest. She's still waking up from the anesthesia, so wait about an hour before you see her."

After interrogating Deirdre, Dunn and the Sheriff found Joe in the waiting room. Brian slept with his head on Joe's lap and Katie divided her attention between cartoons on the TV and a coloring book on the coffee table in front of Joe.

The Sheriff put his hand on Joe's shoulder. "Mr. Conrad, you need to speak to us out in the hall."

Joe glanced from the Sheriff to Dunn.

"Sorry, Joe," Dunn said. "Deirdre Claire's story is a little different from yours."

"What's wrong, Daddy?" Katie asked. She was struggling not to cry.

Joe patted her shoulder. "Don't worry, honey. I'll just be a few minutes. You watch Brian."

Joe gently lifted Brian's head and slipped a pillow under it as he slid off the sofa. He followed the Sheriff out to the hall as Detective Dunn held the door open.

"I might have to take you in, Mr. Conrad," the Sheriff said matter-of-factly.

Joe looked at Dunn. "What the hell's going on?"

"She says you pulled the gun on her, after calling her and asking her to come up and meet you at the cabin. She's claiming that you and Sara had planned on killing her and burying her up here, so she wouldn't make any claims on the manuscripts."

Joe laughed. "That's ridiculous!"

"She sounded pretty convincing," the Sheriff added. "Says she tried to wrestle the gun away from you and you fired the shots, not her. Says *you* wounded your wife, and that's when you beat her up and stuck her in the trunk."

"You're not buying that bull, are you?"

Dunn shrugged. "I found evidence linking Deirdre to the man who fell off the clock tower, so I'm sure she's guilty, but you have to remember, Joe. This isn't the first time you've been accused of beating up and kidnapping women."

Joe stepped backward and let himself lean against the cool plaster wall of the hospital corridor.

"Un-fucking-believable."

"Whose gun is it?" the Sheriff asked.

"Hers!" said Joe. "She pulled it out of her pocket and pointed it at Brian's head."

"I've radioed in the serial number," said the Sheriff, "so if it's registered, we'll at least have that much."

"What if it's not registered to anyone?"

"Then it's your word against hers," admitted Dunn.

"But Katie saw it all. Ask her."

"We might," nodded the Sheriff. "Course, if her mom and daddy were planning to kill somebody, she just might lie to protect them."

Joe shot the sheriff a hateful look. "You obviously don't know my daughter. Detective Dunn can vouch for her. Hell, he can vouch for all of us, can't you?"

"Well, Joe," said Dunn. "It's not quite that simple. We've got to sort out the evidence."

"Jesus Christ," Joe huffed. "Just ask Sara when she wakes up."

Sheriff Rodell nodded. "Oh, we will, believe you me. But then again…"

"Then again what?"

"Well, if you and her were going to kill Ms. Claire, your wife would probably lie about it, don't you think?"

Joe shook his head. "Unreal. So just because this woman makes a ridiculous accusation, you can't trust my family. Not even my daughter, who's too young to know how to tell a lie."

The Sheriff shrugged. "Kids lie all the time."

"Joe," Dunn piped in. "I've convinced the Sheriff to hold off putting you into custody until Sara's released from the hospital."

Scowling at the Sheriff, Joe yelled, "You're going to arrest me?"

"Not yet," said Dunn. "He figures you won't try to run with two small children. That gives me time to share the evidence I found earlier with the Sheriff here."

"What evidence?" asked Joe. "Who has it?"

"Evidence linking Deirdre with Benedict Anderson, the man you killed in Berkeley."

"I didn't kill him. He fell off the damn clock tower after trying to kill me, remember?"

"We'll sort it all out over the next few days, Mr. Conrad," said the Sheriff. The skepticism in his voice was not encouraging. "Meanwhile, do not leave your sister-in-law's cabin. I expect the hospital will release your wife tomorrow and we'll need to take you into custody then."

"You're going to arrest me based on what *that* bitch says?"

"No need for that kind of language, Mr. Conrad."

"If you'd seen her holding a gun to your two-year-old's head, I'm pretty sure you'd call her worse than that!"

"We'll continue to investigate, Joe," Dunn said. "Stay calm and take care of those kids. What'd the docs say about Sara?"

Joe's eyes filled with tears. "She lost a lot of blood, but the wound isn't that deep. If I'd gotten her to the hospital sooner..."

Dunn put his hand on Joe's shoulder. "You made a dangerous drive in almost half the time it normally takes. No ambulance or even life-flight could have gotten her here sooner. Don't blame yourself."

Joe looked Dunn in the eyes. "But I do blame myself, Ryan. I got myself into this whole mess and put my family in danger again. I just wish Jack Claire hadn't sent those damn manuscripts to me in the first place. Why the hell didn't he just send them to one of his granddaughters?"

The sheriff chuckled and Dunn gave him a look that caught Joe's attention.

"What?" asked Joe. "Is there something you're not telling me? Something more?"

"Oh, you might say that," the Sheriff chuckled smugly.

"You might as well know, Joe," Dunn said, still holding Joe's shoulder.

"Know what? Tell me, damn it!"

"Well," Dunn began. "Deirdre Claire now says that she suspects *you* killed her grandparents."

"What!"

Dunn nodded. "She says you found the Shakespeare papers and mailed them to yourself."

Joe fell back against the wall again. "Jesus Christ! She's more diabolical than I imagined!"

"Well," the Sheriff said. "One of you is. That's for damn sure."

CHAPTER 32

Then lofty Love thy sacred sails advance,
My sighing seas shall flow with streams of tears…
From "Reason and Affection"

Joe walked back into the waiting room. Katie sat on the floor helping Brian play with small wooden railroad cars, and when she looked up, trying to be brave, trying not to show her fear and worry, Joe covered his face with his hands.

"Oh, Daddy," Katie said, standing. She started to cry again and ran over to Joe, throwing her arms around his neck when he knelt down to grab her.

Joe opened his eyes as Brian was attempting to stand. He wobbled, trying to get his balance, and then fell back onto his padded behind. The startled look on his face made Joe laugh.

"Your brother's so cute sometimes," Joe whispered.

Katie turned around, trying to stop herself from crying, and looked at Brian sitting on the floor. "He's cute enough," she admitted, choking back her tears. "For a boy."

Suddenly, the door to the waiting room swung open behind them, and Joe turned to see who it was. Sara's sister Suzie rushed in with Bill Morgan behind her.

Relief washed over Joe like a cool wave.

An hour later, Sara, in a semi-private room with everyone crowded around her bed, sat up, sipping Hawaiian punch from a straw and smiling at her children.

"Does it hurt?" Katie asked.

"I've had bee stings that hurt worse than this, honey," she said, touching her daughter's cheek.

"Joe," Suzie said. "I swear to God, if you get my sister into a situation like this again, *I'll* kill you myself!"

"Aunt Suzie!" Katie scolded.

Joe turned toward Detective Dunn, grinning. "You heard her, Ryan. If anything happens to me now, you know where to start your investigation."

Bill Morgan put his arm over Susan Taylor's shoulders, saying, "Don't worry, Suzie. If you *do* kill him, I'll get you off."

"On what grounds?" Sara laughed.

Bill and Suzie said simultaneously, "Justifiable homicide!"

Later that evening, Joe and Suzie took the kids to a nearby coffee shop for dinner, letting Sara rest. Sara had told Joe to take the kids back to the cabin, but they didn't want to leave her until visiting hours were over at 8:00 P.M.

When they got back to Sara's room, a nurse was checking her blood pressure. She recorded the numbers on a chart and then felt Sara's toes for a pulse.

"You're doing great," the nurse said, patting Sara lightly on the foot. Glancing at Joe, the nurse said, "Odds are, she'll be ready to go home tomorrow."

"That's great news," Joe said.

Bill Morgan stepped into the room as the nurse was leaving. "Good news. Ryan had his friend from the SFPD fax a report up to the Sheriff. They're holding Deirdre Claire at the Sheriff's office until someone from the Berkeley PD comes to transport her back down to the Bay Area."

"So does that mean I'm free to go?" asked Joe.

"You bet. I had a pleasant chat with the Sheriff. He'd rather not be accused of making a false arrest. I convinced him that the lawsuit Suzie and I would bring could bankrupt the city of Tahoe."

Joe turned to Sara. "Are you really doing better?"

"Yeah. I'm great. Ninety-nine percent. Why?"

"I should drive down to Stockton in the morning, then. I mean, if you're really all right. I've missed too many classes already, and this is the last week of the session. I give the final on Thursday."

"Are you serious?" Susan said.

"No, Suzie," said Sara, turning toward her sister. "Joe's right. If you can stay here tomorrow to help me when I'm released, then he should go."

"Get your priorities straight, Joe," Suzie said.

"Suzie, please. If you stay with me tomorrow, then I'll be fine."

Suzie scowled at Joe and then turned and smiled at Sara. "All right. I can stay."

In the morning at 5:00, Joe called the hospital from the cabin and asked the nurse about Sara's condition. The report was good, so he showered, dressed and drove the two and half hours to Stockton in time to meet his students. He collected their research papers and half-heartedly reviewed material for the final exam.

After class, he checked his voicemail. Dozens of messages from reporters who wanted his side of the story. Some had been left Monday, asking about his brush with the mercenary at the U. C. Berkeley campus. The recent calls were about the shootout at the cabin. Ignoring these calls, he dialed the hospital at Lake Tahoe and learned that Sara had been released an hour earlier. Suzie answered the phone when he called the cabin's landline.

"How is she?" Joe asked her.

"Well, despite the fact that she has a hole in her leg and she'll be on crutches for a week, she's just dandy. How are you?"

"Tired, but otherwise fine, Suzie. Can I speak to her, please?"

"You want her to get up and come to the phone, really, Joe? We just got her settled into a chair with her leg propped up and you want her to—"

Suzie's voice stopped abruptly and Sara said hello.

"How are you, honey?" Joe asked.

"I'm fine, Joe. Really. The doc gave me good pain meds and it doesn't hurt anymore. Been drinking lots of fluids, so I feel great. We're closing up the cabin and Suzie's driving us home. Should be home for supper."

Joe closed his eyes and said a little prayer of gratitude. "I'll have something ready by the time you get home. I'm leaving the office now."

"Okay," said Sara. "See you soon."

Before leaving the office, Joe made one more call.

"Hello, Smitty."

"Lad!" Jonathan answered. "So glad to hear from you! It's been all over the TV. How's your wife? And the children?"

"All doing well. How about you?"

"You mean my head? The concussion? Oh, lad. Fully recovered, though I must admit, I haven't had the heart to look at those damn manuscripts. Not in all this hellish chaos."

Joe grinned. It was good to hear the old man's voice. It wasn't Jack Claire's, but close enough.

"Well, what are you waiting for, Smitty? Get back to work! What would Sylvia say if she knew you were slacking off?"

Jonathan half laughed, half cried. "I will. I will get back to work."

"Good. We've got a lot of unanswered questions and a lot of interested reporters, so we'd better get our facts straight."

"Yes. Back to work. And Joe?"

"Yes, Smitty."

"I'm so glad you're all right. Grown a bit fond of you, lad."

"Me, too."

Joe hung up and smiled. He looked at Jack Claire's picture and shook his head. Jack couldn't have known the consequences of his actions, the results of the choices he'd made for his son. Or how they had affected his granddaughter.

Then Joe felt a pang of guilt as he thought about his own children. How had *his* choices affected them? Only time would tell. As he packed his students' papers into his briefcase, turned off the light and locked the door to his office, he wondered what the future would bring.

Part VI:
A Comedy of Errors

CHAPTER 33

What cunning can express
The favour of her face?
To whom in this distress,
I do appeal for grace.
From "What Cunning can Express"

Seeing Suzie's car pull into the driveway of their little house on Tenth Street, Joe rushed from the kitchen and went outside to greet his family. Katie had freed Brian from the car seat by the time Joe reached him, so he swooped Brian up in his arms and Katie hugged his waist.

"Mommy's so much better now," Katie said.

Joe turned to help Sara stand up on the crutches, and when she was propped up, he hugged her with one arm while holding Brian in the other. He kissed her harder than he had in weeks.

"You look better," he said. "Got your color back."

"I feel fine. Hungry. But fine otherwise. What's for dinner?"

Joe laughed. "Broiled chicken breasts in lemon and white wine, with button mushrooms and artichokes."

"Sounds delicious," Sara said, smiling up at him.

Suzie stepped around the car and gave Joe a reluctant hug. "Did you make enough for me?"

"Of course" Joe said. "Saved the neck and gizzards for you."

"Very funny," she replied, slapping his arm and smiling in spite of herself.

Katie tugged at Joe's sleeve. "You cooked lizards, Daddy?"

Sara laughed and bent down to kiss the top of Katie's head. "Not lizards, honey. Gizzards."

"It's like the chicken's stomach," Joe answered. "Aunt Suzie's a typical attorney—she enjoys taking every piece till there's nothing left!"

That earned Joe another slap across the arm.

After dinner, Joe helped Sara onto the sofa in the living room and propped up her leg. He went back into the kitchen, did the dishes and cleaned up while Suzie played with Brian and Katie. Joe stepped back into the living room, wiping his hands on a dishcloth.

Craning her head to look at Joe, she asked, "What are you smiling at?"

"I'm just glad to have my family all together, safe and sound."

"Well, mostly sound," Suzie said. "Your wife still has a hole in her leg. Of course, it matches the one in your head. What were you thinking?"

Joe shrugged, grinning. His sister-in-law's rant wasn't going to ruin his mood.

After helping to put the children to bed, and helping her sister change into a cool cotton nightgown, Suzie left and Joe breathed a sigh of relief.

In the bedroom, Joe handed Sara her pills and a glass of water.

"Are you really better?" he asked.

"Yeah. Stop worrying. The doctor said I'll make a complete recovery. I'm young and strong and healthy. Really just a minor wound. Didn't even hit the bone. He said the bullet lost a lot of its force by going through the wall before it hit my leg."

"You looked pretty bad when I got you to the hospital. I was afraid I'd lose you."

"Come here," she said.

Joe climbed across the bed and kissed her. She stroked his temple, saying, "You aren't going to lose me. Not for a long time."

Later, as he watched Sara sleep, Joe read his students' research papers at the small desk in the corner of the bedroom. By 5:00 in the morning, he'd finished twenty-two of the thirty papers. He opened the blinds and looked at the sky, already growing light. The crescent-shaped moon hung in the west just above the dark trees, disappearing as the dark azure sky brightened. Exhausted, he climbed into bed to grab a little sleep before class.

At 7:00, the alarm pulled Joe out of a nightmare—someone shooting into the children's room, punching holes in the walls, letting in pinpoints of light that came closer and closer to the children.

He lurched awake, heart pounding. Sara was snoozing quietly. Joe rubbed his face and climbed out of bed. Before showering, he looked in on Brian and Katie. Both were still asleep.

In the shower, Joe felt groggy, hung over. Something nagged at him, but he couldn't clear his mind.

While brushing his teeth, Joe looked into his reflection in the mirror as the thought became clearer.

"Oh, shit," he whispered. He rinsed out his mouth, wiped his face on a towel and went into the bedroom for his cell phone. Sara was sitting up.

"Good morning," she said, wincing.

"You in pain?"

"Just a little. Can you bring me my pills?"

"Sure" Joe grabbed the bottle, shook two pills out and handed them to Sara. Then he took the empty glass from the nightstand and went back to the bathroom for water.

After giving Sara the glass, he grabbed his phone and walked into the kitchen to start a pot of coffee. He also punched in the number for Detective Ryan Dunn.

Dunn answered after the third ring.

"What is it, Joe?" He sounded annoyed.

Joe glanced at the clock on the stove. It was almost 8:00. "Did I wake you?"

"No. I've been awake for a few hours."

"I just thought of something. Thought I should ask you about it."

"What's on your mind?"

"It's something Deirdre Claire said when she was holding the gun on me. She said she'd been offered millions for the Shakespeare papers."

"Yeah? So?" Dunn asked, sounding impatient.

"Who was offering her money?"

Dunn stayed quiet.

"I'm wondering if we're still in danger, Ryan. Whoever was offering Deirdre Claire money is still out there. Maybe looking for another guy like Benedict to get his hands on the manuscripts."

"Yeah, I've thought about that, too. But this time, I don't think you have to worry. With all the TV coverage, whoever was trying to purchase the papers from Deirdre Claire has probably destroyed the evidence. Shredded papers, burned correspondence."

"But can we be sure? Can we be sure my family's safe?"

"You can't ever be certain of anything, Joe. You know that."

"Can you find out who was behind all this? Who contacted Deirdre Claire?"

"Give us a few days or weeks, and we'll probably find something." The exasperation in his voice was obvious and Joe couldn't understand it.

"You can start by interrogating Deirdre Claire. You know, really put the screws to her. Hell, waterboard the bitch, as far as I'm concerned."

Ryan Dunn laughed. "Put the screws to her?" he repeated.

"Yeah. You know. The same way you grilled me when you thought *I* was guilty."

"No," Dunn said, sounding exhausted. "No, we won't be able to get anything out of her, Joe."

"Why not? Did she lawyer up?"

"She's dead, Joe."

"*Dead?*" Joe's heart pounded fiercely. "How is she dead?"

"Escaped from the jail and stole a car."

"Jesus, Ryan. How'd she do *that*?"

"It's her own damn fault," Dunn said. "Too smart for her own good."

"What do you mean?"

"She played that Sheriff, just like she played…a lot of men. If she hadn't worked her magic on him, he would have followed procedure. Taken her clothing and put her in a jumpsuit. Locked her up where she would have been watched more closely. Stupid bastard probably thought a beautiful, rich bitch like her would sue his ass, if he didn't treat her like royalty, so when she complained of heart trouble, they took her to the hospital. She was able to slip out of the examination room and steal a car from the parking lot."

"How'd she die, then?" Joe asked.

"Driving too fast on Highway 50 up to the summit. Didn't make a turn. Car plummeted down the cliff and she burned to a crisp.

Joe stayed quiet for a moment, thinking. That feeling was still tickling the back of his neck.

"Are you sure it was an accident? Not another murder?"

"Yeah, pretty sure."

"Because it could have been someone tying up the loose ends. You know, the person who was going to pay her for the papers."

Ryan chuckled again. "Tying up loose ends? You've got a helluva way with words, Joe."

"You know what I mean."

Joe heard a strange squeaking noise and turned to look at the doorway from the hall. Sara was swinging herself into the kitchen on her crutches.

"What is it, honey?" she asked. "You sound worried."

"It's Ryan Dunn," Joe told her. "He says Deirdre Claire's dead."

"Oh my god," said Sara. She shook her head and said, "Well, I can't say I'm sorry. Not after what she did to Brian."

"And to you, don't forget."

"I've got to go," Dunn said over the phone.

"Okay, Ryan. Thanks for the information." The call ended and Joe closed his phone, looking at it. "It's weird. He sounds sad."

Joe looked into Sara's eyes.

"It's got to be depressing, dealing with death all the time, the way he does. I'm sure it just gets to him sometimes."

"Yeah," Joe agreed, rubbing the back of his neck.

CHAPTER 34

The lunatic, the lover, and the poet
Are of imagination all compact:
One sees more devils than vast hell can hold.
From *A Midsummer Night's Dream*

Later that morning in his classroom on campus, Joe finished grading papers as his students wrote their final exams. When the last student, Lauren, closed her Bluebook, she handed it to him, saying, "We've all been watching the news."

"Oh?" Joe said. He pushed back his chair to stand, anxious to leave.

The two of them, student and teacher, walked out of the classroom together.

"It's weird to see your own professor all over TV. Like you're a celebrity or something."

"Or something," Joe agreed. "Does it…worry you?"

Lauren laughed. "No! It's totally awesome! I mean, here we are taking this course about crime and murder and stuff, and there you are, all over the news, like, actually killing people."

"I didn't kill anyone, Lauren."

"What about that dude you pushed off the tower at Berkeley?"

Joe looked at Lauren's face.

"Well, he *was* trying to kill *me,* you know."

"No, I know." The young woman nodded. "It was like self defense, totally justifiable homicide."

They had reached his office door across from the staircase. Joe stopped and faced the girl as she spoke.

"And then that woman supposedly escapes from jail. That's like totally weird."

Joe nodded. "Yeah, it's pretty weird, all right."

"I always think the police did it, when someone dies like that."

Joe shook his head. "I have it on good authority, she really did die in a car accident."

"Still, Professor," Lauren said, smirking. "Your body count's growing."

Joe just looked at her, unable to reply.

She added, "You'll have to add another chapter to your book."

With that, the student spun around and walked down the stairs. Joe watched her disappear. Events had happened so quickly over the past several days, he hadn't had a chance to think, to put it all into perspective.

Joe took the exams to his office and put them inside his briefcase. Before shutting down his computer, he checked email. There was one from his literary agent.

> **Hi Joe,**
>
> **Random House is going to publish 10,000 additional copies of Tragic Flaws.**
> **I negotiated an advance of $5,000 against royalties. They're sending you a check minus my 15%.**
>
> **We should talk about another book. Strike while the iron's hot. Call me asap. Hope your family is well.**
>
> **Martha G.**

He decided not to call Martha yet—he couldn't even think about writing a description of the events of the last few days.

He wanted to be done with it—go home, do some work, be with

his family and be done with it. He shut down the computer, turned off the light, closed and locked the door, glad he wouldn't have to return for two weeks.

Back in Davis, Joe found the house empty. Sara was resting in a lounge chair in the back yard, watching Katie and Brian play in a small plastic pool. Trees provided broken shade and Sara seemed relaxed, sipping iced tea and smiling at the children. Her crutches lay on the grass next to her.

"I'm glad you're home," she said.

"So am I." He bent down and kissed her.

"Daddy!" Katie shrieked. She jumped out of the little pool and ran over. Joe lifted her up and hugged her. "This is almost as much fun as the big pool."

"Good," Joe said. He looked over at Brian, who climbed out of the pool with some difficulty and waddled over to clutch Joe's leg.

"You two are getting your father's good clothes all wet," scolded Sara.

"It doesn't matter," Joe said, hugging his children. He closed his eyes and felt how substantial and real the living bodies of his children were. And the world made sense again.

By midnight, he'd graded the students' finals and submitted their grades on line. As he clicked on the command, he looked over at Sara asleep in bed. Glancing back at the screen of his laptop, he read the words, **Final Grades Successfully Submitted.**

Tempted to awaken his wife to celebrate, he opted instead to finish the bottle of Riesling they'd opened at dinner. In the kitchen, he poured a tall glass and sipped it as he strolled down the hall into the children's bedroom. Brian and Katie slept peacefully. All was well.

The fragrance of steaming coffee awoke him at 7:00. A cup was sitting on the desk next to the bed. Joe sat up and sipped it. The wine had left him with a dull headache, but the hot coffee washed it away. Finally, he showered and dressed, and then found his family eating together in the kitchen. Sara stood at the stove cooking scrambled eggs. She'd left the crutches in the bedroom.

"So you're headed back to Berkeley? You and Dr. Smythe?"

"Yeah." Joe fed a spoonful of eggs to Brian, who was pretending he didn't want them. "Now we can work in peace."

Sara put the plate of eggs down in front of him and then set another plate down for herself. "If you say so." She took a bite, but he could tell she was trying not to show the concern she obviously felt.

"I won't go, if you don't want me to, Sara."

"Well, I'd rather have you home with us, but if you think it's important."

"Really, I can stay. If your leg hurts—"

"No. I'm fine. Almost good as new."

Joe sipped orange juice and put the glass down. "Oh, by the way. Martha emailed me yesterday. Said Random House is printing ten thousand more copies of my book. With all the publicity, they think people will want to buy it again."

"Great," Sara said sarcastically. "Just what we need. Reopen old wounds."

He tried to ignore the comment, but the image of Sara bleeding into the dirt outside the cabin appeared in his mind.

"Are you sure you're okay?" he asked her.

"Fine." She forced a smile. "Didn't even need the pain meds this morning."

"We're so close to figuring this thing out, I feel like I've got to take advantage of my time off. Once the fall semester starts…."

"No, I know."

"I hate to leave you, though."

"Katie's here. She can help with Brian."

Hearing her name, Katie looked up from her Harry Potter book. "That's right, Daddy. I can help Mommy."

Sara looked at Joe, grinned, and then crunched down on a piece of toast.

In Berkeley, Sylvia's worktable was covered by dozens of opened books. When she saw her visitors, she stood up and rushed over, hugging Jonathan first, then patting Joe on the shoulder.

"I'm so glad you're both okay. I've been worried sick."

"It's been a hellish week!" Smitty said. "Especially for poor Joe and his family."

"What's the matter, Joe?" Sylvia asked him.

"I was just thinking about Jack. He couldn't have known his own granddaughter was behind his wife's death. At least, I *hope* he didn't."

"Well," Sylvia said, "he must have suspected *something*, on some level. Which explains why he sent the manuscripts to you instead of his granddaughters."

Joe looked at Smitty, who nodded.

"Have you heard from Jack's other granddaughter?" Smitty asked. "She's not involved, is she?"

Joe shook his head. "I don't know. Deirdre didn't mention her, and Detective Dunn doesn't seem to think so."

Sylvia took Joe's hand. "The next few weeks are going to be very hard on her. Should you reach out in some way?"

Joe looked at Smitty.

"I don't think that would be a good idea," Smitty answered. "Let the police sort it out."

Joe nodded. "But I think I *should* involve her in the decisions about how to deal with these papers."

"Not right away, I hope." Sylvia squeezed Joe's hand before letting go.

"No, of course not. Once the dust has settled."

"Yes, lad. Let's figure out what these papers mean first."

As if that was their cue, they turned and looked at the briefcase Joe had already placed on the worktable.

After working for three hours, they broke for lunch and walked down to the Indian restaurant where they'd eaten before. Both Jonathan and Sylvia brought books with them. Once they'd ordered, Jonathan turned to Sylvia.

"What'd you find?"

"Something very interesting from Ernesto Grillo, a professor of

Italian language and literature who taught at the University of Glasgow. He grew up in Italy, studied at Bonn and St. George's College at Cambridge. Quite a scholar of Italy, Italian literature and more importantly, quite knowledgeable about Shakespeare."

Joe sipped his water and listened.

"Go on," Smitty begged.

"Grillo was so impressed by Shakespeare's knowledge of Italy, he argues that Shakespeare had to have visited Italy—Padua and Verona. He points out that Italy is referenced about eight hundred times in the plays, Rome about four hundred, Venice over fifty. Details only someone who'd spent time there could know."

Joe put down his glass, saying, "But I thought Will Shakespeare never left England?"

"Quite right, lad. No record of it, anyway."

"But Grillo says the evidence in the plays proves he must have visited Milan, Verona, Venice, Padua and Mantua between the autumn of 1592 and the summer of 1593."

"But didn't he get a few things wrong?" Smitty asked. "I mean, doesn't he describe characters travelling by water between cities that were landlocked?"

"Ah," smiled Sylvia. "Those places *are* landlocked now. But they weren't *then*, not in the late 1500s. There were canals, and only someone who visited Italy at the time could know that."

"Wait a minute," said Joe. "You mean the facts that Shakespeare gets wrong in his plays about Italy actually weren't wrong?"

"Correct," replied Sylvia. "Modern scholars based their claims on *their* knowledge of Italy today, not on the way Italy actually was in the sixteenth century. We discussed this before, remember?"

The waiter placed a glass of white wine in front of each of them and they suspended their discussion until he left.

Smitty looked at Sylvia. "So Grillo, who grew up in Italy, says the author of these plays must have spent time there."

Sylvia nodded, sipping her wine.

Joe asked, "Did Grillo know about de Vere?" He took his first sip of the chilled wine as he waited for her answer.

"No," Sylvia said, smiling. "That's the beauty of it. He thought he was praising William Shakespeare for his expert knowledge of Italy, Grillo's homeland. He couldn't have suspected that his praise actually helps prove that the man from Stratford *didn't* write the plays."

"We need to find out when Edward de Vere was in Italy," added Joe.

"That can be *your* job," Smitty said. "Read Allen Nelson's book on de Vere and find out when he was in Italy."

Joe shook his head, then took another drink of wine, grinning.

"Don't look at me," Smitty said, smiling. "I live on a fixed income!"

Their plates of food arrived. Joe ate enthusiastically, realizing that his appetite had returned. It felt good to eat and laugh with these friendly colleagues. They fell into a comfortable silence, enjoying the spicy food and washing it down with the cold white wine, each of them, Joe suspected, musing about Sylvia's revelations.

Over coffee, Sylvia turned to Smitty.

"And you, Jonathan? What did you learn this morning?"

Smitty smiled.

"Ah," he said, dabbing the corners of his mouth with his napkin. "It's always bothered me that the courtiers were unwilling to attach their names to their writing. It's so hard for us to understand the taboos of their times. I wanted to see what writers of the day said about this."

Sylvia smiled. "That's why you brought Webbe's book?"

"Yes." Smitty nodded, opening it to a page he'd marked. "Listen to this. Webbe is discussing the nobles and their literary circle. He writes, 'I may not omit the deserved commendations of many honourable and noble Lords and Gentlemen in Her Majesty's court, which, in the rare devices of poetry, have been and yet are most skilful'—and here's the kicker—'among whom the right honourable Earl of Oxford may challenge to himself the title of the most excellent among the rest!'"

Joe reached over and lifted the front of the book. "What's the title?"

"*A Discourse of English Poetry.* It was published in 1586."

"Where'd you find it?" asked Joe.

"In our special collections in the library."

Joe examined the page Smitty had just read aloud. "This is what a lawyer would call corroborating evidence."

"Right you are, lad, but listen to this." Smitty opened another book and started to read. "So as I know very many notable Gentlemen in the Court that have written commendably, and suppressed it agayne, or els suffred it to be published without their owne names to it: as if it were a discredit for a Gentleman, to seem learned, and to show himselfe amorous of any good art."

Joe shook his head. "It seems so schizophrenic of them, to love literature and to hide the fact that they wrote it."

Sylvia touched his arm. "Don't make the same mistake other scholars made, Joe. Let's not impose our modern values on the people of the sixteenth century."

"Listen to this," Smitty urged. "'And in her Majestys time that now is sprong up another crew of Courtly makers'—he means 'poets' there—'Noble men and Gentlemen of her Majesties own servantes, who have written excellently well as it would appear if their doings could be found out and made publicke with the rest, of which number is first that noble gentleman Edward Earl of Oxford.'"

"Wow," said Joe. "De Vere, *not* Shakspeare, was considered the best writer of the time. What's that book, Smitty?"

Smitty handed it to Joe, saying, "George Puttenham's *The Arte of English Poesie.* Published in 1589."

Sylvia nodded. "Contemporaneous praise. As Joe says, that *is* the kind of corroboration people should find convincing."

"There's another mention of de Vere later," Joe said, running his finger over the page. "Puttenham's discussing who deserves the highest praise among the nobles. Listen to this: 'The Earle of Oxford and Maister Edwardes of her Majesties Chappel for Comedy and Enterlude.'"

"You know what Francis Meres wrote in 1598?" asked Sylvia, looking at another book. "Meres wrote, 'The best for comedy among us be Edward Earl of Oxford."

"Yes," Smitty nodded. "I recall reading that years ago and wondering how he could have ignored Shakespeare. I figured he was just doing what was politically correct at the time. You know, praise the nobles to stay in their good graces."

"If you really want to be convinced," Sylvia added, "read this. It's the Preface to Bartholomew Clerke's translation of *The Courtier*, which de Vere wrote in 1571—in Latin, by the way." She slid the book over to Jonathan and he began reading. "It essentially lays out the principles of honor and duty described in Shakespeare's plays."

"Yes," Jonathan nodded. "I remember reading something about this years ago. De Vere's Preface is not included with all printings of *The Courtier*, is it?"

Sylvia nodded. "No, it's not. And that's unfortunate. It's a remarkable piece of writing. Spells out aesthetic principles for writers. I found it, though, in one of the books we have in our special collections." Her eyes lit up. "In fact, do you remember what Gabriel Harvey wrote about it, Jonathan?"

Smitty furrowed his brow, but then shook his head. "Not sure. "

Sylvia beamed. She could hardly contain her excitement or catch her breath. "I now know how de Vere chose his pen name!"

Joe looked from Sylvia to Smitty, and then back at Sylvia.

"Go on," he urged, watching the smile pull at her sensual lips.

"Gabriel Harvey wrote praise for de Vere's Preface. There were a couple of really remarkable lines." Sylvia opened another book to a place she'd marked. "Listen: 'Pallas striking her shield with her spear shaft will attend thee.'" She glanced up. "He was referring to Oxford." Sylvia read the quote: "'Thou has drunk deep draughts not only of the Muses of France and Italy, but has learned the manners of many men, and the arts of foreign countries.'"

She smiled at Smitty, and then at Joe.

Joe said, "That line about Phallas striking her shield with her spear—that might explain why de Vere chose his pseudonym."

"Not 'Phallas', Joe," corrected Smitty. "Pallas."

"But there's more," added Sylvia. "Harvey used a certain Latin phrase to describe de Vere. Would you like to know what it was?"

"Yes, of course," said Smitty, nodding.

Closing her eyes and wearing the smile of the Cheshire cat, Sylvia seemed to chant the phrase: "'Tela vibrat'."

"Tela vibrat?" repeated Joe

"Tela vibrat," said Smitty, grinning. "Of course! Translated, it means 'spear shaker'."

Sylvia read the lines. "Gabriel Harvey wrote of de Vere, 'Thine eyes flash fire, thy countenance *shakes spears*; who would not swear that Achilles had come to life again?'"

Joe's jaw dropped. "Wait. You're kidding, right? He really wrote that de Vere's countenance *shakes spears*?"

Smitty nodded and grinned his Buddha smile, closing his eyes.

"Well that's the answer," Joe said. "Isn't it? I mean, that explains how Edward de Vere chose his pen name."

"It sure supports our case," Sylvia agreed.

Joe nodded. "So then, this guy from Stratford turns up, named Shakspear, which is close enough to Oxford's chosen nom de plume of Shake-speare, and the rest is history."

Jonathan chuckled. "Yes, lad. The rest *is* history. De Vere was quite a patron of the theater, paid the salaries of many players. It's not difficult to imagine him paying the man from Stratford to be his front."

"Shouldn't we be writing this down?" Joe asked.

Sylvia nodded and took a last pull of her tepid coffee. "Yes we should, Joe. This is the start of our article."

"Article?" Smitty chuckled. "You mean book! By the time we're finished, we'll have a book-length manuscript, I'm sure."

Sylvia patted Smitty's wrist. "True, true. But let's start with an article. Maybe for the *PMLA*. A three-way collaboration."

Joe reached for his wallet, asking, "You, Smitty and who's the third author."

"Why, you, of course, Joe."

"*Me?* I'm not a Shakespeare scholar!"

"You are now, lad. You've just been drafted."

When they were on Telegraph Avenue halfway back to campus, Joe's cell phone rang. He looked at the screen. "It's Sara," he told Smitty. He ducked into a doorway and covered his other ear as he answered the phone.

Sylvia and Smitty looked at the books Smitty was carrying while

Joe talked. After he closed his phone, Joe stepped next to Jonathan and grabbed his shoulder.

"Sara says two FBI agents are at our house. Says they don't have a search warrant but asked if they could look around."

"Did she let them?" Sylvia asked.

"She wasn't sure what else to do."

"Do you want to head home, lad?"

Joe looked down into Smitty's concerned face. "I don't know, I don't know. I don't have anything to hide, but..."

"But what?" asked Sylvia.

He turned and held her gaze. "I didn't have anything to hide last time either, but the cops still found enough to make me look guilty."

"We can leave if you want to," Smitty said. "This can wait."

Joe shook his head in disgust. "I'm so fucking tired of being hassled by cops and killers!"

Sylvia burst into laughter. "*Hassled by cops and killers*? How many people can say *that*?"

Smitty tried not to laugh, but he couldn't help grinning.

Joe looked at them, wanting to laugh but ready to cry. "It's just so fucked up, Sylvia. Excuse my French."

Sylvia stopped chuckling long enough to say, "It's not from the French, Joe," she said. "It's Anglo-Saxon."

All three burst into laughter. Joe clutched Smitty's shoulder for support as he nearly doubled over. People on the sidewalk stepped around them as if they were crazy.

"Oh!" Joe laughed. "You want to hear the best part?"

Smitty reigned his laughter in, but Sylvia kept it going as she nodded.

"You know who sent the FBI?"

Smitty quietly shook his head, while Sylvia worked to control herself.

"No, Joe," she said. "Who?"

"You'll love this. Melinda Sloan."

"Melinda Sloan?" asked Smitty. "Isn't that—"

"Yeah," Joe laughed sarcastically. "Deirdre Claire's sister."

CHAPTER 35

Bid suspicion double-lock the door.
From *Venus and Adonis*

Hearing that Deirdre Claire's sister Melinda had asked the FBI to investigate Joe sobered all of them quickly. They'd been intoxicated by the excitement of discovery, more than by the wine they'd had with lunch, but as they pushed through the crowd on Telegraph Avenue toward campus, they remained quiet.

The music and incense and chatter that surrounded them in the heart of Berkeley, which had seemed so vibrant on their way to lunch, now seemed to Joe like the irritating buzz of insects. Odors of urine mixed with stale wine; chanting merged with folk singing, Reggae, and rock. He felt dizzy, claustrophobic, hemmed in by tourists and local freaks whose body odors and marijuana smoke and exotic perfumes converged in a nauseating miasma that sickened him.

Relief came from the cool air-conditioned atmosphere inside Sylvia's spacious office. Joe opened a bottled water and took a long pull, feeling the cold water wash down his throat. He'd considered stopping in the men's room to splash cold water on his face, but plopped down in the overstuffed chair instead, closing his eyes and enjoying the chilled air.

"Thank God for air conditioning," he said.

"What do you want to do, lad? Head back?"

Joe shook his head. "I told Sara to have one of the agents call me. If one of them doesn't call in a few minutes, I'll call Sara. I want to find out for myself what the hell they're looking for."

Sylvia waved her arm over the manuscripts spread out across her worktable.

"They're looking for these, Joe. They'll probably confiscate them, take them as evidence."

Joe glanced at Smitty, who nodded.

"Can they do that? Take the papers from us?"

"No, lad. Not until they have a search warrant."

"To get a search warrant, they'll need evidence of a crime," added Sylvia.

"Well, there's lots of evidence of a crime!" Joe scoffed. "A few murders, kidnapping, not to mention breaking and entering."

"Yeah," said Sylvia. "What I mean is, they'll need evidence that *you* were involved in those crimes."

Joe shut his eyes and said, "Here we go again."

Smitty stepped over and placed his hand on Joe's shoulder.

"Call your attorney."

Joe sat up, tugging his phone out of his pocket. "I'm calling Sara first. I'm going to talk to one of those FBI agents. Then I'll call Bill Morgan and get him over there."

After two rings, Sara answered.

"Are the agents still there?" He listened to her answer as he looked at Smitty and Sylvia. "Okay, put one of them on. Then call your sister and Bill Morgan. Tell them to drop what they're doing and get over to the house."

Joe waited patiently as he listened to silence. At least he wasn't hearing Katie or Brian crying in the background. He recalled the morning raid on his home years earlier when the SWAT team arrested him—the terrified look in Katie's eyes as a large man in a black uniform, wearing a black helmet with a face guard, handed his daughter to Sara.

"This is Agent Lott." The deep voice pulled Joe from his memory.

"This is Joseph Conrad, Agent Lott. May I ask what the hell you're doing searching my home without a search warrant?"

"Calm down, Mr. Conrad. We simply asked if we could look around and your wife gave her permission. That's all we need."

"My name's on the lease, too, and I *don't* want you in my house. Understand? I repeat, I do *not* want you searching my home without a warrant."

"Technically, we only need one occupant's permission."

"Are you sure about that?"

"Well, we're pretty much done anyway."

"My lawyer's on his way, so you can debate the point with him."

"We'd like to handle this informally, sir. If that's possible."

"Handle what?" Joe asked. "What is it you're investigating?"

"A woman came into our Sacramento office yesterday. She told us about the deaths of her grandparents in Louisiana and now the death of her sister here in California, and all the suspicion that's been cast upon her sister. Because this involves documents that originated in one state and found their way to another, it becomes a federal problem."

"A *federal* problem!" Joe looked at Smitty and Sylvia, his heart pounding.

"Yes, sir. I'm afraid so. Mrs. Sloan asked us to look into the matter. I hope you can understand her concern. She's lost three family members in as many weeks."

Joe closed his eyes again. He could picture Melinda Sloan's sad face at Jack's funeral.

"I do understand her grief. Her grandfather was a very close friend." Joe tried to visualize the last time he'd seen Jack Claire alive, but all he could see was the black and white photo on his desk. "What exactly are you looking for? Maybe I can help."

"Your cooperation would be very much appreciated, Mr. Conrad. Can we meet in person?"

"When? Today?"

"Yes. If possible."

"I'm in Berkeley, at the campus."

"That's what your wife told us. You're meeting with a Dr. Sylvia Williamson. She's some kind of expert?"

"I'd rather not involve her." Joe looked at Sylvia, who looked down at the papers as if trying to hide her concern. "What do you need? What are you looking for?"

"Well, truthfully, we aren't entirely sure. We'll need to look at these Shakespeare documents."

"Are you planning on confiscating them?" Joe tried to keep the panic out of his voice.

"No, not necessarily," the agent responded.

"Because Jack Claire sent those papers to me."

"So we've been told."

Joe recognized the tone of suspicion in the agent's voice. He'd heard it before. Trying to control his anger, he said, "I'm not about to turn these documents over to you."

"I understand your concern. The papers are very valuable. And they're in your possession right now. If you turn them over, then the courts could get involved. And if the courts get involved, well..."

"Is Melinda Sloan contesting ownership of the manuscripts? Is that why she put you guys onto me?"

The agent stayed quiet for a few seconds. Joe knew he was considering how to answer.

"Let's just say, she'd like us to verify that her grandfather really did send them to you."

"Is she accusing me of stealing them?"

"No. She hasn't said that."

"But she's suggested it?"

"Well, Mr. Conrad, we're all a little curious."

Joe closed his eyes and tried to think. It felt as if he were being pulled down into quicksand and the weight was already pressing against his chest. He opened his eyes and looked at Smitty. The look on Smitty's face was not hopeful. Sylvia had gone to her desk and was sitting with her back to Joe, looking at a few pages of the manuscripts.

"I won't meet you today," Joe said finally. "We're working down here and I don't want to interrupt that again. We've already had quite a few interruptions."

"Go on." The agent sounded tense, as if he didn't like being told what to do.

"I'll meet you tomorrow in my attorney's office. Bill Morgan. How's ten a.m.?"

"Ten o'clock tomorrow morning in Bill Morgan's office? Sure. Fair enough."

"You can get his address from my wife. Bill's office, I mean."

"We know where it is."

"Okay," Joe said. "Tomorrow morning."

Smitty smiled and nodded at Joe.

"One more thing," said the agent. "Do you have something from Dr. Claire that proves he sent the papers to you? A letter perhaps?"

"A letter? No. He didn't send a letter with the papers. Just the papers themselves."

"*No letter?*" The agent's skepticism was clear. "Nothing telling you what to do with those documents? Don't you find that a little odd?"

"I imagine Jack was in a bit of a rush when he mailed them to me. I think he was being chased by the same asshole who nearly killed me here in Berkeley, me and my friend, Dr. Jonathan Smythe. Maybe you read about it, Agent Lott?"

"Yes, sir. I have read the news accounts. For what they're worth."

"For what they're worth? What's that supposed to mean? The stories are correct. Maybe a few minor details are missing, but those stories are pretty accurate."

"I'm sure they are, as you say, pretty accurate. Journalists have a different standard of investigation than FBI agents, though. We need concrete evidence. Something tangible. Do you have something tangible, Mr. Conrad?"

Joe's heart raced. It was the murder investigation from his past all over again. "The only evidence I have," he said, "is the box the papers came in."

"The box?"

"Yes, Agent Lott. The box Jack mailed to me."

"Let me ask you an important question, Joe," the agent said. "How is it addressed?"

"How is it addressed? What do you mean?"

"Did Dr. Claire use printed address labels or did he write your name and address out by hand?"

Joe smiled. "By hand. He wrote my name and address in his own handwriting."

Sylvia turned around, a smile gracing her face. Smitty smiled too and closed his eyes.

"Well, then." The agent paused. Joe could hear his own heart beating. "Please bring that box to the meeting tomorrow. It's what we call evidence."

Joe chuckled. "Yes, sir. I will."

"And bring a few samples of the manuscripts, too, if you don't mind. I'd like to examine them."

Joe's heart tightened. "Are you planning to keep them?"

"Let's try this," said Agent Lott. "How about you bring some of the manuscripts and I give you a receipt for them. We send the documents to the FBI lab in Virginia and have them tested. Our guys can examine the ink, the paper, the penmanship. That's the kind of thing you guys are doing anyway, isn't it? This way, we can all say you're cooperating with the investigation and if our labs at Quantico come up with some stuff that helps in your scholarship, then you've got independent—you know—confirmation. That might be helpful for your research, don't you think?"

Joe listened quietly, trying to read the man's voice, trying to determine if Agent Lott was like his friend Detective Dunn. His voice sounded sincere, if a bit detached, as if he'd rather be doing something else.

"Here's what I'll do," Joe said finally. "I'll bring some sample pages and we can chat in front of my attorney for awhile. If I feel you're a reliable enough guy and I can trust you, then I let you see the papers. But I'll definitely bring the box they came in."

"Fair enough," the agent said. "One more thing. Try not to handle that box any more than you have to. We'd like to have the fingerprints preserved as much as possible."

Joe nodded and smiled. "That will do it, won't it? If the box has Jack Claire's prints on it and his handwriting, then that's the tangible evidence you need to corroborate my story."

"Sounds like you've been through this before, Mr. Conrad. Yes, that type of evidence will help put you in the clear."

CHAPTER 36

Small to greater matters must give way.
From *Antony and Cleopatra*

After his conversation with the FBI Agent, Smitty and Sylvia settled into their research and note taking, as Joe outlined the timeline of Edward de Vere's life and travels. By five o'clock, Joe reluctantly pulled Smitty aside and suggested they drive back to Stockton.

"Right you are, lad," Smitty said somberly. "Lost track of time. Licia will be expecting me."

"We're going to call it a day," Joe told Sylvia.

She looked up from her books and notes, rubbed her eyes and nodded. "I'm going to keep working. Dinner plans at eight, so I can put in a few more hours."

"Are we making progress?" Smitty asked her.

"Yes, I think so." She forced a smile, but her concern was apparent. "When can we rendezvous?"

"Well," Joe said, "assuming all goes well with the FBI, let's plan to meet here Monday morning."

Smitty nodded. "Good. Sylvia and I can work on our own. We'll compare notes Monday. What will you do, lad?"

Joe let out a sarcastic laugh. "If I'm not in jail, I'll finish Greenblatt's book and wade through Ogburn's to finish the timeline."

Sylvia stood and walked over, saying, "You don't really think they'll arrest you, do you?"

Joe shook his head. "I don't know. With Deirdre Claire out of the picture, it's hard to say where the investigation is going. I'll give you both a call tomorrow after the big meeting."

Sylvia reached over and gave Joe a friendly, sympathetic hug.

Traffic between Berkeley and Stockton was light, even through Livermore. When they reached Smitty's house, Joe went inside with him and grabbed the empty box Jack had sent, carrying it carefully by the edges of the flaps.

"Hope that does the trick," Smitty said, escorting him to the door.

"Me too," said Joe.

He heard the door shut behind him, heard the click of the deadbolt, and wondered if he'd see Smitty again any time soon.

The next morning, Joe drove to Bill Morgan's office in the heart of Sacramento, leaving the kids in front of the TV and Sara on the sofa reading the end of her Nicholas Sparks book. She hadn't used the crutches in the last twenty-four hours, but Joe noticed them leaning in the corner behind his easy chair. Otherwise, the members of his little family seemed content, all of them still in pajamas. He hated leaving, but he'd gotten himself into this mess…

At Bill Morgan's office building, Joe found not only Bill Morgan but also Suzy, and it was one of the first times he was actually relieved to see his sister-in-law.

"Morning, Joe," Morgan said.

"Good morning," he replied, wondering if Bill's deletion of the word "good" in front of "morning" indicated something ominous. He set the cardboard box down on a small table, stepped over, gave Suzy a perfunctory peck on the cheek and started to sit down beside her.

"Don't sit," Bill Morgan instructed as he pushed his chair back and stood up. "The others are waiting for us.

Suzie pushed her chair back and stood.

"Should I bring the box and manuscripts?"

"No," Bill said. "Leave them here for now. We'll decide after the meeting whether or not to turn them over."

Joe followed Bill Morgan into the hallway and down to a room that held a long oak table and a dozen chairs. Little else was in the room. A credenza with bottled water and glasses sat against the far wall, a colorful large painting of farmland at sunset hanging above it.

Three people sat at the far side of the table, their backs to the bank of windows. Two large, serious-looking men in business suits flanked a sad-looking middle-aged woman dressed in a black suit. One man looked just a little older than Joe, perhaps in his mid-thirties and had a pale baby face framed by short jet-black hair. He wore thin silver-rimmed glasses that nearly disappeared against his pale face. The flesh of his cheeks, chin and neck seemed so smooth that Joe wondered if he even needed to shave yet. The effect brought a smile to Joe's face, but the smile quickly faded as he glanced at the other man.

Looking tall and fit, even while sitting, he was probably in his mid-fifties, his medium-length salt and pepper hair slicked back, framing the tanned, rugged features of his face. Joe noticed a small scar above his left eye—a line that ended with a pock-mark, making the scar look like an exclamation mark, but also giving his left eyebrow the appearance of constantly being raised, as if he were perpetually in doubt. Joe pegged him as the FBI agent. And the way he was returning Joe's stare made Joe nervous, so he turned to look at the piece of colorful art on the far wall.

"Beautiful painting," Joe said. "Who's the artist?"

The two men and the woman he recognized as Deirdre Claire's sister turned to look at the painting, giving Joe a moment to compose himself.

"The artist?" Morgan pulled out a chair and placed his hand against the small of Suzy's back. "Actually, it's a woman who lives in Davis. Melissa Chandon. Have you seen her work before?"

The question caused everyone to turn their attention back to him. He shook his head and sat down next to Suzy. Bill pulled out a chair on the other side of Joe.

"Did you bring the box?" the man sitting across from Bill Morgan asked.

"Agent Lott?" Joe asked.

"Yes." He half stood and reached over to shake Joe's hand, and Joe returned the gesture. The man's grip was crushing.

Joe looked at Melinda Sloan as he sat back down. "I'm so sorry about your grandparents," he said. "They were wonderful people."

"Thank you," she answered. Her eyes were red but she seemed to be holding back tears. "What you said at my grandfather's service was wonderful. I remember it clearly. Simple but eloquent."

"Thank you," Joe responded. He felt his own eyes tearing up and choked back a sigh.

She added, "Grandpap would have loved the quote from *Hamlet.* It was his favorite play. Yours, too?"

Joe nodded and tried to smile.

The man sitting to Melinda's right—baby-face—stood up and reached over. "I'm Doug Hollister."

Joe half stood again and reached over, believing the man was going to shake his hand. Instead, the man handed Joe a business card.

"I'm with Fowler, Rubinstein and Kositsky. Ms. Sloan has asked us to represent her interests here in California."

Joe sat down and examined the card.

Bill Morgan spoke up. "And what does Ms. Sloan believe her interests to be, here in California?"

"Well, to start with," the lawyer responded, "she's recently lost three family members, apparently because of some documents that belonged to her grandfather. Those documents are now in Mr. Conrad's possession, and we'd like to be sure he came into them legally."

Joe snorted. "You're kinda blunt."

"The only reason," Morgan replied, "your client knows that the manuscripts once belonged to Dr. Claire is Joe's admission during the investigation of the man who attempted to murder him."

"I understand that," said the other attorney.

"He easily could have withheld that information and your client would have been none the wiser."

"True enough. But Mr. Conrad *did* admit the papers came from Dr. Claire. That makes it a different matter altogether."

"My client's honesty is now being used against him."

"As you should know, counselor," Hollister said sarcastically, "a suspect's admissions during an investigation of a crime can and are used against him."

Suzy cleared her throat and said, "Excuse me, but Joe Conrad is *not* suspected of a crime. Your client's sister, on the other hand—"

"Wait, wait," said Joe. "Let's not get into a shouting match here."

"I agree," said Melinda. "Let's keep it civil."

Joe turned and looked at Melinda. "I don't know why Jack sent the papers to me, I've racked my brain trying to figure it out, but he did. All I can assume is that he suspected someone might hurt you or your children, after what happened to Mrs. Claire, and he probably thought sending the Shakespeare papers to California would get them out of the killer's crosshairs."

Terry Lott leaned forward. "Do you think Jack Claire suspected his other granddaughter, Joe? Suspected her of hiring this mercenary, Benedict Anderson?"

Joe shook his head, staring into the green eyes of the FBI agent. "I honestly don't know. I keep hoping some letter will turn up explaining everything to me, telling me what he wanted me to do with the papers. I'm sure he knew I wasn't qualified to, to authenticate them. Not without help."

"But," Melinda Sloan said sympathetically, "he had his reasons for sending the documents to you. He must have seen in you some quality that made him trust your judgment."

"*If*," began Doug Hollister, "if he really *did* send the papers to Mr. Conrad. We haven't really verified that, yet, have we."

"No," agreed the FBI agent, "we haven't. So let me ask again, did you bring the box?"

Joe looked at Bill Morgan, who nodded, and then at Suzy Taylor. She shrugged her shoulders with a scowl on her face, which made Joe smile.

"Calm down, tiger," Joe whispered as he stood. "It's in Bill's office."

Joe followed Bill Morgan out into the hallway and back into his office where he removed the loose manuscripts, placed them on the small table and picked up the box. They returned to the meeting room and Joe put the box on the table in front of Melinda Sloan.

"Do you recognize your grandfather's handwriting?" Lott asked her.

She stood up and examined the mailing address.

"It looks like Jack's handwriting to me," Joe said, "but I can't be absolutely sure."

FBI Agent Terry Lott and the attorney Doug Hollister also stood and inspected the penmanship.

She nodded. "At first glance, it sure looks like grandpap's handwriting."

"We should have a handwriting expert examine it, though," said Hollister. "Are we all in agreement on that?"

Bill Morgan nodded. "I have no problem with that. Joe?"

"No, of course not," Joe said. "I have no problem with it, either."

"Can I take the box, then?" asked Agent Lott.

Joe shrugged and nodded. "I guess so."

"As long as we get a receipt," added Suzy.

"Even if the handwriting *is* Dr. Claire's," Doug Hollister responded, "how can we be sure he wasn't *forced* to address the box to your client."

"That's insulting," Suzy said with disgust. "Joe Conrad was nowhere near Baton Rouge on the day Jack Claire died."

"But," Hollister shot back, "Benedict Anderson was. And who was Benedict Anderson working for?"

Joe laughed. "That's easy. He was working for Deirdre Claire."

"How can you be so sure, Mr. Conrad?" Hollister asked him.

"Because she told me so," Joe replied. "She confessed to me when she was holding a gun to the head of my two-year-old!"

"Please!" Melinda yelled. She stood up and clutched her hands together, as if praying. "Please, please keep this civil!"

"I'm sorry," Suzy Taylor said, "but if you're going to allow your attorney to make accusations against my brother-in-law, then you're going to have to hear the truth—the whole truth, no matter how ugly it may be."

Joe turned to Melinda. Seeing the pain on her face, he said, "Your sister was evidently not who you thought she was. She was a very calculating and vicious woman."

Melinda shook her head and fell back down into her chair. She covered her eyes. "I always knew she was ambitious. And, yes, even calculating. I know she blamed grandpap for our father's feelings of inferiority. I just didn't realize how deep it was—her anger and resentment."

Terry Lott pulled a white handkerchief from the inside pocket of his jacket and handed it to Melinda Sloan.

A knock on the meeting room door made all of them turn to see who had stepped in. Detective Ryan Dunn had been standing in the doorway listening, the door half open.

"I can supply a few answers," he said.

Joe looked at his friend, the detective, feeling a rush of relief.

"Who are you?" asked Hollister.

Dunn introduced himself to the attorney and made it clear that he and FBI Agent Lott already knew one another.

Without being invited to do so, Dunn pulled the chair away from the head of the table and sat down. He opened a manila file folder and held up a paper.

"This is a photocopy of a cashier's check made payable to Benedict Anderson, the man who fell to his death when he was attempting to murder Mr. Conrad."

Dunn handed the paper to Doug Hollister, who examined it carefully.

"This isn't official," Hollister said.

"No, that's true. But this isn't an official investigation here today, is it. The DA said it was all right to show it to you—*un*officially."

"Where'd you find this?" Hollister asked.

"In Deirdre Claire's desk drawer."

"Could it have been planted there?" Hollister leaned toward Ryan Dunn—he wasn't giving up.

"Could've, I suppose," Dunn admitted. "But there's lots of evidence pointing to Deirdre's guilt."

"Did you have a valid search warrant when you searched the home of my client's sister?"

Dunn leveled his gaze at the attorney. "You're sort of an asshole, aren't you, pal."

Hollister pulled away, his mouth dropping open. Then he managed to say, "Just looking out for the best interest of my—"

"Okay," Melinda said. "That's enough." She placed her hand on her attorney's arm. "I didn't want to do this. Not like this. Not now. Certainly not the day before my sister's funeral. My husband thought it was important. He said those papers are probably very valuable."

"They probably are," Hollister agreed.

She turned to him and said, "You know, at this point, I really don't care. Maybe I will later. Maybe I'll get that greedy streak my sister had. And my husband, God love him." Her Southern accent was growing stronger as she allowed her authentic emotions to show. "But right now, I just want to bury my sister and put this ugly episode behind me."

She stood up and held out her hand to Joe, who stood and reached across the table. They didn't shake hands, just held on to each other.

"I'm sorry to put you through this, Joe. I heard Grandpap speak about you a few years ago when you were having that other trouble. He knew you were innocent. I could hear the affection in his voice when he spoke of you."

"I loved your grandfather, Melinda," Joe said, choking back his tears.

"I loved him, too." She let go of Joe's hands and turned toward Ryan Dunn. "You're a cop and you seem to know Joe."

"I do," Ryan said, standing up.

"You think he's innocent?"

Dunn smiled and nodded. "I wouldn't call Joe Conrad innocent exactly. But if you mean, did he have something to do with your grandfather's death, I'd have to say absolutely not. There's no evidence at all linking him to that crime."

"What about stealing the Shakespeare manuscripts?" Hollister asked.

Dunn tightened his smile, his jaws working, as he stared at the attorney.

"No," he said sharply. "No evidence he stole anything."

Melinda turned around and looked at the FBI agent. "What do you think, Agent Lott? Does Joe seem like a plausible suspect for any of these crimes?"

"On the record, I have to withhold judgment until I have time to examine the evidence for myself."

"What about off the record, Terry?" Dunn asked.

Lott chuckled. "Off the record, Joe Conrad strikes me as one of the unluckiest lucky bastards I've ever met."

Joe snorted, unsure how to react. "What the hell do you mean by *that*?"

"I mean, who ends up embroiled in one murder case after another, gets his name cleared, and then winds up with a treasure that could be worth millions of dollars?"

Suzy laughed, too. "It's what I was telling you before, Joe," she said. "You're a magnet for trouble."

"A lightening rod is more like it," Dunn added. "But as Agent Lott said, he's a pretty damn lucky guy."

"We'll see how long his luck holds," Hollister said.

"Put a sock in it, Doug," Bill Morgan told his colleague.

"You two know each other?" Joe asked.

"Oh, yeah," Morgan replied. "We've run into one another a few times. Suzy—I mean, Ms. Taylor—knows him better."

"We've faced off a few times in court," she admitted.

"Not lately," Hollister added.

"Who usually won?" asked Joe. "When you faced off before?"

"Out of professional courtesy," Suzy said, "I decline to answer. I don't wish to embarrass such a fine adversary."

Joe and Bill Morgan chuckled, but stopped upon seeing Melinda's face. She struggled to grin, but her lips quivered and her eyes filled with tears. One slipped down her cheek.

"I'm glad we can end this on a friendly note," she said. "But I think I need to leave."

The attorney stood up and started to walk behind Detective Dunn. Melinda followed but stopped abruptly.

"Joe," she said softly. "I know this seems strange to ask, but Deirdre's funeral is tomorrow afternoon. We don't expect many people, maybe a few from her San Francisco store. My husband and kids will be there—they're flying in this evening. If you feel up to it, it would be lovely for you to come, too. That way, we could get to know each other better. We're having a simple service at a small Catholic chapel in midtown. Because it may have been a suicide she can't—she can't have a full mass."

Joe looked at the pained expression in the woman's face. He dropped his head and looked at the surface of the mahogany table. Then he closed his eyes and tried to visualize himself sitting through the service.

Finally, he looked up into her eyes. "I *would* like to get to know *you* better. I'd like that very much. But I have to decline. You have to understand what Deirdre did to my family. The fear my children felt."

Melinda nodded. "I understand."

Detective Dunn stood and blocked her path, taking something from his sports coat pocket. "Before you leave, Mrs. Sloan, I'm sorry, but I've been asked to get a DNA sample."

"What?" She stepped back, stumbling against Doug Hollister. "For heaven's sakes, why?"

"The Coroner wants to confirm that the body we have is really your sister's. It was burned pretty badly and we don't have dental records."

"I object," Hollister said loudly.

Dunn shot him an unhappy look. "I figured you would. I can get a warrant if I have to, but this way is easier."

"Is it painful?" Melinda asked. "Do you have to take my blood?"

Dunn shook his head. "Naw. Just have to swab the inside of your mouth. Won't hurt a bit."

Hollister held up his hand. "Maybe you should get a warrant." He made eye contact with Melinda. "This could be some sort of trick to make *you* look guilty."

"I can promise you, Mrs. Sloan, it's no trick. Before the Coroner signs off on releasing your sister's body for tomorrow's service, he's got to confirm its identity."

Melinda nodded. "Okay, what do I do?"

Dunn pulled a single-sided Q-tip out of a small test tube and stepped forward. "Just say awe."

The woman blushed, but opened her mouth and allowed the Detective to swab the inside of both cheeks. Then, looking a little humiliated, she walked out of the room, followed by Doug Hollister.

The rest of them sat back down. No one said a word for several minutes. Joe looked out the window, across the rooftops of lower buildings at the trees and farmland to the south. The sky shone bright blue as the sun rose to its noon-time zenith.

"I'd still like samples of those manuscripts," Agent Lott said, breaking the quiet.

Joe looked at him, trying to read his stoic face, then looked at Bill Morgan.

"Okay," Morgan said. "As long as we get a receipt for those, too."

The FBI agent nodded.

"Well," Suzy sighed, "I guess that just about clears everything up." She stood, stretched her arms, and then patted Joe on the shoulder. "I could use a cigarette."

Joe pushed his chair back. "Man," he said. "I feel like I've been through the ringer."

"Now you can go home and relax, Joe," Bill Morgan said. "Spend a little time with those beautiful babinos."

"There is one more matter," said Lott.

Joe felt the FBI Agent's eyes locking on him.

"In the report, it says that Deirdre referred to her client, her buyer, someone who'd upped the price he was willing to pay for the documents, after news leaked that you and your colleagues had found them to be authentic. At least, preliminarily."

"Yeah, that's correct," admitted Joe.

"So," Agent Lott added. "Who's the client?"

Suzy sat back down. "Could Joe still be in danger?" she asked, looking back and forth from one lawman to the other.

"No way of knowing, yet," Dunn admitted. "Probably not. Now that the police are involved and there's been so much publicity."

"Still," the FBI agent said. "It would be nice to know who set all this in motion."

Joe looked at Detective Dunn, who was looking at FBI Agent Terry Lott. Both men nodded, frowns tugging at their rugged lips. Joe Conrad put his two hands flat on the top of the table, then slowly lowered his head and rested his forehead on the backs of his hands.

"Will this nightmare ever end?" he said to anyone who would listen.

CHAPTER 37

Men's judgments are
A parcel of their fortunes; and things outward
Do draw the inward quality after them,
To suffer all alike.
From *Antony and Cleopatra*

Joe looked at his sister-in-law, then at Ryan Dunn at the head of the table. "What should I do?" He searched the face of the FBI agent sitting across the table, and finally turned to look at Bill Morgan on his right. "I don't want my family in danger, I don't want to put my colleagues in danger. And, hell, *I* don't want to be in danger anymore."

Agent Lott spoke up. "Let me ask you something, Joe. Now that you and your pals have had a chance to look the manuscripts over, who do *you* think is behind these crimes?"

Joe shook his head. "No idea. I was surprised as hell that Deirdre Claire hired that guy, Benedict."

Suzy touched his arm. "Did the Claire woman say anything that might give you a clue who she was working for?"

Joe shut his eyes and tried to recall the conversation he'd had in the cabin, but all he could see was the crazed expression on the face of the woman holding a gun to Brian's little head.

"I don't remember very well," he said opening his eyes, hoping the vision would disappear. "She said something like, since you've done your research, the person I'm working for has raised the reward. I wasn't thinking about what she was saying, I was trying to figure out how to get my kids away from her before she shot them."

"Of course," Bill Morgan added, "it's quite possible the person or persons who contacted Deirdre Claire had no idea she'd hire a killer."

"That's the defense attorney talking," Dunn scoffed. "But you might be right. From our investigation so far, all we know is, Deirdre had been offered an enormous sum of money for those papers and the person offering the money wanted it to be handled discretely. That doesn't give us much to go on. We're hoping her phone records and emails will fill in the blanks."

"From what you've told me," Agent Lott said, "Deirdre Claire is the one who reached out to these people. She somehow learned that her grandfather had the papers and went in search of a buyer."

"Well," Dunn said, "We know how she first learned of the Shakespeare papers. Her grandfather had asked a mutual friend at the Metropolitan Museum of Art in New York for help. Deirdre had a close relationship with this man, Marcus Eccles. They were having an affair. Eccles had been one of Jack Claire's students."

Suzy chuckled. "Dr. Claire's students seem to have a knack for trouble, don't they."

"Suzy," Joe replied. "Jack Claire had thousands of students over his career. Two of us get into trouble, and you think it's a trend?"

"I'm teasing," she said, squeezing his hand the way Sara did sometimes.

"Would this guy at the Metropolitan know?" Agent Lott asked. "This Eccles?"

"He might," Dunn answered. "I called him yesterday. He hasn't been very cooperative so far. He was cheating on his wife with Deirdre, so he's not inclined to help."

"That's one reason it's good we're involved," Lott said flatly. "The police here in California don't have jurisdiction in New York. But now that we've established the inter-state nature of this conspiracy, the FBI has jurisdiction. *We* can squeeze this guy's nuts—sorry, Ms. Taylor."

"Squeeze away!" Suzy laughed. "If it'll get Joe out of trouble and get my sister and her kids out of harm's way, then rip those puppies off."

"And this from an officer of the court?" Bill Morgan laughed.

"Think, Joe," Dunn said. "Who pops into your head when you think about who might want those manuscripts?"

Joe closed his eyes and tried to visualize Deirdre Claire at the cabin, talking calmly at first, then the maniacal look in her eyes, the intensity in her voice, the steady, confident way she held the gun, the way she'd tried to manipulate Dunn and the way she had manipulated the Tahoe Sheriff.

"Only one person comes to mind," he said, finally. He opened his eyes. "It's crazy."

"Go on," Dunn prodded.

"Well, when I think about how cunning and manipulative Deirdre Claire was, how ambitious she was, the only person who even remotely reminds me of her is Hayden Crawford, the Assistant Chair of the department at LSU."

Terry Lott wrote the name down in a notebook he'd pulled out of his suit jacket pocket. Joe noticed Dunn writing the name down, too.

"But it doesn't make sense," Joe added quickly. "I mean, first of all, Hayden was right there with Jack at LSU. He could have searched the offices much more easily than this Benedict clown did."

"Maybe," Lott said. "But sometimes it takes a pro."

"But also," Joe added quickly, "Hayden Crawford doesn't have that kind of money. I mean, what did Deirdre Claire say? The offer had gone up to, what, forty million dollars? Hayden isn't rich. Besides, even if he were wealthy and if he knew about the Shakespeare manuscripts, he would have simply offered to help Jack authenticate them." Joe shook his head again, as if the gesture would erase Hayden's name from the notebooks of Detective Dunn and Agent Lott. "No, it's just not plausible."

"We've got nothing else, yet, Joe," Dunn said. "It's as good a lead as any."

"Where's Hayden Crawford now?" Lott asked. "In Baton Rouge?"

"No," said Joe. He felt his cheeks blush and he wasn't sure why. "He's on vacation in France."

Agent Lott and Detective Dunn glanced at each other. Joe could swear Lott's left eyebrow arched more than before.

"Where in France?" Lott asked.

"Somewhere in southern France," said Joe. "Let me think for a minute. Carcisonne, I think."

Lott again looked at Dunn, who nodded.

"Wait," said Joe. "What's *that* look for?"

"When will Hayden Crawford get back?" asked Agent Lott.

"I'm not sure," said Joe. "Two weeks, I think. But why does that seem suspicious?"

The FBI agent said, "It's just a weird coincidence that he's out of the country when all this is happening."

"No," said Joe. "He takes his family to Europe every summer. Has for years. Usually to France or Spain. Sometimes Italy. Always for four weeks."

Lott and Dunn exchanged knowing looks again and wrote in their notebooks.

"The fact that he goes to Europe so often," Lott said, "implies he has expensive habits."

"Gives him motive, Joe," Dunn added.

Trying to sound like one of the guys, Suzy said, "I'm starting to like this guy for the brains behind this whole scheme."

"No, no, no," Joe insisted. "Yes, he's manipulative and ambitious, but he's basically a good man. I'm sure of that." Joe looked both of the other men in the eyes, trying to convince them. "Don't get me wrong. He's not my favorite person—a pretentious jerk at times. But I don't think he's dishonest. Or capable of contracting a murderer."

"But, Joe," Ryan Dunn said softly. "You met Deirdre Claire, didn't you? When you went back for Dr. Claire's funeral?" Joe nodded. "Did *she* strike you as the kind of person who could commit murder?"

Joe thought about it for a few seconds. "No, not at all."

"People can surprise you," Agent Lott added.

"They sure can," Dunn agreed. He closed his eyes and Joe examined his face. He looked sadder than Joe had ever seen him.

"So," Joe sighed. "This is all well and good, but it brings me back to my earlier question. What the hell do I do now? I mean, if there's still someone out there who would do anything to get his hands on these manuscripts, how do I protect my family?"

"Well," Lott said, "you could simply turn the papers over to the FBI. We can hold them until the investigation is concluded."

"The FBI can keep them here in their Sacramento office," Dunn added. "That way, you and your colleagues could still do your research. Couldn't you?"

Joe shook his head. "I don't know. I'd have to ask Sylvia and Smitty."

"Of course," Lott said, the irritation in his voice obvious, "you can continue to ignore the danger and just keep on doing what you've been doing. Maybe you'll be safe."

"Or," Dunn added, "maybe you won't because whoever's after those papers will contract another mercenary to steal them, no matter who gets in the way."

Joe felt his stomach tightening. He felt nauseated and looked at the waste-paper basket by the door.

"There's another option," Bill Morgan offered.

Joe looked at him. "Please. What?"

"Give the papers away."

Joe's mouth dropped open. "What do you mean? To the cops?"

"No," Bill said, grinning. "Donate some of the plays to other universities, like Stanford and Harvard. Let other scholars get involved."

Suzie nodded. "Not a bad idea. Disperse the threat. If the manuscripts are in one location, it's easier for someone to steal them. If they're spread out across the country, well…"

"And why limit yourself to the U. S.?" Morgan added. "Send some to a museum in London. Send some to Oxford and Cambridge. I mean, Joe, how many plays are there? Over thirty, right?"

Joe nodded. "Yeah. And the two long poems. And the bound copy of the First Folio."

"That might actually work," Lott said.

"I agree," Dunn added. "Isn't there a Shakespeare library down in L. A.?"

Joe nodded. "Yeah. The Huntington."

"So be a hero," Suzy said. "Drive down to L.A. and donate one of the plays. Get yourself on the news."

"I've *been* on the news, thank you very much. And I'd be giving away a million dollars, potentially," Joe said.

"Yeah," Dunn responded softly, "but you might save the lives of Sara and the kids in the process."

"And the Folger," Bill Morgan added. "In D. C."

"That's right," Lott said, nodding. "The Folger Shakespeare Library. It's not far from FBI Headquarters."

Suzy touched Joe's arm. "Maybe Agent Lott could be entrusted with the task of transporting a manuscript or two back there to Washington, D. C., for you, Joe."

Joe scanned the room of faces. All looked expectant, waiting for him to agree. *What would Smitty do?* "Let me talk it over with Sylvia and Smitty. We discussed donating some of the papers to other institutions eventually, but I think we wanted to do the research first to, you know, make sure they're genuine. We've already begun outlining an article—maybe even a book."

"But Joe," Suzy said, "is an article worth the lives of your children or Sara?"

"Of course not." He felt his cheeks burn. "But this is important work. I mean, come on, it's the find of the century! Do you just give that away?"

"Yes, if it'll save lives," said Suzie.

Joe surveyed the faces again, hoping they'd understand.

"You'll have to decide that for yourself, I guess," Bill Morgan said.

"But remember, Joe," Suzy said. "Your friend, Dr. Claire, gave those papers away, didn't he? He was a Shakespeare scholar, too."

"And don't forget," Dunn added. "He waited until it was too late."

CHAPTER 38

When I was fair and young then favour graced me;
Of many I was sought their mistress to be.
Ascribed to Queen Elizabeth

On the drive back to Davis, Joe called Smitty. He told Smitty he'd given the FBI agent some of the manuscript pages. "Agent Lott handled the papers carefully. I saw the concern in his eyes," said Joe. "I think this is a man we can trust."

"Good. I'm glad the business with Jack's granddaughter turned out well," Smitty said. "She could have stopped our work entirely."

"Yeah, she seems reasonable. I'm worried what will happen when her husband's had a chance to work on her."

"Her husband?"

"She implied that he's anxious for her to claim ownership of the manuscripts."

"Oh, I see," said Smitty, a note of sadness in his voice. "Well, maybe we should consider giving her one or two of the plays."

Joe chuckled. "That's exactly what the others suggested. In fact, they suggest giving quite a few of the manuscripts to other universities and libraries."

"Yes, that's reasonable. In time."

"They suggest sooner rather than later."

Smitty stayed silent for a moment. "Why?" he managed.

"They think another mercenary might be hired to steal the papers. They think we—all of us—could still be in danger."

"I see." Smitty stayed quiet again. Joe could picture his face, eyes closed, forcing the muscles of his face to relax as he considered the possibilities. Joe heard him exhale. "These papers, our research—it's too important. Of course, I don't want anything to happen to you or your family. Nor to Sylvia. But this is the most exciting research project I've ever been involved with. So, for me at least, it's worth the risk."

Now it was Joe's turn to think. Traffic on the Causeway over the wetlands was light, but the glare of the afternoon sunshine made it hard to concentrate.

"Let's think about it, Smitty. I'll talk it over with Sara. You should give Sylvia a call, too."

"Very wise suggestions, lad. I'll expect to hear from you before dinner."

Joe pulled the earphone out of his ear. The coastal range in the distance was shrouded by the haze of a wildfire near Lake Berryessa. The smoke made Joe think of the cliché, "Where there's smoke, there's fire," which made him think there might be something to the suspicions of Bill Morgan, Ryan Dunn and Agent Lott. And as much as he hated to admit it, even his sister-in-law might be right. His family *could* still be in danger. So could Smitty and Sylvia.

The question was, what to do about it.

When he walked through the front door, Joe found Sara in a sundress over her swimsuit and the kids dressed for the pool.

"Daddy!" Katie shrieked. She ran over and jumped up into his arms. "We're ready to go swimming."

"I see that," he said, kissing his daughter. "What about mommy's leg?"

Sara held her leg up. The large bandage had been replaced by a Band Aid.

"The wound's all closed up and feeling fine. Watch." She walked around the living room barely limping. "I want some sun. I *need* some sun!"

"Don't you want to hear how the meeting went?" Joe asked, looking at Sara.

"Suzy called. I know all about it."

"I should have known."

"Might be good for us to get out of the house, Joe." Some of the joy leaving her face. "You know, be around other people."

Joe nodded. "I see your point. Give me five minutes to change."

The pool at North Davis Park was packed with people escaping the heat. They managed to find a spot in partial shade. Katie quick-walked across the hot pavement and jumped into the shallow end where Joe and Sara could watch her.

Joe spread out his towel and sat down next to Sara. He looked out over the pool filled with children splashing, sunlight shimmering on the water.

"Your leg's really okay?"

"Yeah. It's healing up nicely. No redness. No infection. Hardly any pain. A little stiffness," she said. She raised her leg up and bent it a few times. "See?"

Joe leaned forward and kissed the Band Aid.

"Suzy and I hatched a plan while you were driving home," Sara whispered. Brian lay asleep on a towel-covered pad between them.

Joe sighed. "Okay. What's your plan?"

"Well, hear me out before you object."

"I will." He smiled.

"And don't make that face!"

"What face?" His grin widened.

"*That* face. That condescending expression that tells me you think my ideas are cute and you're going to patronize me by listening."

"Jeez, Sara. Okay."

"The newspapers haven't revealed where these priceless papers are located, right? They've implied they're in Berkeley. That's good for us, right, Joe?"

Joe nodded. "I guess so." He glanced at Katie, who was splashing another girl while both of them giggled.

"The problem before, with going to Suzy's cabin, was there was a connection—a family connection. That's how the Claire woman was able to find us, right?"

"Where are you going with this?"

Sara smiled broadly. "Funny you should ask. We're going to Disneyland."

Joe burst into laughter. "Disneyland? Are you serious?"

"Think about it. We could leave tomorrow. Stay someplace where no one could find us. Be away from all this craziness for a week."

"A week? That'd be expensive."

"So what?" Sara said, a note of anger in her voice. "Aren't you going to make millions from these damn Shakespeare papers? Isn't *that* why you were willing to put us at risk?"

"It's not just about the money, Sara. This is important work. It could change everything we know about Shakespeare."

Sara leaned across the toddler's sleeping body. She clearly wanted to whisper something in Joe's ear, so he leaned toward her as well.

"I don't give a shit," she whispered. "I just want to keep my family safe."

"So do I, honey."

Frowning, she turned away.

"Let me think about it. It's a good idea—really—but let me mull it over, okay?"

Sara nodded and lowered herself onto the towel, her eyes hidden behind sunglasses.

He looked at the pool again and watched Katie play with the other children. She was laughing and having fun without a care in the world, the way a child is supposed to act. Nothing like the fear that had distorted her face only days earlier when she had seen a gun held to her baby brother's head and had seen blood oozing from her mother's leg.

Joe stood up, lay his phone on the towel and walked over to the pool. He stepped into the water, splashed some on his chest, then dove forward and started swimming laps. The exertion cleared his mind.

Sara was right. They needed a dramatic change, something cheerful to replace the trauma of the last week. He climbed out of the pool, walked over to Sara, and, dripping water on her, leaned down and kissed her.

Sara sat up. "Hey. Dry off first."

"Okay," he said.

"Okay? You mean it?"

"It's what families do, right? They go on vacation."

Sara stretched up and kissed Joe, inviting his tongue to play with hers.

After drying off, Joe called Smitty. He told him the plan. They would stop at the Smythes' house in the morning so Joe could take one of the manuscripts with him to the Huntington. They would put most of the other plays in a safety deposit box. While Joe and his family were in Disneyland, the police investigation could continue.

"In a week's time, the police should have most of the loose ends tied up, don't you think?"

"One would expect so, lad."

"I need your advice. How do I approach the Huntington Shakespeare Library?"

"Just give them a call. They'll be delighted."

"Here's the thing. I don't mean to sound greedy, Jonathan, but spending a week at Disneyland is going to be expensive."

"Yes, of course."

"We already blew our vacation money on the trip to Louisiana for Jack's funeral."

"I see," Smitty said. "How much were you expecting to ask for the play?"

"Well, that's just it. I have no idea."

"Let me call Sylvia. She knows people at the Huntington."

"Great, Smitty," Joe said. "Thanks a lot."

"You've thought this through, haven't you?"

"What do you mean?"

"Well, you're worried about the buyer Jack's granddaughter contacted, right?"

"Yes," Joe chuckled. "That's the whole point of getting out of town. Why?"

"It's a remote possibility, but I feel I have to mention it, Joe."

"Okay." He braced himself, completely perplexed.

"The people that the Claire woman was going to get millions of dollars from when she turned over the manuscripts?"

"Oh, crap," said Joe. "You think it could be someone at the Huntington?"

"Sylvia and I discussed it. The Huntington Library is one possibility."

Joe looked at Sara, his heart sinking as she turned away. He knew she'd heard the fear in his voice.

"I'm afraid to ask, but who are the other possibilities?"

"The Folger in D. C. They've been accused of a few underhanded tactics in the past. I wouldn't put it past them to buy up all these papers so they can sit on them. The people at the Folger are pretty committed to their man from Stratford."

"Would they do such a thing, Smitty?"

"Well, you'll need to read about the way they handled the Ashbourne portrait."

Joe recalled something about the controversy, about the painting actually being a portrait of Edward de Vere but repainted to look like Will Shakespeare. He didn't know how the Folger had been involved, though, so he filed Smitty's comment away for later.

"Okay," Joe said. "I'm planning to take some books with me anyway."

"Read the first few chapters of the book on Oxford by Paul Steitz," advised Smitty. "I'll loan you a copy."

"I will," Joe responded. "Who else should I worry about?"

"Who has the most to lose, should the man from Stratford-upon-Avon turn out to be a fraud?"

Joe wasn't in the mood for riddles—he wanted a beer. "I don't know, Smitty."

"The people who run the Shakespeare exhibits in Stratford, of course."

Joe laughed. "You can't be serious. Would they—whoever *they* are—hire someone to steal the manuscripts? Could they even afford to?"

"Oh, yes, lad. It's big business. A huge tourist attraction, just like Disneyland. You think they want to lose all that business? Have the tourists head to de Vere's home instead?"

Joe felt overwhelmed. Instead of finding his way out of trouble, he was sinking deeper into a quagmire he barely understood.

"Of course, there's one other important possibility."

Joe waited, hearing only the silence, fearing Jonathan Smythe's next words.

"I give up. Who else could be behind this?"

"Think about it, Joe. The same people who must have been behind the cover up before, assuming Edward de Vere, the seventeenth Earl of Oxford, is the real author."

Joe laughed. "Those people are dead now, Smitty? That happened four hundred years ago."

"But the royal family still covers up scandals, don't they?"

Joe huffed, but felt his heart stop.

"Are you really saying, you think Queen Elizabeth—*today's* Queen Elizabeth, in the twenty-first century—could be behind this? C'mon, Smitty."

"She has money, power and resources, lad."

"But why? What would be her motive?"

"Perhaps the same as before, to hide an embarrassing truth about the *first* Queen Elizabeth, the so-called Virgin Queen."

Joe huffed again. "You're saying de Vere might have slept with Queen Elizabeth and *that's* why he hid his identity as the writer of these plays?"

"Perhaps," the older man responded, his voice going very calm. "Maybe de Vere *was* the Queen's lover. That's a possibility. But there might have been another relationship, an even stronger bond, an embarrassing one that the Queen desperately needed to conceal before she could assume the throne."

"Meaning what, that they were married?" Joe tried to make sense of it. He hated his ignorance and wished he knew more about the British monarchy. "Is *that* the big scandal the monarchy's been covering up all these years?"

"No," Smitty said. "I don't think they were married, but given the age difference, there's another possibility."

Joe closed his eyes and tried to do the math. "De Vere was born in 1550 and the Queen in 1533," he said. "A seventeen-year difference."

"Approximately, yes. Elizabeth was sixteen, I believe, when de Vere was born."

"You don't mean what I think you mean, do you?"

"Yes, lad. Edward de Vere just might have been Queen Elizabeth's illegitimate son."

Part VII: All's Well That Ends Well?

CHAPTER 39

Time shall unfold what plaited cunning hides.
From *King Lear*

When Joe's cell phone rang on Sunday morning, he didn't expect trouble. But FBI Agent Terry Lott had bad news.

"The person who's after the documents isn't giving up. I can't get into details, but some chatter came my way. Someone's searching for another gun for hire."

Joe's heart raced as he listened. "Searching for another gun for hire? What's that even mean?"

"It means you and your friends are still in danger. The good news is, we don't believe anyone like Benedict has actually accepted the offer."

"What should I do?"

"Don't say where, just in case your phone is bugged, but I understand you're taking your family away. Is that right?"

"Yeah. How'd you know?"

"Spoke to your sister-in-law, Suzie. I think that's a wise move. I also think it would be a good idea to put the documents in a secure location. If you'd like, you can bring them to the Sacramento FBI office. If you don't want to do that, at least put them in a safety deposit box."

"That's the plan."

"I'm continuing to work the case, but I have to be honest. With threats from terrorists coming in every day, this is a low priority. You need to take the best precautions you can. Understand? Be careful."

Joe closed his eyes and nodded. "I'll do my best."

He found Sara reading the newspaper in the living room as Katie read the comics and Brian watched TV. He quietly pulled her into their bedroom. When he told her the news, she started to cry.

"What are we going to do, Joe?"

He held her in his arms, feeling her tremble with fear.

"I've got an idea. I think you and the kids should go. I'm going to stay here and keep working with Jonathan and Sylvia. That way, *I'll* be the target, not you."

"You don't want to come with us."

"Of course I do, Sara. But I think it's better for you and the kids if you're away from me."

"I don't see why you can't come with us?"

"If there is another guy out there, he'll come after me, Sara. And if I'm with you and the kids, then all of you will be in danger."

"Just like before." She cried harder and slapped Joe's shoulder. "I told you not to get involved again, didn't I."

"It's too late for I told you so."

A knock came to the door and then it opened. Katie looked up at Joe and Sara with a worried expression. "Aunt Suzie's here. She wants to see you, mommy."

"Great," said Joe. "Just what we need."

Sara slapped Joe's shoulder again. "She's here to help."

When Sara walked into the living room, Suzie reached out and held her.

"You've been crying," she said. "And I know why." She glared at Joe over Sara's shoulder.

"How?" asked Joe.

"Agent Lott told me what's going on and asked me to keep an eye on you guys."

Sara pulled away from Suzie. "Joe wants to stay here and be the target, he says, while I take the kids."

"Daddy," Katie said. "Aren't you coming with us?"

Joe looked down and put his hand against Katie's cheek. "I don't think so, Katie. It might be better for you if I stay here."

Sara spun around and glared at Joe. "That's really noble of you, Joe, but do you really expect me to watch two kids by myself in Disneyland?"

Suzie touched Sara's shoulder. "That's why I'm here. I can help. I'll take next week off and come with you guys."

Sara's shoulders shook as she cried again. "Oh, you don't have to do that."

"I want to. It'll be fun to spend time with my niece and nephew."

"Can you really take the time off?" Joe asked her.

"You bet. I've got lots of vacation coming."

Joe looked at Sara. "That would solve our problem, wouldn't it?"

Sara nodded and smiled though her tears.

Joe and Sara spent the rest of the morning planning the trip, making reservations, packing for the children. Staying busy helped keep Joe's mind off the possibility that another mercenary was hot on his trail. But later, while taking a break over coffee, Joe looked at Sara and said, "I've got one more errand before I can leave. It means I have to be gone for a few hours. Will you be okay?"

"Sounds important," Sara responded. "We'll be fine."

Joe sprinted to his bedroom, changed into dress clothes, grabbed his keys, kissed the children goodbye, and then jumped in the Mustang.

Traffic was light, so he reached Smitty's house in record time. Having called during his drive, Joe found Smitty waiting outside, the small wooden box in hand. Jonathan walked briskly to the car and handed Joe the box through the window.

"See you tomorrow for brunch," Smitty said.

Joe placed the box on the passenger's seat and sped away.

He found the little Catholic church in midtown Sacramento easily. The service for Deirdre Claire was still going on when Joe pushed into the cool darkness of the chapel. Perhaps a dozen people sat in the front rows. He quietly slipped into the last pew. A priest was swinging incense around the casket—Joe wondered if he knew that Deirdre may have taken her own life. Maybe priests in California were not as strict as they were in the South.

Joe had missed the eulogies. *Just as well*, he told himself. An altar boy pulled a staff with a cross atop it out of a stand and walked in front of the casket. Six men stood up and clutched the bars on each side of the casket, rolling it out of the church behind the lone altar boy and the priest. Joe watched Melinda Sloan and a man he presumed was her husband stand and follow the casket.

A chill went down Joe's spine as the coffin holding Deirdre Claire rolled by him. Then he glanced up at the red eyes of Melinda Sloan. She nodded and smiled as she walked by.

Outside in the heat, Joe watched as the coffin was loaded into a hearse. The others stood on the sidewalk talking and hugging. He saw Melinda step away and look up at him, so Joe walked down the steps toward her.

"Thank you for coming after all," she told him, reaching out her hand.

As they had the day before, they simply held hands, somehow connected.

"I have something for you," Joe said. He noticed her glance at the wooden box, which was about the size of a school binder. "This is one of the boxes your grandfather sent me. Inside are the manuscripts of two complete plays."

Melinda let go of Joe's right hand and took the box.

"Which plays?" she asked, her voice thin. Her furrowed forehead told him she wasn't sure how to react.

"I gave that some thought," said Joe. "I decided a tragedy and a comedy would be appropriate. *King Lear* seemed like an obvious choice. Do you know the play?"

The woman nodded, a wry smile tugging her lips apart. "Which daughter am I?"

"The good one," Joe answered. "You're a good granddaughter, at least." He saw Melinda's husband walking toward them, a concerned look on his face.

"And the other choice?"

"Ah," Joe said. "Something lighter. *The Merry Wives of Windsor.*"

"Good," she laughed. "I was afraid you'd picked *Taming of the Shrew*!"

Joe laughed.

Melinda nodded toward the hearse, saying, "She wasn't always like that, you know. When we were growing up, Deirdre was very caring, very protective of me."

"Listen," he said, "I need to get going. Just promise me that you'll handle those papers with care."

"Of course," Melinda answered. "As if Grandpap had given them to me himself."

Being reminded of Jack brought a flood of emotion to Joe's heart. He felt his eyes tear up.

The sound of screeching tires caused everyone outside the church to look at a sedan that had raced around the corner and slammed to a stop in front of the hearse. A few seconds later, a Coroner's station wagon turned the corner and pulled in behind the sedan.

"This can't be good," Joe said.

He watched as Ryan Dunn stepped out of the sedan and, after slamming his car door shut, jogged up the steps toward Melinda and Joe.

"Bad news, folks," he called as he approached. "We've got to take the body back."

"What?" Melinda waved for her husband. "I don't understand. The Coroner's office released the body to the funeral parlor last night."

"Yeah," nodded Dunn. "The night shift screwed up. They thought they could release the body because the DNA samples had been collected. The thing is, they hadn't been tested yet. Coroner checked the results this morning. The DNA doesn't match."

"Jesus Christ, Dunn," said Joe. "Does that mean that Deirdre is still alive?"

"Looks like it."

Melinda's husband had come up the steps and put his arm around Melinda.

"What's going on?" he asked.

Dunn reached over and held the other man's arm. "The woman in the coffin isn't your sister-in-law."

Melinda Sloan started sobbing. "Then where is she? Where's Deirdre?"

"We don't know," Dunn answered. "Probably on the run, trying to get as far from here as possible."

The four of them turned to see the coroner and some others pulling the casket out of the hearse.

"This is all too horrible," Melinda said, catching her breath between sobs.

"Then who's in the coffin, Ryan?" Joe asked.

"No idea. We'll have to check missing persons up around Tahoe."

Joe pulled Dunn aside as Mr. Sloan helped Melinda down the steps to the waiting black limousine.

"Do you think Deirdre would come back here, looking for me?"

Dunn shrugged. "I wouldn't think so. Too risky. But..."

"But what?"

"Deirdre Claire isn't normal. She's probably a sociopath, so who knows what the hell she might do."

"I thought this was over," Joe said.

"Doesn't look like it," Dunn responded. "Meanwhile, keep your family safe."

Joe chuckled. "I thought I was."

"Get them away from here, would be my advice."

"They're going to Disneyland with Sara's sister."

"Disneyland?" Dunn chuckled. "That's not a bad idea. Probably the best place for them, with all the security cameras and guards they've got. Yeah. I like it."

Joe nodded. "Glad it meets with your approval."

During the drive home, Joe received a call from Sylvia.

"Good news. My contact at the Huntington says they're willing to pay $200,000 for one of the manuscripts, on the condition that they verify its age."

"Two hundred thousand? I don't mean to sound greedy but is that enough?"

"Probably not," Sylvia replied. "But remember, the manuscripts haven't been authenticated yet. If these are the original handwritten plays of Shakespeare, then each one could be worth a million bucks. Maybe more."

"Which play do they want?" he asked.

Sylvia laughed. "Well, they want all of them. But I told them *A Midsummer Night's Dream*."

Joe chuckled. "How apropos. So how's this work? We give them the manuscript and they give us a check?"

"Well, not the full amount. They're willing to give you a check for $25,000 as a deposit. If they can date the manuscript and verify the handwriting using their own experts, they'll pay you the rest."

"Sounds fair to me, but what do *you* think?"

"It's a win-win for everyone. Based on what I've told them, they're very anxious to examine these papers."

"Really? I thought they'd be, I don't know, angry—disappointed that Will Shakespeare is being knocked off his pedestal."

"Not really," Sylvia said. "You see, even if they still believe their man from Stratford was the author, the fact that de Vere might have written out the plays in his own hand still makes it a curiosity. They can claim that de Vere copied Shakespeare, which increases the status of the man from Stratford."

"De Vere, the forger?" Joe considered the possibility. "Why would he bother?"

"It's going to take time and hard work to convince the skeptics. The research is just beginning, and we have you to thank."

"Well, don't forget Jack Claire and you and Smitty."

"Yes, but, Joe, you're the one who was brash enough to go forward with releasing the de Vere manuscripts. You could have sat on them for years, after all."

"Whether I did it out of brashness or stupidity has yet to be determined."

"I say it took courage and insight," Sylvia answered. "That's my story and I'm stickin' to it."

When he got home, Joe took Sara outside and sat her down in the lawn chair.

"I've got some bad news."

"What could possibly be worse than what we've been through?"

"Deirdre Claire isn't dead."

Sara jumped to her feet. "What!"

"Dunn did a DNA test on the body they found in the car that crashed. It isn't a match for Deirdre."

"Christ, Joe, does this mean she'll come back for us?"

Joe shook his head. "Dunn says it's unlikely. He thinks she's probably on the run, trying to get as far away as possible."

"God, I hope so. I'm not sure I have any fight left in me."

Joe grabbed Sara in his arms and held her close. "I do. I have enough fight for both of us. I won't let anything happen to you or the kids."

Sara looked up into Joe's eyes, crying. Joe wiped the tears off her cheeks and kissed each eye softly.

"I love you, Sara. I won't let anyone hurt you again."

"You promise?"

"I promise."

They kissed deeply, and Joe held her tight. Finally, Katie opened the back door and stepped onto the back porch.

With Brian peering around her, Katie yelled, "Jeez, you two. Get a room."

On Monday morning, they packed Suzie's car, and Joe followed in the Mustang as they drove south to Stockton. Alicia answered the door.

Joe introduced his family and Suzie.

"Come in," she said. As the children strolled inside, Alicia gestured toward the living room. "I'm so glad you can stay for lunch."

Sara held Brian, while Joe walked Katie into the dining room. Smitty was standing at the table, gingerly placing a manuscript into a new white cardboard box.

"Nearly finished, lad. I've held out *Julius Ceasar, Hamlet* and *Romeo and Juliet,* just as we discussed."

"Should we take the box to the bank now or after brunch?"

"I say work before pleasure, lad. What's your thought?"

"Let's get this over with," said Joe. "But first let Katie see inside before you seal it." Joe picked Katie up and held her so she could see.

"Can I touch them, daddy?"

"It just feels like paper, Honey."

"Oh, but Joe," Smitty added, smiling, "she's never touched four-hundred year old paper before."

"All right." Joe smiled as Katie placed her hand inside the container and rested her palm on the top manuscript.

Then she noticed the three other manuscripts still stacked on the table.

"Put me down," she said. She stepped over to the first stack of handwritten pages and read the title. "*Romeo and Juliet.* I've heard of that one before."

"It's a very sad story," Joe said. "Romeo and Juliet die in the end."

"Really?" Katie asked looking up at her father. "That's like you and mommy."

Sara laughed. "What in the world do you mean, Katie?"

"You and daddy almost died when mean people tried to keep you apart." Katie blushed, realizing she might have said something wrong. "Isn't that right, daddy?" Her voice shaking, she said, "Mommy almost died when that mean lady shot her leg and you almost died when I was little and that bad man shot you in your side."

Joe knelt down and hugged her. "That's all over now." He wiped a tear off her cheek. "Remember where you're going?"

Katie reached up with her fist and wiped another tear away from her eye. She forced a smile and said, "Disneyland."

"I see why they need this holiday," Smitty said. He patted Joe on the shoulder. "Good for you, lad. Time away from all this."

They stood in silence for a minute. Then Joe held the flaps while Smitty taped the box closed.

Joe picked up the box and looked at Sara. "We'll be back soon," he said.

He and Smitty went to the car, and Joe placed the box in the trunk, while Smitty climbed in the passenger's side. After closing the lid, Joe looked up and down the street. There were a few cars parked along the curb, but they appeared to be empty.

Still, the hair on the back of Joe's neck bristled as he climbed in and started the engine. As he pulled away from Smitty's house, he watched his rearview mirror to see if anyone followed.

In fifteen minutes, they were inside the bank, walking toward an attractive woman sitting at a desk. As they crossed the lobby, Joe glanced back to see if anyone had followed them inside. When she noticed Smitty, the attractive woman smiled and pushed away from her desk.

"Hello, Dr. Smythe."

"Why so formal, Paula?" Smitty said. "You don't need to put on airs in front of Joe, here."

She shook Joe's hand. "I'm Paula Vanderbilt. Smitty thinks of me as his personal banker."

Joe shifted the box so he could shake hands.

"I'm Joe Conrad," he said. "Smitty thinks of *me* as his chauffeur."

Paula's hearty laugh put Joe at ease. "But in reality you're an instructor at CLU, right? That's what Smitty told me. And I've also read about your brush with danger in Berkeley. That was pretty amazing."

Joe nodded and followed Paula back to her desk where he and Smitty read over and then signed papers making them co-owners of a large safety deposit box.

Inside the vault, Joe slid the cardboard box into the metal safety deposit box, pushed the drawer in and closed the door. He locked his key and removed it. Smitty turned and removed his key, and then Paula Vanderbilt did the same. The bulk of the Shakespeare-de Vere manuscripts were secure.

Smitty looked at Joe and smiled. "Do you feel better now, lad?"

Joe looked around at the walls of safety deposit boxes and at the heavy chrome vault door. "I wish I could say yes."

Paula chuckled. "If it makes you feel any better, we've never been robbed."

When they had left the vault, the three of them stood together in the bank lobby.

"How's Alicia feeling?"

Smitty glanced at Joe, then back to Paula.

"Oh, much stronger."

Paula looked at Joe. "You know she's been fighting ovarian cancer, don't you?"

Joe shook his head, glancing at Smitty.

"Been in remission for nearly six months," Smitty said. "Almost back to her old self. Even helping again in the flower garden."

"I wish you had let me know. I wouldn't have gotten you involved in this mess."

"Nonsense, lad. We're having the time of our lives."

The brunch Alicia had prepared offered everything from scrambled eggs to crepes and quartered sandwiches, as well as mixed fresh fruit, orange juice and glasses of cold milk. They ate greedily.

After the meal, Alicia led Sara and the children on a tour of the back yard so the kids could work off some energy before being trapped in the car for the five-hour drive. Suzie and Joe stayed and chatted with Smitty, who pulled a book from his shelves.

"This is the book by Paul Streitz that I mentioned."

Joe read the tile out loud: "*Oxford: Son of Queen Elizabeth I.* Published by Oxford Institute Press?"

" Is that in England?" Suzie asked.

"No, it's in New England. Connecticut."

"Oh," replied Suzie. "I thought it might be a propaganda piece, you know, commissioned by the descendants of Edward de Vere."

"Not exactly. Streitz is not a typical Elizabethan scholar, but he has fairly good credentials. And the book is researched well enough, though there are some problems. Still, he makes a rather strong argument."

"Really?" Joe asked, sipping coffee from a china teacup.

"The princess Elizabeth would have been sixteen when pregnant with Edward. At her coronation, de Vere marched in the procession and carried Elizabeth's banner. You have to wonder why," Smitty added. "She was twenty-five and he was only eight, so yes it *is* possible that Elizabeth was de Vere's mother. That would explain a lot!"

Smitty opened the book to an etching showing de Vere in his role as Lord Great Chamberlain. "This shows Edward later as an adult carrying the sword of state before Queen Elizabeth."

Joe nodded. "The connection between Queen Elizabeth and Edward de Vere seems pretty clear."

Suzie spoke up. "But that was then. You really think today's Royal Family offered millions to Deirdre Claire?"

Smitty shook his head. "I don't know. But we have to consider it."

Joe chuckled. "Why wouldn't they just send one of their own agents after the papers? You know, someone from Her Majesty's Secret Service?"

Smitty shrugged. "It's a possibility, Joe. Someone was willing to pay a lot of money for the manuscripts. Whoever wants them also wants to keep the whole matter quiet."

Sara returned from the back yard with Alicia and the kids. "I guess we should get going."

Joe loaded Brian into his car seat and kissed his forehead. Then he held Katie and kissed her cheeks. "Have fun with Mickey, okay?"

"I will, daddy. I wish you were coming, too."

"So do I, but you'll have fun with mommy and Aunt Suzie."

He helped Katie with her seatbelt and then shut the door. Sara hugged him hard, saying, "I'm mad at you, but please stay out of trouble, okay?"

"I will. You guys have fun."

Joe watched Suzie pull away and waited to see if anyone followed them. No one did. As the car disappeared around the corner, he felt a pang of guilt and fought the feeling he might never see his family again.

CHAPTER 40

No profit grows where is no pleasure ta'en;
From *The Taming of the Shrew*

On Tuesday morning Joe's cell phone buzzed next to the bed, waking him. He was reluctant to answer until he saw that it was Sara calling.

"Are you all right?" he asked. "Why didn't you call last night?"

"By the time we got into the hotel, we were starved, so we went to dinner. Then the kids wanted to swim. It was really chaotic."

"But you're there safe and sound?"

"Yeah, we're fine. Heading to breakfast and then—"

"Don't say where you are, in case someone's listening, okay."

Sara chuckled. "Jeez, you're more paranoid than I am."

"The FBI agent said to be careful, Sara." There was an uncomfortable silence.

"How'd it go at the Library yesterday? Did you make the exchange?"

"Yes. The people at the—"

"Don't say the name, okay?"

"Okay, okay. Anyway, Suzie handled it. Signed a document, acting as your attorney, and collected a check, which we got to the bank just before closing."

"Wow. That's the most we've ever had in our account."

"Yeah. Now we can enjoy being here without worrying about money." The relief in her voice was clear. "What's on your agenda?"

"Continue the research, I guess."

"Gee, *that* sounds like fun," she replied sarcastically.

"Sara, please understand."

"I do. Actually, Suzie defended you on the drive down."

Joe laughed. "That's a surprise."

They said goodbye, and Joe put down the phone.

After a quick breakfast, Joe drove to Stockton and picked up Smitty. On the way to Berkeley, Smitty was beaming with excitement, but wouldn't "spill the beans," he said until they could meet with Sylvia.

In Sylvia's office, the three of them sat around the work table, sipping coffee, until Joe couldn't take it any longer.

"Okay, what's the big secret?"

"Well," Sylvia began, leaning forward. "I met with my guy in our chemistry department. Analysis of the paper and ink confirms that it was from the sixteenth century. In fact, the paper is definitely a kind used in London and among the wealthier classes. My handwriting expert also confirmed that, in his opinion, based on the samples we supplied him, the handwriting is definitely de Vere's. We've now got credible, independent evidence—it all comes back in support of Edward de Vere as the author of the plays."

"Fantastic!" yelled Joe. He raised his hand and Sylvia gave him a high five. "That's really terrific news."

Smitty clapped his hands together. "I could hardly contain myself, but I wanted Sylvia to tell you herself. And there's more."

Grinning from ear to ear, Joe looked from Smitty to Sylvia. "More?"

"Have you heard from your family?" asked Sylvia.

"They dropped off the manuscript yesterday afternoon. Now they're at Disneyland."

"How about you? Are *you* up for a trip?" Sylvia asked.

"Maybe. Where?"

"We're going to England, lad! London, Stratford-upon-Avon, Oxford."

"Yes," Sylvia said. "And on the way, we'll stop in Washington, DC.

I've already arranged a day inside the special collections areas of the Folger Shakespeare Library."

"Whoa. Even with the check from the Huntington, I can't afford all that," Joe said, blushing.

Sylvia put her hand on Joe's forearm. "I have university funds to cover the trip," she said. "You won't be out a penny."

"For all three of us?"

Sylvia beamed. "Yes."

Joe looked at Smitty.

"See, lad? I told you Sylvia was amazing."

"I don't know. I only have two weeks before classes start. Besides, should I really leave Sara and the kids?" Joe looked from Smitty to Sylvia and back.

"That's up to you," said Smitty. "We'll probably get back about the same time they do."

"Seems like a good idea to me," added Sylvia. "If your FBI friend is right, then wouldn't it be harder for someone to track us down?"

Joe closed his eyes and tried to sort it out. "When do we leave?"

"Tomorrow," said Sylvia. "I've reserved rooms at the Washington Hilton and made an appointment at the Folger. We'll have eight hours to do research. The next morning we leave bright and early for London. We'll need to take a couple of the manuscripts with us, as well as the bound copy of the *Folio*."

Joe put his fingers to his lips, trying to think about the trip and its implications, worried that Sara wouldn't want him going without her.

"You know, Joe," said Smitty. "You should consider donating one of the plays to Oxford University."

Sylvia nodded. "The more scholars have a chance to look at these manuscripts for themselves, the more quickly they'll come to realize the truth about the authorship."

Joe nodded. "I've been considering something, and I'd like to know what you two think."

"Go on," said Sylvia.

"Since we're going to England anyway, what about returning the bound copy of the *First Folio* to the de Vere family?"

Joe watched Sylvia and Smitty exchange glances. They smiled simultaneously.

"That's a great idea," nodded Sylvia, "as long as we can show it to the people at the Folger first and let them photograph it for their archives."

"You'd be giving away a small fortune, Joe. Will you be okay with that?"

"De Vere's descendants should decide what to do with the *Folio*, not me. I feel guilty enough profiting from the plays."

"You don't need to, lad. Not after the hell your family's been through."

"Still," Joe said, "with Jack's death and all the others, it's a mixed blessing."

CHAPTER 41

Kindness in women, not their beauteous looks,
Shall win my love.
From The Taming of the Shrew

"You should go," Sara said. "The kids and I will be fine. They're having a blast."

"Are you sure?"

"Yes, absolutely."

"Don't *you* want to see England?"

"Eventually. But I'm enjoying the time with the kids."

Joe busied himself packing and making calls. He wanted Bill Morgan to know their plans, and then he called the FBI agent at Bill's suggestion and was surprised by the Agent's request that they meet in DC.

"Things are moving fast," Lott said. "I'll be in DC myself and we're tracking leads on who was offering the money to Deirdre Claire. I'll have some answers for you in a couple of days. Give me a call in DC and we'll meet at my office."

Joe hung up and turned his attention to packing. Then something occurred to him. He found his passport in the middle drawer of his desk and tossed into his suitcase.

Giddy as a child, Smitty chatted incessantly while they drove from Stockton to SF International, where they met Sylvia. The flight from San Francisco to DC was smooth, and before Joe could fully believe what was going on, they'd checked into the Hilton and had gotten a cab to the Washington Mall, where the Washington Monument gleamed against a deep blue sky.

Tucked behind the Library of Congress, the Folger Shakespeare Library was a rather nondescript, oblong building that seemed unimpressive to Joe.

After climbing out of the cab, Sylvia walked between Smitty and Joe. "Most of the holdings are below ground. It's much larger than it looks."

After Smitty and Sylvia showed their Folger cards and vouched for Joe, they were granted access to the grand research halls. The high ceilings, dark wood panels, rows of impressive bookcases, and massive oil paintings on the walls inspired a reverence for all things literary and scholarly in Joe. They searched for an empty table—most were filled with scholars quietly working and tapping on the keyboards of their laptops.

Sylvia and Smitty visited a card catalogue as Joe looked on. They walked to a counter in the center of the great hall, handed a dozen requests slips to the clerk and waited. In ten minutes, several four-hundred-year-old books and yellowed manuscripts surfaced from the bowels of the library and were handed to the scholars.

Incredible! thought Joe, amazed by the speed and expert handling of the materials.

They carried the ancient books and papers to a table, and Joe watched the expressions on his colleagues' faces. They grinned with anticipation, gently cracking open the books. Smitty handed the most impressive looking volume to Joe, flashing that all-knowing Buddha grin as he allowed Joe to pull the heavy book from his fingers.

The text was Edward de Vere's *Geneva Bible*, and Joe saw the resemblance at once. He opened his briefcase and removed the copy of the *First Folio*, placing it on the table next to the other book.

Folger Shelfmark 1427 (STC 2106): The 1570 de Vere Geneva Bible. Provided by the Folger Shakespeare Library, Washington, DC.

The bindings of the *First Folio* and de Vere's *Geneva Bible* were identical—the same cover, the same silver protectors on the corners, the same silver medallion in the center with a wild boar and a crown over its head. Joe looked at Smitty and then at Sylvia, whose knowing smile mirrored Mona Lisa's grin.

"These two volumes were bound by the same bookbinder for the same family," Sylvia said. "No doubt about it."

"Open the Bible," whispered Smitty. "Let's examine the inside pages."

With the others looking on, Joe gingerly opened the cover of the bible and thumbed through the first ten pages or so, then he folded the book open in the middle. Several passages were neatly underlined, as if someone had used a ruler.

"Do you recognize that line, Smitty?" Sylvia pointed to an underlined verse in the Bible. Joe looked over Sylvia's shoulder and read the verses from *Wisdom*.

"'He will take holiness for an invincible shield. He will sharpen his fierce wrath for a sword and the world shall fight with him against the unwise.'"

"Yes," whispered Smitty. "It's from *Henry VI, Part 2,* isn't it?"

Sylvia glanced up, a puzzled look on her face. "Oh. Maybe. I was thinking Richard II when Bollingbroke says, 'To reach victory above my head, Add proof unto mine armor with thy prayers and with thy blessings steel my lance's point."

Too loudly, Joe asked, "You have that memorized?"

"Shhh," hushed Sylvia, smiling up into Joe's face.

He blushed, looking around the reading room. Other scholars glanced up, more surprised than annoyed, and went back to their reading.

"Yes, it's one of my favorite passages."

Sylvia thumbed through the Bible's pages, stopping to read an underlined passage here and pointing another one out to Smitty, who nodded knowingly. Then they saw an odd doodle in the left margin of a page. It looked like an elongated capitalized S in cursive with a few lines and an upside-down question mark underneath.

"What in the world do you suppose that means?" Smitty asked.

"I have no clue," whispered Sylvia. "It looks kind of like a seahorse holding a spear. Weird."

Joe leaned down to get a better look. "I've seen that before."

Smitty and Sylvia turned up and stared at him. "Where?" asked Syliva.

"In one of the manuscripts. Wait. It's in one of the plays we brought."

Joe opened his briefcase again and pulled out the handwritten copy of *The Tempest.* He placed the manuscript on the table next to the Bible and turned over each sheaf of the rag paper. "Here," he whispered. He put his finger under the image.

The identical mark lay in the margin next to lines of dialogue by Ariel, which Smitty whispered as he read them aloud. "'The fire and cracks Of sulphorous roaring the most might Neptune Seem to besiege, and make his bold waves tremble, Yea, his dread trident shake.'"

"Is that supposed to be Neptune holding a trident, then?" asked Joe.

"Maybe," whispered Sylvia. "It doesn't really matter, though. What matters is the same doodle appears in this handwritten manuscript and in de Vere's Bible. Let's keep looking."

Joe turned over new pages and the three of them noticed similar fists in the margins of the play and in the Bible. The fists were adorned with familiar lace cuffs and five dots, like the points of a crown.

Page after page held similar fists in the margins.

Sylvia turned the pages of the Bible. She stopped, pointed to one fist in de Vere's Geneva Bible that was identical to one in the margin of *The Tempest.* All three scholars looked at each other.

Sylvia whispered, "This could be the smoking gun! The evidence skeptics need to admit de Vere is the true Bard."

"You're convinced then?" Smitty asked her.

"There's simply too much evidence now to deny it, Jonathan. Don't you agree?"

Smitty stood up straight and stretched, then rubbed his eyes under his glasses. "I'm fairly certain, but I want to continue the research."

"Oh, of course," whispered Sylvia. "Agreed. I'm just bowled over by the similarity in the marginalia."

"As am I," Smitty said.

Then he pulled the chair out for Sylvia and grinned. She laughed quietly and took a seat in front of Edward de Vere's *Geneva Bible*, while Jonathan pulled out another chair beside her and sat down.

Seeing his friends reconciled, Joe leaned between them. "This looks like a good time for me to duck out and meet Agent Lott," he whispered. "I'll leave you two to continue your work."

They both nodded and set to work laying out their notepads.

With its mammoth overhang, the FBI building reminded Joe of the Kaufmann Fallingwater House designed by Frank Lloyd Wright. He paid the driver and walked briskly into the building, pausing a moment before crossing over the FBI seal on the marble floor.

A row of security tables and metal detectors stood in front of him, and he went through security just as he had at the airport. Beyond the security checkpoint stood a bank of windows—bullet-proof glass, he suspected—and behind the glass were clerks who looked like bank tellers. Joe approached an open window and explained who he was. With a few taps on the keyboard of his computer, the security clerk said, "Agent Lott will be down in a moment to escort you upstairs. Here's a Visitor's badge. Be sure to keep it on while you're inside the building."

"Okay," Joe said, pinching the clasp open and snapping it shut on his shirt pocket.

"Do not take the badge off at any time, for any reason," the clerk said sternly.

For a few minutes, Joe stood awkwardly inside the lobby, looking up at the security cameras that stared back down at him

He was beginning to feel the whole trip had been a mistake when he heard his name echo off the marble walls and turned to see Terry Lott walk from the elevators toward him, his arm outstretched.

"How was your trip?" Lott asked, shaking his hand.

"Pretty smooth."

"You're staying at the Hilton?"

Joe nodded. "How did you know?"

"It's my job to know."

"That's kind of scary."

"Actually, your attorney told me. I spoke to him yesterday."

"Oh, okay," said Joe. "Mystery solved then."

"Well, not quite."

"What do you mean?"

"C'mon," Agent Lott said, placing his large hand on Joe's shoulder. "I'll tell you upstairs."

Joe followed Lott to the elevator and they stood together in silence as they rode up to the fifth floor. The doors opened to a large office abuzz with men and women in their cubicles talking on phones and reading computer screens. Most wore white shirts or blouses and dark slacks. What struck Joe were the holsters and pistols strapped to every agent's waist—male and female alike. Lott led Joe through the outer office to a small conference room with a view of the street. He shut the door once Joe had stepped inside and taken a seat.

"What's this about? You're starting to worry me. Have you tracked down Deirdre Claire yet?"

Lott sat down across from Joe, his back to the window.

"No sign of Deirdre Claire, but we *have* been able to identify three buyers who were contacted by her. One is a private barrister in London who works for the Royal Family. He hasn't confirmed it, but we're sure he's actually making offers on behalf of Prince Charles."

"Wow!" Joe laughed. "Prince Charles? Really?"

"Charles has been deeply involved with historical preservation, usually landmark buildings, but sometimes important works of art and literature, so it makes sense. You'll want to meet with his attorney when you're in London."

Lott slid a copy of an email across to Joe. It was from the barrister's office:

Please advise the person in possession of the manuscripts that we would surely make a reasonable offer upon inspection. Have said person ring our offices when convenient.

Joe looked at the address and telephone number after reading the message and nodded. "The Royal Family. Pretty cool. I'm taking some of the manuscripts with us to England, so I'll schedule a meeting."

"The next number we identified came from here."

"Here?" Joe asked. "As in FBI Headquarters?

Agent Lott laughed. "No. Here in DC. The number belongs to the curator at the Folger Shakespeare Library."

"That's interesting. They acted pretty uninterested this morning when they were having us sign in. It surprised me, frankly."

"It's a ruse. They want to lowball you on the price."

"Oh," chuckled Joe. "Like buying a used car."

"Yeah. A used car worth a million bucks. Only they'll probably offer you ten grand to start with."

"Sounds like you've done a little research of your own."

"Deirdre Claire was pitting buyers against one another, to drive up the price."

"She seemed like the type. Very sly."

"You want my advice?"

Joe nodded. "I'll take all the advice I can get."

"Don't take less than a hundred grand for any of the manuscripts. The people at the Folger will tell you the papers are potentially worthless, nothing more than forgeries."

"All right. I'll hold out for as much as I can get, but Sylvia made a good point."

"What's that?"

"She said, the more scholars have a chance to examine the papers and authenticate them, the more they'll increase in value."

"That's probably true. But trust me when I tell you the Folger has enormous assets. Of course, the papers are in your hands, so you can do with them what you wish."

Joe sensed something in Lott's voice. "Has the ownership come into doubt?"

"As a matter of fact, yes. The barrister from London—his first communiqué raised that very issue. I learned about it a couple of days ago and asked people in our legal department to give me their opinion."

"And?" Joe asked nervously. He felt his chest tighten.

"Since the papers were mailed to you from someone close to you, Jack Claire, you own them outright."

"That's a relief."

"Well, let me clarify. Someone can always challenge your ownership. We still don't know exactly how Dr. Claire got the manuscripts, but your possession and consequent ownership is well established. A judge or jury would see it that way, too. I'm ninety percent sure."

Joe breathed a sigh of relief. "I'll settle for ninety percent."

"I said there were three buyers, remember?"

Joe nodded. "Who's the third one?"

"This is where it gets dicey. We can't be sure, but we think it's someone from the Middle East."

"The Middle East? Why would some Arab be interested?"

"For the same reason they buy anything else. Because they think they can make a killing on it."

"A killing?"

"Sorry. Poor choice of words. They often buy underpriced works of art—paintings, vases, statues—and they probably believed they could get the papers from Deirdre Claire for a million bucks and turn them around for twenty times that much."

"Wow," said Joe. "Maybe I should deal with them, then."

The neutral expression on Lott's face soured. "Trust me, Joe. You do *not* deal with these people. They'll offer you five million dollars for the whole lot, get you to a place they can control, and we'll put your face on a milk carton three days later."

Joe started to chuckle, but Lott's face silenced him.

"These are bad people, Joe. How in the world Deirdre Claire found them, or how they found her, we have no idea. But you don't want them in your life. In fact—"

"What?"

"While you're travelling in England, be careful. Also, it might be a good idea for your wife and kids to stay someplace where they can't be kidnapped."

"Kidnapped?"

"These folks are accustomed to getting what they want. They might decide to take your family and exchange them for the papers. Of course, once that happens, you'll never see your family again, even if you turn over the documents."

"Oh, great!" Joe slumped in his chair. "Sara's going to kill me."

Lott grinned.

"Are you yanking my chain, Agent Lott?"

"A little."

"Jesus Christ, that isn't funny."

"Don't get me wrong. I wasn't joking about the Arabs. They can be as ruthless as the Russian mob. But I doubt they'll really come after you now."

"Why not?"

"Too much publicity," said Lott dryly. "Besides, you've given a few pieces away."

"Yeah? So?"

"You've broken up the set. The thirty plus plays are much more valuable if all of them are together."

Joe nodded. "Any clue as to how much the whole set would be worth, if it were sold altogether?"

"Do you really want to know?"

"Of course."

"Our forensic accountants and appraisers estimate that the set, if it were auctioned off all together, would be worth half a billion dollars."

Joe's heart skipped a beat. "Billion with a *b*?"

"You heard right, Joe. Five hundred million dollars. Maybe more."

"Jeez. I could have been another Bill Gates."

"Nah. He's worth fifty billion."

"Still," Joe said, "I coulda been a contender."

CHAPTER 42

I am all the daughters of my father's house,
And all the brothers, too.
From *Twelfth Night*

Trying to blend in, the tall Asian woman, dressed like an Administrative Assistant in her thirties, strolled out of the neighborhood into Hyde Park in London and walked casually to the lake. Geese slept quietly around the edge and slender young office women on their lunch breaks, their tops off, sunbathed in their bras as young men pretended not to stare. How different it was, she noted, from her previous life in Hong Kong.

The woman, her long, jet-black hair piled neatly on her head, strolled around the lake and came to a vendor selling bags of popcorn for a pound. No other customers were standing close by. She pulled a silk handkerchief with a 100 pound note inside from her pocketbook and handed it to the vendor, who in turn handed her a bag of popcorn without speaking. The vendor did not make change.

She pinched a few kernels of the popcorn and popped them into her mouth. The smooth, tight burgundy dress caressed her lithe body as she walked back toward the path that led out of the park. By the time she had reached the neighborhood where she'd parked her Jaguar, she'd eaten or dropped a third of the popcorn from the bag.

After unlocking her car, the woman climbed inside, closed the driver's side door and glanced around before removing a folded note from the popcorn bag. She looked in the rearview mirror, ostensibly applying fresh lip gloss to her full, sensual lips, but in reality checking to see who might be watching her. Then she once more looked around before opening the note.

NH Museum 1:30

She had an hour. Good. She could grab some sushi before the meeting and get the taste of stale popcorn out of her mouth. She knew just the place near the Natural History Museum. Her parents had taken her there years ago, when it was a simple Chinese restaurant, and she had continued to return, watching as it metamorphosed into a trendy, upscale sushi place. Still, it held some sentimental value, she supposed. Now that her parents were dead.

As she drove away, she wondered how profitable this new mission would be. And who she'd have to kill.

The grand main lobby of the Natural History Museum, with high windows and beautiful arched ceilings, hummed with the footsteps and voices of tourists from all over the world. The woman from Hong Kong made her way through the impressive lobby to the Darwin Exhibit and found her contact standing near the white marble statue of Charles Darwin. The tall, well-dressed man smiled when he noticed the woman walking toward him.

"Mr. Talcott. How nice to see you again."

"Ms. Lee. A pleasure."

They shook hands and strolled toward a bench near a dark corner of the hall. After they had seated themselves, the man held out a manila envelope. The woman took the envelope casually and opened the clasp. She tugged a stack of photocopied newspaper stories out and began to read as the man spoke.

"My client would like you to recover as many of the manuscripts as possible."

The woman he called Ms. Lee scanned the pages before speaking.

"So, it's off to California, then?" she asked.

"As it turns out, the subjects are arriving in London tomorrow."

"Oh?" Ms. Lee smiled. "How convenient. Are you sure?"

"Yes." Talcott looked like an attorney in his crisp, tailored suit. "I called the woman's office at Berkeley. Her assistant—a jealous little twit, it seems—was furious that Dr. Williamson was taking her newfound friends to London without him."

"He gave you their itinerary?"

"Yes, including their hotel. It's written on the last page. Hence, our contacting you, Ms. Lee, instead of someone in the states."

"I see." She continued reading the articles. "This Joseph Conrad the papers speak of, he killed a professional in California?"

"Sheer luck, by the looks of it." He reached over and touched the woman's forearm. "Still, it serves as a good reminder to be careful, even when dealing with amateurs. Your father learned that, didn't he."

She studied the man's face. "My father was betrayed by the very government he'd worked for all his life."

"No need to remind me, Ms. Lee. I handled your father's affairs for your mum after she returned, as you well know."

The woman pulled her arm away. "Yes, you handled everything, as I recall."

"Mae Lee, I have only ever tried to be a good friend to you and your mum."

"Indeed you did. And when mother would have nothing more to do with you, your attention drifted my way."

"I treated you very well, didn't I?"

"Like most Englishmen, you treated me like a whore. That's why I work for people like your client and not you."

Mr. Talcott shook his head in a scolding manner. "Bitter girl."

"Sweet and sour," she answered sarcastically. "Like your pork." She pointed to the photos of Joe, Smitty and Sylvia. "And how should I deal with them?"

Talcott grinned. "Cleanly. He doesn't want to be bothered by some nuisance in the future, understand?"

The woman stood and smoothed her satin burgundy dress. She picked up the papers, slid them back inside the envelope, and glared at Talcott.

"Be sure the funds are in my account by tomorrow."

Talcott rose and smiled. "Consider it done."

CHAPTER 43

What plague is greater than the grief of mind?
The grief of mind that eats in every vein…
From "Grief of Mind"

The longest, most uncomfortable flight Joe Conrad had ever been on was the flight from Washington, D.C., to London. He watched jealously as Smitty and Sylvia slept. Both used inflatable neck pillows and took sleeping pills. Joe tried to read, but the snoring of his colleagues cut at the edges of his temper like a hacksaw on rusty metal.

Joe finally drifted into a restless sleep—his first in almost forty-eight hours—only to be jarred awake by the captain's announcement that they'd be landing at Heathrow in twenty minutes. Looking out the window across Smitty's chest, he saw a gray dawn bloom in a milky sky over a dull, flat landscape. Upon landing, the jet rolled and bounced intolerably before reaching the gate.

The line moved tediously through Customs. Smitty grinned patiently, as did Sylvia in the line on his right. Their patience annoyed him.

Finally, the three of them stood outside and waved up a taxi. After loading the trunk with their suitcases, Joe climbed in on the passenger side, while Smitty and Sylvia settled in the back.

"Brace yourself," said Smitty. "It takes a good forty minutes to reach London."

"Forty minutes!" barked Joe. "I shouldn't have come."

"Joe," Smitty whispered, "what's the matter? I've never seen you so distraught."

"I told you what the FBI guy said, right? Gangsters from the Middle East. The Russian mafia."

The driver looked at Joe, concern wrinkling his forehead.

"Calm down," said Sylvia. "I'm sure your family's fine."

"I should have called from the airport. Why doesn't my damn cell phone work over here?" Joe leaned between the seats to look Smitty in the eyes. "I'm worried. Agent Lott made light of the mafia thing, but the more I think about it…"

"You're exhausted," Smitty said, a look of sympathy wrinkling his eyes. "You need to sleep."

Joe turned around and faced forward, looking out the windshield at the misty, overcast morning.

They drove on in silence through the low farmlands and suburbs outside London. As the clouds gave way to sunshine, the roads widened and grew more crowded, and the buildings grew taller. Joe nodded off again and awoke as the taxi pulled up outside their hotel. They approached the front desk with their rolling suitcases in tow.

Joe put his hand on Smitty's shoulder while Sylvia spoke to the clerk at the front desk. "I'm not checking in until I've spoken to Sara."

He made a collect call, and soon Sara was on the line.

"Jesus, Joe, it's one in the morning."

"Oh," he said. "I don't know it was so late."

He heard Sara yawn. "Why are you calling?"

"To make sure you're okay."

"Oh, we're fine," Sara said. "Everyone's asleep. Brian's in the bed next to mine and Katie's in with Suzy."

"Has anyone bothered you? Any strangers?"

"No, honey." She said nothing for a few seconds. "Why do you ask?"

"I told you about the Middle Eastern buyer that Agent Lott mentioned, right? He also mentioned the Russian mafia."

"You said he played down the risk."

"Now I'm wondering if *I* played it down. Maybe I made less of it than I should have."

Sara said nothing. Joe could visualize her—thumbnail in her mouth, brow furrowed, worried now, thinking about her options.

"You know, Sara? I'm going straight back to the airport. I can be back in California in twelve hours."

"You're having an anxiety attack or something. We're not in danger. You just need rest."

"I should come back home. My place is with you and my children."

"I'm glad you feel that way. But we're fine. Get something to eat, grab a shower and take a good, long nap. Call me when you wake up. When you're clear headed."

Joe closed his eyes and tried to imagine Sara and the children in the hotel room. "Are you really all right? No one's standing there with a gun to your head, right?"

Sara chuckled. "No, Joe. No gun to the head, no Russia mafia. Just a couple of tired kids who need their sleep, just like their father."

Joe turned toward the front desk and watched Sylvia and Smitty stroll in his direction. Sylvia held up a white card—his room key, he figured.

"I guess I'll stay," he told Sara.

"Good night, Joe." Her voice sounded amused or annoyed—he couldn't tell. "Sweet dreams."

And with those words, she hung up.

The initial silence on the telephone sounded eerie, ominous. *The absence of life*, thought Joe. But he hung up the receiver, despite the urge to call back.

Sylvia handed him the plastic room key and a pill.

"What's this?"

"It's a sleeping pill," she answered. "Get some rest. You'll feel a hundred times better."

Suddenly, the idea of climbing between cool sheets overwhelmed him. His shoulders slumped, his eyelids grew heavy, and he could barely feel his legs.

"Maybe you're right. I *do* feel exhausted."

Joe allowed himself to be guided to the elevator, towing his suitcase behind him, and before it seemed possible, he had shed his clothes, leaving them strewn across the carpet, and slipped into the bed and into the black sleep it invited.

CHAPTER 44

Beauty provoketh thieves sooner than gold.
From *As You Like It*

After sleeping for nearly twenty hours, Joseph Conrad awoke a stranger in a strange land, in a room black as night, uncertain where he was or how long he'd been there. He threw back the covers and stumbled to the bathroom, squinting after turning on the light. The bathroom was not familiar. He splashed cold water on his face and inspected his two-day growth of stubble, rubbing his cheeks and chin. *Rip Van Winkle has got nothing on me.*

After wiping off his face, he looked around the room, turning on the light by the bed. Slowly, the fog cleared. A red light on the phone was blinking. He had two messages.

The first was from Smitty. "We've discovered something very significant. Call my room when you wake up. I'm in 517."

The second message was Sara. "Joe. Hope you got some sleep. We're headed back to the park. No Russian gangsters in sight. Please don't call again. Email instead, when you can. Your collect call cost over fifty dollars! Love you."

Joe put the phone down, stretched and yawned. Whatever demons had plagued him before seemed to have evaporated. *Russian mafia! Really, Joe.* "You're losing it, man," he told himself.

He stepped over to the window and pulled open the heavy curtains. Sunlight streamed in. He saw the enormous Ferris wheel, rotating slowly, majestic beside the sparkling, muddy water of the Thames. Below him sidewalks bustled with people and streets were crowded with cars driving the wrong way. The lively scene made him laugh.

Somehow he knew Jack Claire was watching.

"I'm in London! Jesus Christ, Jack, I'm in London!"

A knock at the door startled him. Smitty. He padded across the lush carpet and peeked out the spy hole, seeing an attractive Asian woman's smiling face. He looked down at his bare chest and pajama bottoms. Was there a robe in the closet?

The hell with it, he thought. He opened the door a crack.

"Yes?"

"Sorry to disturb you, sir." Her articulate British accent surprised him. "My name is Yu Mee. I'm a concierge here at the hotel. May I come in?"

Joe noticed her musky perfume and full red lips. He smiled but shook his head. "I'm not dressed yet. Just got up. Jet lag."

She smiled confidently. "I can see you're in pajamas. Really, it's fine."

Joe glanced down and felt his face turn red. "Well, let me grab a robe." He stepped away from the door and opened the closet. A white terrycloth robe hung inside and he quickly pulled it on as the attractive woman stepped in and closed the door. He moved out of the way as he tied the belt. "I'd offer you coffee, but I—"

"Oh, please," the woman said. "Allow me."

She grabbed the small coffee pot and stepped around Joe again, brushing by him, tossing her fragrant hair against his cheek as she hurried into the bathroom and turned on the light.

Joe looked her up and down. Over her left breast was a magnetic plastic name tag.

YU MEE PRENTICE
GUEST SERVICES

"You're last name is Prentice?"

"My father was British."

Her tight black dress left little to the imagination. He could see the outline of her firm breasts, the flat, muscular stomach, her shapely hips and tight calves.

Suddenly wishing he'd brought Sara with him, Joe sighed and walked over to one of the chairs at the little round table. The woman poured water into the small black coffee maker. She tore open a package of coffee with her teeth and placed the filter containing coffee inside the funnel of the maker, slapping it shut. Then she spun around and smiled at Joe, her hands smoothing her dress.

"There we go. Good, strong coffee in five minutes."

She stood in the lamplight as if she enjoyed the way Joe was studying her. Her confident grin made him self-conscious.

"So, what can I do for you, Ms. Prentice?"

She took a few steps closer, saying, "Oh, no. You've got it backwards. I'm here to ask what I can do for you."

The way the woman's hands were pressed against the front of her tight dress, her fingers with their bright red fingernails pointing toward her groin, made Joe feel uneasy. *Is she for real?* he wondered.

"I, I'm not sure," he managed. "What did you have in mind?"

She waved her hand in the air and then flipped her hair, looking above Joe as she took a step closer. "Well, the concierge can provide many things for you. We can arrange personalized tours of all the major museums and art galleries. We can get tickets for any live performances you'd care to see in London, from live theater to rock music, or even a gentleman's club."

She gazed down at him, within reach, her eyes softening.

Joe laughed. "I'd better stay away from gentleman's clubs. Those sorts of place got me into some trouble once before."

"Oh?" She smiled. "*That* sounds intriguing."

She was standing close enough that Joe could again smell her strong, sensual perfume and it was having its desired effect.

"Wouldn't you like a relaxing massage? It's a lovely way to begin the day."

"No, thank you."

Joe stood up, then stepped around her and reached for the coffee pot as it gurgled the last few drops. He poured some into the black porcelain cup and then held the pot up as if to offer the woman a cup.

"Would you still like some coffee?"

She pouted. "Sure. Coffee would be nice."

Joe poured a second cup. "Do you take anything in it? Creamer? Sweetener?"

"Yes. One packet of both, actually." She stepped closer, standing beside Joe, her shoulder rubbing against his. "But *I* should be doing this for *you*. That's my job. To make your stay here as pleasing as possible."

"That's all right." Joe opened packets of creamer and sugar, dumped the powder into the cup, and then stirred the coffee a few times before handing the cup to woman.

"Thank you." She held the cup to her lips and allowed the steam to rise into her flaring nostrils. "Don't you just love a good hot cup of coffee?"

Joe chuckled. "Yes." He stepped away, closer to the door. "You know, Ms. Prentice. I'm sort of here on business, so I'm not sure I'll have time to visit a museum or attend a show."

The woman stepped closer. "Can't I tempt you with *something*?"

Joe chuckled and shook his head. "Trust me. You *have* tempted me."

"Have you been to London previously?"

"No, this is my first trip."

"Then you must do some sight-seeing while you're here. Look. I have an idea. I can get you passes to the London Eye."

Joe shook his head. "The London Eye?"

"It's really our hottest new attraction. The Millennium Wheel?"

"Oh. The giant Ferris Wheel? I can see it out the window."

"Yes, yes. It's called the London Eye. Don't ask me why."

Joe walked to the window, holding his coffee in his left hand, and he tugged open the curtains and peered out. She joined him at the window, her arm brushing against his.

"There it is. Look." She pointed to it, her delicate hand hovering close to Joe's lips. "You really should ride her. You'll absolutely adore it."

Joe stepped away from the woman's hand. "Maybe I will be able to squeeze in a tourist attraction while I'm here."

She placed her hand on Joe's shoulder. "Are you quite sure I can't do anything for you?"

Joe looked down into the woman's eyes.

"Quite sure."

"I promise you won't be disappointed."

Joe stepped away. "I'm afraid my wife would, though."

"Well, in that case—"

The woman walked over to the low dresser and set her coffee cup down. Joe thought she was going to leave, but instead she turned and stared at him, the expression on her face both sad and seductive.

Joe raised the hot coffee to his lips. Now her persistence made him uneasy.

A knock at the door startled both of them, causing Joe to burn his lips on the coffee. Annoyed, he yelled, "Come in"

The door opened and a maid—a young Indian woman—looked inside wearily. "Housekeeping. Is this not a good time?"

"It's an excellent time!" Joe called out. Then he noticed Jonathan standing behind the maid's cart.

"You're finally awake! Good. Sylvia and I are about to have breakfast."

"Great, Jonathan. I'll join you. Soon as I jump in the shower." Joe nodded, holding the other woman's stare. "I'm just finishing up with this woman from the hotel." Looking at the maid, he said, "Maybe you two know each other? Ms. Yu Mee Prentice?" The Asian woman spun around and walked briskly to the door. Joe followed as she stepped around the maid and disappeared down the hall, leaving behind only the fragrance of her sensual perfume.

The maid looked bored as she stared at Joe, awaiting instructions. "Do you want me to clean now or come back, sir?"

Joe smiled. "Come back in thirty minutes."

The expressionless maid stepped into the hallway and pushed her cart out of view as Jonathan stepped inside, closing the door behind.

"Joseph! You're a married man."

"It wasn't like that, Smitty. I think she might have been trying to rob me."

"She didn't look like a thief to me. She looked like...well, you know what she looked like."

"I'm telling you, there was something not quite right about her."

"Where *are* the papers?"

Joe motioned to the bed. "In the briefcase between the mattress and the box springs. I slept on them."

Jonathan shook his head. "This won't do. It won't do at all. Why don't you hop in the shower and I'll make arrangements for the papers to be kept in the hotel safe."

Joe looked into Jonathan's blue eyes. "Do you think that's wise?"

"Yes. Much better than hiding them under the bed."

"All right." Joe grabbed clean underwear and a pair of slacks from his suitcase and stepped into the bathroom, closing the door. After showering and drying off, he opened the door to let the steam out and saw Smitty sitting in the chair by the window.

"Did you call the front desk?"

"It's all arranged. They have security boxes and we can put the briefcase in one when you come down for breakfast."

"Security boxes?" asked Joe.

"Like a safety deposit box in a bank. You'll have your own key, so no one else can get in."

The idea of not having to lug the papers around London lifted a weight from Joe's shoulders. "Sounds good. Give me a few minutes to shave and finish dressing and I'll join you in the lobby."

Jonathan left and Joe went to work making himself presentable.

Twenty minutes later, Joe and Jonathan sat at the Concierge desk in the lobby. A frumpy, overly made-up woman in her mid-fifties, her reading glasses hanging from gold chains at rest on her matronly bosoms, shook her head.

"No, I'm terribly sorry. We do not have a Chinese girl name Yu Mee Prentice working here."

"As you suspected, Joe," said Smitty.

"I think she might have been trying to rob me."

The woman's face seemed not to register the concern Joe and Smitty felt.

"I'm sure it was just some sort of misunderstanding. Nothing to be concerned about."

Joe shook his head. "No, she definitely had a purpose. It wasn't just a misunderstanding." He tried to make the Concierge, whose name tag identified her as Victoria, understand how potentially serious the encounter might have been. "Maybe you should notify hotel security and the police. You probably have her on your security cameras."

"Really, Mr. Conrad. I'm quite sure it wasn't anything."

"Have you had problems with prostitutes?" asked Smitty.

"Excuse me?" the woman responded, her voice climbing an octave.

"She offered to give the lad a massage."

"Oh, I see." Victoria blushed, straightened the pamphlets on her desk, and then placed her glasses up on the bridge of her nose, as if they afforded a barrier between her and the foul topic under discussion. "Well, candidly, yes." She leaned forward and dropped her voice to a whisper. "All the major hotels are experiencing it. The ladies follow single gentleman up to their rooms and then offer their...services."

Jonathan sat back. "That's it, then."

Joe rubbed his neck. "Maybe. But I had a bad feeling about her."

"You were right to," Victoria whispered. "They've been known to let their accomplices into the room after they have the hotel guest in a compromised position, so to speak. They excuse themselves to powder their noses and then let their friends in. The hotel guest is photographed, beaten and robbed."

"Then," Joe said, "you *should* inform hotel security to review their tapes and give a photo of this woman to the police."

Victoria wrote some information on a notepad. "You're absolutely right. I certainly will. You're in room 519?"

Joe nodded.

"Consider it done, Mr. Conrad." Victoria finished writing and then removed her glasses once again.

A few minutes later, they met the hotel manager and went into a large backroom that had impressive-looking, silver-faced safety deposit boxes covering one wall.

"Not to worry, gentlemen," a fit, middle-aged manager said. "We've held millions of pounds in these security boxes and hundreds of jewels without there ever being a problem. Your property will be safe."

Joe glanced at Smitty.

"They'll be fine, lad," Smitty assured him.

Joe put the Shakespeare papers in one of the boxes and slipped the long, flat key into his pocket. Smitty patted Joe on the shoulder and they stepped out of the back office into the bustling hotel lobby. The mid-morning guests were checking in and the front desk was quite active. They walked through the lobby to the restaurant. Sylvia sat at a table munching on a piece of toast.

"Feeling better, Joe?"

"Much. Sorry for going off on you guys."

"No problem," replied Sylvia. "You've been through a lot."

Joe took a seat as Smitty poured him a cup of coffee. Then Smitty sat down.

"Joe, we've discovered something that really needs investigation."

"Oh?" Joe sipped his coffee and eyed a thick piece of toast, a square of butter melting into the craters of its surface. "Can I have that?"

"Sure, Joe," Sylvia answered.

Smitty leaned forward. "But listen. There's a pub in St. Albans that we must visit today. Evidently, there's a wall-painting we should examine."

"St. Albans?" asked Joe as he spread the butter. He took a bite and while chewing asked, "Where's St. Albans?"

"It's in Hertfordshire, about thirty-five kilometers from here."

"Thirty-five kilometers? How much is that in Am-MARican?" he asked, imitating George Bush.

Smitty chuckled. "About twenty miles."

Joe spied strawberry jelly and scooped a glob onto his toast, spreading it around with the back of the spoon. Then he took another bite.

"How do we get there? Rent a car?"

"No, lad. We hop on a train. The tube's across the street."

Joe glanced around the room. "Where's the damn waitress?"

"I think we need to let Joe eat before we hop the train, Smitty."

Smitty grinned. "It's a buffet. Help yourself."

"Why didn't you say so?" He stood and looked over at the spread of food on the table behind Sylvia. Then he leaned down and mimicked Arnold Schwazenegger. "I'll be baack."

CHAPTER 45

When I was at home, I was in a better place:
But travelers must be content.
From *As You Like It*

The train ride took thirty minutes and showcased the backyards of impoverished homes before the train reached an open patch of countryside. The interior of the train smelled of stale cigarette smoke. Still, Joe soaked up the atmosphere along with the scenery.

Once the train stopped at St. Albans and they climbed down, Joe looked around and asked, "Where to from here?"

"City center," said Sylvia, glancing at a map. "We're looking for the White Hart Hotel."

Walking behind the others, Joe asked, "What's at the White Hart Hotel again?"

"A wall-painting that illustrates a scene—the hunt scene, in fact—from *Venus and Adonis*."

"Oh? And what's important about that?" asked Joe as they walked hurriedly down the sidewalk.

"The experts say the scene was painted in 1600," Sylvia explained.

Joe glanced at Sylvia, who was smiling a knowing smile of her own. "I know you're going to tell me why this painting is important eventually, so I'll just keep my mouth shut until you do."

Sylvia laughed. "Let's see it first. If it really is the hunt scene from the poem, then it might be proof of authorship."

"Of Edward de Vere or William Shakespeare?" asked Joe.

"Neither, lad. Remember our earlier discovery? The capitalized letters in the *Rape of Lucrece*?"

"Honestly, so much has happened in the past two weeks, I can't recall."

"Here we are," chimed Sylvia. "The White Hart Hotel and Pub."

The building in front of them was a three-story whitewashed structure in the Tudor style. Dark wood reinforced the outside white walls and three dormer windows looked out on the street.

They entered to find a small, dark, cool establishment filled with rich aromas from foods steaming and baking in the back kitchen. A few people sat at tables in the restaurant and looked up as they let the door close behind them. Smitty approached a pleasant-looking gentlemen in shirt and tie who looked, it seemed to Joe, like Anthony Hopkins in *Remains of the Day.*

"Excuse me," said Smitty, stepping up to the man. "Pardon me, but can you show us the mural?"

"Americans?" asked Anthony Hopkins' twin.

"Yes," answered Smitty, holding out his hand. "I'm Dr. Jonathan Smythe and this is Dr. Sylvia Williamson, from U. C. Berkeley, and—"

"Cal? You're from Cal?" asked the man of Sylvia.

"Yes, I am."

"My nephew did an exchange at Cal. He's turned us into fans of your American football."

He reached over and pumped Sylvia's hand enthusiastically.

"Is this your husband, then?" He looked at Joe.

Sylvia chuckled. "No, this is a colleague, a fellow college professor. We're all interested in the mural."

"Oh, college professors. I might have guessed. You look the part, don't you."

"I'm Joe Conrad." They shook hands.

"Studying Francis Bacon, then, are we?" asked Anthony Hopkins.

Joe suddenly remembered the capitalized FRA and B that Smitty had shown him when they first began studying the papers. "Yes, we are."

"Well, come on in and I'll show you."

"And who are you, sir?" asked Sylvia.

"My name's Ross. I do a little cooking here."

Joe followed behind as the four wended their way between tables. Suddenly, they were face to face with an enormous painting in three panels. The colors had faded and some of the paint was blotched, but the image of a fallen nobleman with an angry boar standing over him was quite visible.

Gesturing grandly at the mural, the cook named Ross announced, "I give you the hunt scene from *Venus and Adonis*!"

"Lovely," said Smitty. "Simply lovely."

Sylvia took her digital camera from her bag and started to photograph the mural, but stopped abruptly. "Is it all right to take some pictures?" she asked.

"Yes, yes, of course. No charge. Just as long as you stay for lunch."

Smitty smiled. "Of course. An early lunch will be nice."

Sylvia took photographs from various angles while they watched.

"So tell me," asked Joe, "how does this painting prove that Francis Bacon wrote the poem?"

"Oh, that's easy," Ross responded. "He lived a few kilometers from here at Gorhambury. He and his fellow Freemasons used to meet here all the time for their Lodge meetings."

Smitty beamed and pointed to an image in the mural. "Look! Look, Sylvia. There!"

Sylvia stepped closer and focused her camera lens at the image.

"What is it?" Joe asked.

"A rose, lad, a rose."

Joe looked perplexed and turned to the cook for help.

"Don't you know about Bacon?" Ross asked him. "Francis Bacon was not only a high ranking Freemason but also a proponent of the Rosicrucian movement."

"Ah," nodded Joe. "And their favorite symbol was—"

"Yes, lad," said Smitty. "The rose."

"You know, of course," added Ross, "Shakespeare mentions St. Albans over a dozen times."

"I didn't realize that," admitted Joe. "But, wait. How many times does he refer to Stratford?"

"An excellent question, lad." Smitty seemed giddy. "Care to tell him the answer, Sylvia?"

"Well, Joe," said Sylvia, looking up from her camera. "How many times can you recall Shakespeare mentioning Stratford-upon-Avon?"

Joe searched the low ceiling of the Inn. "Honestly, I can't recall a single reference to Stratford. But he must have, right?"

Ross laughed. "If the fellows who've been here before aren't lying, then the answer is never."

"Never?" repeated Joe. "Wait. Shakespeare must have mentioned his home a few times in his plays. I mean, almost every writer mentions his home now and then."

"Actually," Smitty corrected, "Stratford-upon-Avon *is* mentioned in passing once or twice, but it certainly is not an important setting in any of the plays."

Joe looked at the twenty-foot mural again with new appreciation.

"I think you've finally convinced me, Smitty," Joe admitted. "All along, I've doubted that Mister Shack-spur, as you call him, didn't really write the plays and the two long poems."

"But now?" asked Sylvia.

"There's just too much evidence against the Stratford man. And in favor of de Vere for the plays, but now Bacon?"

"Ah," said Ross. "So you're Oxfordians, then?"

"Yes," responded Smitty, sounding surprised. "We're leaning that way, at least in terms of the plays. But this mural. It's overwhelming support for Bacon as the author of the long poems."

"Taken with the other evidence, I'd have to agree," nodded Sylvia.

For lunch, Joe ordered a salad and was surprised to see layers of anemic slices of tomatoes sandwiched between a bland white cheese, something akin to Mozzerella, a dab of kippers and something else atop the center. With an oil and vinaigrette dressing, it was edible. He washed down bites of the slimy concoction with sips of lukewarm diet Coke.

Jonathan and Sylvia ate pieces of dry brown beef and mashed potatoes covered in gravy as thick as hot fudge.

"Excuse, me," he said, pushing his chair back. "I'm going to call Sara."

He called collect again and Sara answered.

"Is everything okay?" she asked.

"Yeah. We're in a quaint old restaurant in St. Albans, outside of London. There's an interesting mural here that reinforces the theory that Bacon wrote the two long poems."

"But you're all right?"

"Yeah, fine. How about you and the kids?"

"We're fine, too, but Joe, this is really expensive. I wish your cell phone worked over there."

"So do I, honey, but what can I do?"

"Well, it's good you called. I have a message from that FBI guy, Terry Lott."

Joe's heart skipped a beat. "What's *he* want?"

"Wants you to call him. He has some new information for you."

"Nothing about the Russian mafia, I hope."

"No," laughed Sara. "Do you need his number?"

"I've got his card. Think he'll accept a collect call?"

"Gee, let me think. A chance for the federal government to waste taxpayers' dollars. Hmm."

"Okay, okay. Hug the kids for me."

"I will. We miss you. Stay safe."

"Safe is my middle name," said Joe.

Sara laughed. "I wish that were true."

Joe hung up, fished Agent Lott's card from his wallet, and asked the operator to place the call. She came back on the line and, sounding to Joe like Miss Moneypenny, said, "The agent took your number and will ring you up straight away."

"Straight away?" Joe repeated, smiling at the expression.

"Yes, sir, straight away, so you should hang up now."

He couldn't resist. In his best Sean Connery, he said, "Will do, Moneypenny."

Ten seconds later, the phone rang twice and Joe picked up.

"Who's this?" Lott asked.

"Conrad. Joseph Conrad. Who's this?"

"Are you trying to sound like Sean Connery?"

"Maybe."

"Well, it's awful, so stop it."

Joe laughed. "All right. What does the FBI have for me. I'm in the middle of a major investigation over here across the pond, old Chap, and there's just been an incredible break in the case."

"Are you drunk?"

Joe chuckled. "No. Things are going well and, unless you're about to tell me that the Russian mafia is out to get me, I'm really enjoying myself."

"I wanted to get some information to you, since you're in England anyway."

Joe glanced back at the table and saw Smitty and Sylvia laughing about something. "Shoot."

"Your pal Jack Claire went to England about a year ago, to attend the funeral of a man named Phillip Owens."

"Phil Owens? I know that name. He taught at LSU for a year, some sort of sabbatical."

"Owens and Claire were good friends, so when Owens died, Jack and Maggie went to the funeral."

"Okay." Joe furrowed his brow. "What's it mean?"

"We've contacted the attorney who handled the estate for Phil Owens. Owens left books and manuscripts to Jack."

"Ah! That explains how Jack got the Shakespeare papers!"

"We think so. Shortly after his return to the states, Claire began to make the inquiries that drew his granddaughter's attention."

Joe nodded. "Phil Owens. Makes sense." Joe tugged a notebook out of his hip pocket and wrote down the name. "But it also raises another question."

"Yes it does."

"How did Phil Owens get the papers?"

"Exactly."

"Do you know the answer?"

"No, but Phil Owens was survived by his wife. She still lives in the home, as far as the lawyer knows."

"And where does the widow Owens live?"

"Swansea, Wales. An easy train ride from London, I'm told."

"We're not in London."

"No, I know. You're in St. Albans, just west of London."

"Right you are, Agent Lott."

"And Wales is west from you, so you could make it there in a couple of hours."

"I'll check with the others. I'm not sure they'll want to shake up their plans."

"Okay, but it looks like Swansea's the last piece of the puzzle."

Back at the table, Joe told the others his news.

"I think Agent Lott is right, lad. We should check it out."

Sylvia put her fork down. "Well, at least one of us needs to go to Hadleigh. We've got an appointment this evening with the de Vere descendant."

"When did you set that up?" asked Joe.

"While you were sleeping, lad. You did want to hand over the bound copy of the *Folio*, didn't you?"

"Yes, of course." Joe pushed a tomato off a slice of cheese and then stabbed the cheese with his fork. "I suppose we can go to Swansea tomorrow."

"You and Smitty go," said Sylvia. "I've got meetings at Oxford tomorrow."

CHAPTER 46

He that wants money, means, and content
Is without three good friends.
From *As You Like It.*

From St. Albans, they took the train back to London, and then another to Ipswich, where they hired a car to drive them to Hadleigh. They were to dine with Charles Francis Topham de Vere Beauclerk.

A slender man in his mid-forties stood on the steps of a restaurant, looking a little lost. To Joe, he looked like a cross between Hugh Grant and Cary Grant—average height and build, but kind eyes, genteel features, hair a little too long and graying at the temples. He wore a dark suit, a bright white shirt, and a bold red tie.

"Dr. Smythe," he said, stepping down as he extended his hand.

"Yes, I'm Jonathan Smythe. You must be Charles Beauclerk."

"I am, yes."

The two men peered into each other's eyes, politely assessing one another.

"Let me introduce Dr. Sylvia Williamson and Mr. Joseph Conrad."

"Lovely to meet you both," he said, letting go of Smitty's hand and taking Sylvia's. He held her hand and stared into her eyes. Joe stood to the side, waiting.

"Shall we go in to dinner?" He pulled Sylvia up the stairs and placed his arm in the small of her back.

Sylvia glanced over her shoulder at Joe and rolled her eyes, causing Joe to laugh out loud. After holding the door open for Jonathan and Sylvia, Charles reached out to shake hands with Joe.

"So you're the young man who found my ancestor's manuscripts?"

Joe took his hand and shook it, but Charles tugged him closer.

"I'd like to talk to you about all the papers, not just the *First Folio*."

Joe tried to pull his hand out of the other man's, but Charles tightened his grip.

"Those papers rightfully belong to my family, you know."

Joe suddenly wondered if *this* man was behind the efforts to steal the papers all along. He tightened his grip on the briefcase that held the copy of the *First Folio.* Then Joe pulled away and walked forcefully to the Maître de's stand. The Maître de was already starting to show Sylvia to the table.

The waiter seemed to know Charles Beauclerk well. He opened a bottle of red wine—a cabernet from France—and poured a few splashes into Beauclerk's glass. Beauclerk swirled the wine inside of the glass and then held it under his nose before taking a sip. The aroma brought a slight nod of approval, and he titled the glass to his lips just enough to allow a drop or two onto his tongue. After letting the drops melt on his tongue, Beauclerk opened his lips as if to whistle and sucked air over his taste buds.

"Very nice, Claude," he stated. "You may pour."

Joe chuckled. "In California, we just open our wine and drink it."

"I'm sure that's the way it's done in the states, Mr. Conrad, but here we like to indulge our senses a bit more." He turned to Sylvia. "Don't you sometimes find it necessary to take it very slowly when you're indulging your senses?"

Sylvia laughed. "Yes. My husband and I often exhibit a great degree of patience, when it's needed."

Joe chuckled at Sylvia's rebuke.

"No doubt." Beauclerk leaned back in his chair and lifted his glass, drinking half the wine Claude had poured. "You brought the bound copy of the *First Folio*?"

Joe nodded as he took another sip of wine. "It's in the briefcase."

"Wonderful. Did you know that the two men who financed its publication and to whom it was dedicated were brothers? Philip Herbert, Earl of Montgomery, was the husband of Edward de Vere's daughter, Susan, while the other, William, Earl of Pembroke, had once been a suitor to Bridget, de Vere's other daughter."

Joe, placing his wine carefully on the white table cloth in front of him, glanced at Smitty, who smiled.

"Yes, indeed," Smitty said. "In fact, Pembroke became Lord Chamberlain, which gave him authority over the theatre, and that put him in a position to decide which plays were published or suppressed."

"Quite right," Beauclerk answered.

"We also know," Sylvia added, "that Ben Jonson, who wrote much of the introductory material, was intimately associated with the de Vere family after Edward's death."

Beauclerk pretended to applaud. "Very good. You've done your research."

Smitty cleared his throat. "What do you make of Ben Johnson's reference to the Sweet Swan of Avon in the dedication?"

"Ah." Beauclerk nodded. "Clearly a reference to Mary Sidney, also known as Mary Herbert, Sir Philip Sidney's sister. She married the Earl of Pembroke and gave birth to William and Philip, who financed publication of the *Folio*, as you know."

"What's your point?" Joe asked.

Beauclerk raised an eyebrow and shot Joe an incredulous look. "My point is that publication of the *First Folio* was very much a family affair—*my* family, not the one in Stratford-upon-Avon."

Joe nodded and picked up his wine glass again, gesturing as he spoke. "I think we can all agree that the man from Stratford lacked the education, the access to books and the inside knowledge of court politics that someone like Edward de Vere possessed."

Beauclerk grinned, lifted his glass as if raising a toast to Joe, and drained his wine. Joe nodded and took another swallow of the good red wine before setting the glass down again.

"Mr. Conrad, how is it that *you* came into possession of these papers? Dr. Smythe was a bit cryptic on the phone yesterday. I've been following the news out of the States, of course. But I'm still unclear as to how someone like you wound up with my family's manuscripts."

Ignoring the implied insult, Joe lifted the glass to his lips and sipped the wine. "It's a bit of a mystery to me, as well." He swirled the glass and watched as strands of wine slipped down the inside of the glass. "Nice legs," he said. "Good bouquet."

Smitty cleared his throat. "Joe's mentor Jack Claire sent the manuscripts to him shortly before his death, just a couple of weeks ago."

"Jack Claire? I'm not familiar with that name," Beauclerk said.

"He was the Chair of the English Department at LSU in Baton Rouge, Louisiana," Joe explained, "and an Elizabethan scholar."

"I see. But that still doesn't explain how he got his hands on my papers."

"First of all, let's get something straight," Joe said, placing his glass on the table. "Until I hand them over to you, they aren't *your* papers."

"I must be candid at this point," Beauclerk said. "I've already contacted my attorney to look into the best way for my family to recover what's rightfully mine. We *are* planning to sue you for ownership."

"Well, that sort of ruins the mood, doesn't it," Sylvia said.

Joe could feel his face grow hot with anger. He was tempted to throw his red wine all over the other man's bright white shirt, but he stood up instead.

"I came here in good faith to give you something quite valuable." He bent down and picked up his briefcase, slamming it down on the table in front of him, causing a clatter that made everyone in the place fall silent and stare. Joe snapped open the latches, opened the lid, and lifted the bound copy of the *First Folio* out, tossing it on the plate in front of Charles Beauclerk, who pulled his wine glass out of the way just in time. "We allowed the Folger Library to scan and photograph the pages. Otherwise, it's in the same condition as when I found it. Sue me if you wish, but you'll lose. My attorneys and my friends in law enforcement will see to that."

Joe closed his empty briefcase and walked out of the restaurant.

He heard Smitty and Sylvia say something, but his ears were ringing—he was so furious—as he stormed out into the evening air to catch his breath. Turning back, he looked through the glass of the front doors and saw Smitty walking out, with Sylvia behind him. Then he turned back to the street to find the driver who would take them to the train station. The driver was leaning against the car, smoking a cigarette. When he noticed Joe, he tossed his cigarette away and jogged over.

"You leave something inside the car, sir?"

"No," said Joe. "Our dinner ended early, so we need to go back to the station."

"Already?"

"Yes."

Sylvia pushed open the door and held it for Jonathan. Once Smitty walked through, Charles Beauclerk followed closely behind him.

"C'mon, Smitty," Joe yelled. "We're leaving."

The driver spun around and jogged back to the car, climbing in and starting the engine. Smitty and Sylvia descended the steps and stood beside Joe, while Beauclerk stood on the porch with the light of the restaurant behind him.

"I'll be in touch, Mr. Conrad. Or my lawyers will."

"Go to hell," said Joe.

Joe opened the door to the backseat, allowing Sylvia to climb in first. After Smitty slid in, Joe slammed the door closed and then clutched the handle on the front passenger's door.

Suddenly, a strong hand squeezed his shoulder and turned him around.

"I'm sorry," Beauclerk said. "I can be a real prig at times."

"*Prig?* That's close enough to the word I was going to use."

"Look, Conrad. I *do* appreciate the gesture—your giving me the Folio—but I honestly believe it was my ancestor, Edward de Vere, the Seventeenth Earl of Oxford, who wrote those plays."

"So do I, but that doesn't give you the right to claim ownership."

"Oh, no? Well, who then should the owner be? You? From what I've read, you aren't even a Shakespeare scholar."

"You're right. I'm not."

"So what gives you the right to claim the manuscripts?"

Joe took a deep breath, afraid he might slug the aristocrat before he could speak his mind. "This will be hard for you to understand, but the fact that Jack Claire, a man I loved like a father, believed in me enough to send them to me, knowing he was about to be killed—that's why I'm keeping them. Some of them. At least for now."

Charles Beauclerk looked Joe up and down, sizing him up, Joe thought.

"Can we negotiate?"

"Yes," Joe said, exasperated. "I expected you'd want more of the plays. That's one of the reasons I wanted to meet you in person."

"You've already sold or given away some of them, haven't you."

"Yes, I have. I plan to keep two at my University, I'd like to give two to LSU, where Jack Claire taught. Berkeley wants a couple, and without Sylvia's help, I wouldn't know what the hell I was doing. The Huntington and the Folger have purchased one each. Tomorrow, Sylvia is meeting with people at Oxford, and I know they will want some, as will Cambridge."

"Fuck Cambridge." He held up his hand. "Sorry, sorry. It's just so frustrating to know that proof of the claims I've been making for years is out there, but it's being handed out like candy and I can't do anything to stop it."

Joe nodded. "Here's what Sylvia and Smitty explained to me. The more we get these manuscripts out there for other scholars to examine, the sooner we'll reach a consensus on their authenticity. If what we four now believe is true, then this consensus will confirm your ancestor's legitimate title as the greatest writer ever to have walked the earth."

Charles Beauclerk stared into Joe's eyes as he spoke. He could feel the penetrating gaze looking for the truth somewhere deep inside him where a person's soul might dwell.

"Your argument makes sense. I'll instruct my attorney *not* to file the restraining order that he's written up, blocking you from doing anything more."

"Thank you," Joe said. He pulled out his wallet, fished for one of Bill Morgan's business cards and handed the card to Beauclerk. "Have your attorney call my attorney and we'll work out a way to send you at least two of the plays."

Beauclerk extended his hand. "It's a deal."

They shook hands. Then Joe grabbed the car door, but Beauclerk stopped his arm.

"Are you sure you wouldn't like to dine together now after all?"

Joe shook his head. "After making a grand exit like that?"

Beauclerk laughed. "It *was* rather dramatic."

"Your Great, Great Grandpa would be proud."

"Great, Great Grandpa?" Beauclerk shook his head, not getting Joe's reference.

"The Seventeenth Earl, Chuck. He also had some dramatic flair."

Beauclerk laughed. "Right you are. Yes. Quite a dramatist, that Edward." He shook his head. "I just don't think of him as 'grandpa'!"

Later, on the train ride back to London, with Sylvia's head drooping, Smitty looked at Joe and whispered, "I'm not sure how you manage it, lad."

"How I manage what?"

"You get yourself into one confrontation after another, but somehow manage to get out again."

Joe shrugged. "Luck, I guess."

"Don't count on luck forever."

Sylvia had nearly dozed off, but she took a deep breath and sat up straight.

"What's the plan for tomorrow, then, boys?"

"You're going to Oxford, right?" asked Joe. Sylvia nodded. "Then I guess Jonathan and I will go to Wales to talk to the Owens widow."

CHAPTER 47

All the perfumes of Arabia will not sweeten
This little hand.
From *Macbeth*

Back in his hotel room the next morning, Joe hung up after speaking to the widow of Phillip Owens and turned to Smitty. "She can't meet until tomorrow."

"Too bad." He looked at Joe and shrugged. "What should we do?"

Joe shrugged. "We have an entire day to kill. Want to do some sightseeing?"

"It's your first time to London, lad. What do *you* want to do? The usual tourist destinations, I suppose. Buckingham Palace, the Tower of London?"

Joe picked up a brochure from the nightstand, a picture of an enormous Ferris wheel on the cover. "I guess I'd like to go on the London Eye first. That is, if you're up to it."

Smitty patted Joe's shoulder. "I've been to London several times, but that was before the Millennium Wheel was constructed. So, yes, I'd rather enjoy that."

As they left the hotel lobby and stood on the sidewalk, dozens of tourists passed them walking in either direction—people, it seemed to Joe, from all over the world. A group of Middle Eastern men, a couple from India tugging two small children, a Japanese high school girl, a group of college-aged tourists speaking German—a steady stream of humanity as diverse as any mix of people Joe had seen in Berkeley or the French Quarter. There was something thrilling about the energy of these various people that sent a wave of gratitude through Joe. He had to shake his head and then he glanced at the perfect blue sky, thinking about his mentor. *Thank you, Jack.*

Stepping through the flow of bodies with Jonathan at his side, Joe hailed a cab and they took the short drive to the London Eye. Big Ben chimed ten times as they climbed out of the cab. A long line had already formed for the ride, but it was moving quickly and the two men joined the line as several people pushed in behind them.

Joe opened his brochure and read a few statistics to Smitty. "It says here that the Millennium Wheel is the tallest observation wheel in the world at 135 meters. How tall is that in feet, Smitty?"

Smitty did a quick calculation. "About 400 feet, I'd say."

"It says here they get ten thousand visitors each day."

They watched in awe as the wheel made its slow rotation.

"How many of those capsules are there?" asked Smitty.

Joe glanced at the brochure. "Thirty-two. Says here that each capsules can hold up to twenty-five people."

Smitty smiled and shook his head. "Amazing. The capsule look like spaceships, don't they, Joe?"

Joe glanced up as they stepped closer to the wheel. "Yeah, like little glass submarines about—what would you say—thirty feet long?"

"Yes, that sounds about right. It doesn't stop, does it?"

"No. I guess it turns slowly enough that we can all just walk into a capsule." Still looking up at the looming structure, Joe shook his head. "I really should have brought Sara and the kids. They'll be so jealous when they find out I rode this thing."

"Bring them next time, Joe. You'll be able to afford it."

"Oh, Christ," Joe said, exasperated.

"What's the matter?"

"I forgot my camera."

Jonathan reached into the pocket of his khakis and pulled out a small silver digital camera. "Nothing to worry about, lad. I've got mine."

Before long, they pushed their way into a capsule with at least twenty others. Joe glanced at the people. Husbands and wives from all parts of the world, grinning and laughing with their children, including an overweight family of four talking and laughing too loudly, it seemed to Joe. The father, his beer-belly barely contained in his bright red Hawaiian shirt, yelled in a Texas accent, "This here's better than the one they got at Disneyworld, ain't it, boys?"

Joe rolled his eyes and turned to look out the window, noticing a shy-looking Japanese girl who slowly pushed her way through the crowd toward him.

As the oblong capsule rose in the air, the chatter of two dozen tourists obscured the narration playing over the speakers. Joe and Jonathan stood together leaning against the curved glass, watching as the length of the muddy Thames came into view. They could see the sprawling buildings of Parliament and the Tower of London. As the capsule climbed, all of London spread out below them.

"My God, Smitty. I had no idea London was this big. It's like L.A., isn't it?"

"It does sprawl in all directions, doesn't it."

People standing behind them leaned over to look, some pressing against them.

"Excuse me," someone behind Joe said. He turned. A handsome young man in his twenties leaned forward. "Mind if I have a look?"

"Maybe we should step back and let some of the others have a look," Jonathan said, sounding a little annoyed.

Joe shook his head and stepped back from the glass. The crowd behind jostled him and he noticed Smitty pushing his way back from the glass toward an opening in the center of the car. Someone else bumped into Joe. He turned to see the jet black hair of the Japanese girl whose backpack had hit his elbow.

"So sorry," the girl said in a soft voice. Her head down, she seemed to bow humbly and push away. The pink backpack had the face of a kitten embroidered on it, one eye open and one closed in a wink. Joe chuckled and turned to look back out the window.

In fifteen minutes, the car was almost at the apex of its assent, and now Joe was feeling a little uneasy. The height of the capsule as it neared the top brought a sudden chill to Joe's neck. He pushed his hands inside his pockets and tried to join Smitty in the center of the car where the crowd was thinner.

He felt for a mint inside his pocket. His fingers made out the outline of his plastic hotel room key, the tube of Chapstick and the mint, but something was missing. He felt around in his left pocket. Some loose change and his cell phone that didn't work in England, but nothing else. He felt around in his right pocket again. Something was missing.

The key!

Joe pushed through the crowd and found Jonathan. Trying to keep panic out of his voice, he said, "I think I lost the key."

"Which key?"

"The safety deposit box key, Smitty."

"Damn it, no!"

Joe removed the plastic room key and handed it to Jonathan. Then he pulled out the Chapstick and the breath mint, also handing them to Jonathan. He felt around in the pocket. *Was there a hole?*

Nothing. No hole. No key.

Joe looked around. "The girl."

"What girl?"

Joe looked over Smitty's head and scanned the crowd. "A Japanese girl wearing a pink backpack."

"What about her?"

"She might have picked my pocket."

Then he spotted her, just as she glanced up and saw his face. She turned and looked away, but Joe pointed and yelled, "There she is!"

A few people standing nearby looked at Joe and then in the direction of the girl, but they returned to the windows and resumed taking pictures.

Joe pushed through the crowd, watching as the young woman removed her backpack and pulled a mask out if it. She placed the mask over her mouth. Then she tugged a canister from her pack and pulled a pin from it.

Immediately, noxious white smoke spewed from the canister, filling the capsule as people coughed. Joe tugged his shirt out of his pants and pulled the shirt tail up to cover his mouth and nose.

He glanced at a woman holding a water bottle. Joe grabbed the water and doused his face and shirt tail with it, and then handed it back to the woman, saying, "Cover your eyes and mouth with a cloth and splash water on it."

The woman, her eyes squeezed closed and coughing furiously, dropped the water bottle and pushed away.

Joe turned. The Japanese girl looked familiar now as she pulled a pistol from her pack and pointed it at him. *The Chinese woman from his hotel room!*

The sadistic smile on her face told him she was going to pull the trigger. Seeing her finger move ever so slightly, Joe jerked his body as a shot exploded, its piercing noise ringing inside the capsule.

Joe glanced over his shoulder to see a red stain blooming on the shoulder of a teenage boy's white tee shirt. The big man from Texas grabbed his son and pulled him down to the floor of the capsule. His wife screamed as she saw her son collapse. The Texan stood up and shot a look of hatred at the woman.

"Goddamn it!" He charged toward the Asian woman, who pointed and fired another shot. People in the crowd screamed and moved away. If the bullet hit the man, it didn't stop him. Before she could fire again, the big man fell against the smaller woman, knocking her back and pinning her to the glass wall.

Joe lurched forward, too, and grabbed the gun, pushing the woman's hands up. The gun fired, shattering glass over head. People screamed again, pushing against one another at the far end of the capsule. Smoke billowed out of the bullet hole in the roof.

The Texan buckled and collapsed, rolling onto his back. Joe tightened his grip on the woman's wrists as he saw blood glistening on the large man's red shirt.

The Asian woman landed a knee to Joe's groin. Intense pain shot through him. She tried to knee him again, but he blocked her leg with his own and kneed her in the stomach. She tugged fiercely for the gun and managed to bring it down close to Joe's shoulder. When she pulled the trigger, the explosion hurt Joe's left ear and he heard a scream from behind.

"Oh, God. She's bleeding!" someone screamed.

The woman's panicked voice reminded Joe of Sara when she'd

been wounded. Enraged, he yanked at the gun, spinning the woman around.

When she fired again, the glass in front of her shattered and fell away. She fired again, and again more glass broke, leaving a gaping hole in the capsule that drew in warm summer air. Joe's watery eyes cleared. He saw his chance. He slammed the woman against the guard rail, knocking the wind out of her.

She seemed to go limp and Joe loosened his grip. Then her elbow jerked back, catching Joe's jaw with blinding speed and pain.

Joe's reaction was primal. He pushed his attacker away with all his strength.

As if doing a perfect back dive, the woman tumbled over the handrail and out the window. She disappeared from view, leaving behind the smell of teargas, gunpowder and a faint hint of perfume.

CHAPTER 48

Men's evil manners live in brass;
Their virtues we write in water.
From *King Henry VIII*

Joe and Smitty became very familiar with offices deep inside Scotland Yard. After hours of questioning and many calls back and forth to FBI Agent Terry Lott, the Chief Inspector, a distinguished looking man with graying hair, closed the door to his office and sat down at his desk across from Smitty and Joe. He unbuttoned the coat of his charcoal suit and smoothed his light-gray silk tie.

"Your stories check out," he told them. "We also have several witnesses who corroborate your version." He held up the flat key the woman had stolen from Joe's pocket. "You'll be wanting this back, I suspect?"

"Yes, thank you." Joe plucked the silver key from his fingers. "Did you find it on the girl's body?"

The Chief Inspector nodded. "Yes, along with a small arsenal in her back pack."

"The other passengers," said Jonathan, "the ones wounded, are they all right?"

"Yes. The woman and the boy from Texas had through-and-through wounds. Both were stitched up and released."

"How about the big guy who helped me?" Joe asked.

"His wound is more serious. Spent several hours in surgery. Damaged liver, but last word from hospital was, he'll pull through."

"That's good," chimed Smitty.

"So, who's the dead girl?" Joe asked.

"Something rather disturbing has come to light about your dead Asian girlfriend, Yu Mee Prentice."

"I still can't believe that was the same woman who was in my hotel room. She looked thirty years old yesterday. Today, she looked fifteen."

"I'm going to tell you something now that I will deny. But as you were nearly killed by this woman, I feel you have a right to know."

"Was she working for the Russian Mafia?" Joe asked.

The Chief Inspector jerked his head back. "The Russian Mafia? Good God, no! Why do you ask?"

"Agent Lott told me he found a link between the mercenary in America and the Russian Mob."

"How I wish that were the case. No. What I'm about to tell you cannot leave this room. The woman who posed as Yu Mee Prentice? Her real name was Mae Lee Price. She was the daughter of a couple who used to work for MI6 in Hong Kong before we returned it to China. Her father was killed there. The mother and daughter assumed we had her father killed as some sort of exchange with the Chinese government. They emigrated to England, fearing retribution."

"I don't understand," Smitty said. "Mae Lee was working for the Chinese government?"

"Lord, no. She was working for someone here in England, someone who was, at one time, somewhat close to the British government."

"You're joking," scoffed Joe.

"Wish I were, young man."

"The Queen?" asked Smitty.

The Chief Inspector smiled. "No."

Joe and Jonathan exchanged a look.

"Who, then?" Joe asked. "Prince Charles?"

"No, no. But someone who has a vendetta against Charles and the Royal Family."

Smitty blew out a stream of air. "I don't believe it."

The Inspector shrugged. "As the saying goes, there are more things in heaven and earth…."

"Wait," said Joe. "Who are you talking about?"

Smitty looked at Joe. "Do you know who once owned the most famous department store in London and who might hold a grudge against the Royal Family?"

Joe looked from Smitty to the Inspector. "Are we talking about who I think we're talking about?"

"We've investigated Miss Price before. She hired herself out as a private contractor, doing everything from arranging sex scandals to industrial spying, but we've never had enough evidence to go after her. This time, she had recently been paid a large sum of money, which we managed to trace back to a solicitor who also works for this man whom I will not name."

"But why?" asked Joe. "If this is who I think it is, why act in secret?"

"Yes," Smitty added. "Why not just come out in public and make an offer to buy the Shakespeare documents?"

The Chief Inspector grinned. "Ah," he said. "That is a mystery, isn't it. One can only guess that he wanted to prevent the truth about the authorship to come out."

"I don't understand," said Joe. "Why?'

"Perhaps to own something of value connected with England or maybe to deny Royal family the pleasure of knowing the truth. The manuscripts give him absolute control of the greatest works in the English language, would they not?"

"So all this over the death of his son?" asked Jonathan.

"I think so, yes. Remember. He believes very strongly that his son was murdered for being involved with Diana."

Joe shook his head. "Can you prove any of this?"

The Chief Inspector smiled. "I'm sorry," he said, "prove any of what?"

They were released a short time later and given a ride back to their hotel, where they met Sylvia in the bar. It was eight o'clock at night and she had already consumed several martinis.

"I leave you two boys alone for one day and you practically destroy one of the oldest cities in Europe. Can't take you anywhere!"

Jonathan hugged her and climbed onto the barstool on her left. Joe kissed her lightly on the check and plopped onto the stool on her right.

"Bartender! Another round," Joe called.

"What did you learn at Oxford, my dear?" Jonathan asked.

"The fine scholars at Oxford are going to fight us pretty hard."

"Why?" asked Joe.

Sylvia waved her arm in the air. "They said, and I quote, 'Only a fool would believe anyone but William Shakespeare wrote the plays.' Meaning, my career might be going down the drain, if I can't convince these bloody Limeys."

The bartender scowled as he placed fresh drinks in front of them.

Sylvia took a sip of her martini. "It was naïve of me to think they'd simply believe me. My reputation isn't quite as, as stellar as I thought it was."

"You're reputation is impeccable," said Smitty. He raised his glass. "Here's to Sylvia Williamson's impeccable reputation."

Joe raised his glass. "To Sylvia."

"To my stellar reputation!" She raised her glass.

All three took long sips of their drinks.

"So what's on the agenda for tomorrow, boys? Going to blow up London Bridge?"

The bartender shot a suspicious look at Sylvia.

"Juss joking, juss joking." She was beginning to slur her words.

Joe shrugged. "I guess we're off to Wales tomorrow to meet with the widow of Jack Claire's friend."

Sylvia nodded, sipping her drink. "Well, I'm sure you'll have a whale of a good time in Wales."

Smitty laughed politely. "I've never seen you tipsy before. It's rather amusing."

"RA-ther amusing," repeated Sylvia in an exaggerated English accent. "Hey, you should change your name to Jonah, Jonathan. Then you'll be Jonah inside Wales! Get it?"

"You've probably had your limit," Joe said, laughing. "We better call it a night."

Sylvia nodded. "I think you're right." She chewed her last green olive, then spun around and slid off her barstool, rocking a little as she stood. "Let's call it a night."

Joe swallowed the rest of his drink, and then he and Smitty walked Sylvia to the elevator.

"Hey," she said. "I made a rhyme, didn't I. I think you're right. Let's call it a night. It's a rhyming couplet, isn't it, Jonathan."

Smitty smiled as they helped her into the elevator.

"Shakespeare often ended a scene with a rhyming couplet, Joe. Point that out to your students, okay?"

Joe giggled as they rode the elevator. "I will definitely point that out to my students. Thanks, Sylvia."

The doors opened and the three of them walked arm in arm down the hall toward Sylvia's room. She handed her plastic key to Joe and he slipped it into the slot.

"Here's another one for you. Check it out. Get me to my room quicker, 'cause I'm gonna be sicker."

Joe pushed open the door and helped Sylvia into the bathroom. Standing over the sink, bracing herself with her arms, she looked at herself in the mirror.

"My father used to call me Cleopatra, Jonathan. Did I ever tell you that?"

Smitty stood in the doorway to the bathroom, Joe next to Sylvia at the sink.

"No, I don't think so."

"It's what got me interested in history and literature. And Shakespeare."

"That's wonderful, Sylvia," said Smitty.

"He was a wonderful man, my father. But he was just a man, 'Take him for all in all, I shall not look upon his like again.' Died of an enlarged heart."

"Sorry to hear that," Joe said.

"That's a helluva thing to die of, isn't it. A heart that's too large."

Suddenly, Sylvia heaved into the sink. She straightened up and groaned, then bent over and heaved again. Joe turned on the cold water and washed the vomit down the drain.

"Did you have any dinner tonight?" he asked.

Sylvia straightened up and looked at Joe in the mirror. "Yes. Six lovely, fat green olives. Came with my martinis."

"That explains it."

She leaned over, heaved again, and then bent down, resting her elbows on the counter. Joe grabbed a wash cloth and held it under the running faucet. Then he wrung it out and placed it on the back of Sylvia's neck.

"That feels good."

Joe glanced at Smitty, trying to read the look of concern on his face.

Finally, Sylvia stood up. "Oh, boys, I feel better." She rinsed the washcloth out again and pressed it to her face. "Much better." She smiled and pushed Joe out of the bathroom. "If you two wouldn't mind, I think I'll get to bed."

"Of course." Smitty stepped back into the hall and Joe followed.

"Are you sure you're all right now?"

She nodded and smiled. "Thanks for being here for me, guys." Sylvia held the door as Joe and Smitty stood in the hall. "If you don't mind, I think I'll stay behind tomorrow. You boys go off to Wales on your own, okay?"

Smitty nodded. "Sure, if you say so. But call me in the morning."

She nodded, smiled and slowly closed the door.

Joe looked at Smitty. "Think she'll be okay?"

Smitty nodded. "Give her a day to rest."

Joe walked Smitty to his door down the hall. "She seems really worried about her reputation with the folks at Oxford, Smitty."

Jonathan opened the door to his room and turned his calm, wise face to Joe. "You know what I think, lad?"

Joe smiled, knowing he was about to hear the Buddha-like wisdom of a Zen Master.

"No, Jonathan. What do *you*, in all your wisdom, think?"

"I think the folks up at Oxford are assholes."

Joe burst into laughter.

"Good night, Joe."

"Oh, God," Joe laughed. "Good night, Smitty."

CHAPTER 49

I will believe thou hast a mind that suits
With this thy fair and outward character.
From *Twelfth Night*

After climbing off the train at the Swansea station, Smitty and Joe took a cab to the home of Phillip Owens. A modest three-story row house on the side of a steep hill, it seemed to Joe to stand like the homes James Joyce had described in his short story "Araby," with brown, imperturbable faces. Stepping down to the porch, they saw that the front door was open behind the screen door. Joe knocked on the aluminum door, causing an awful racket.

After a few seconds, they heard a scraping noise from inside the home. Using a walker, an elderly woman dragged herself into the hallway and peered out at the men.

"Can I help ya?" she said with a thick Welsh accent.

"We spoke on the phone a couple of days ago," said Joe. "May we come in?"

"I don't like visitors," whined the woman.

"We've come all the way from America," added Smitty.

"Yeah, so? We've had many visitors from more notorious places than that."

"I was a friend of Jack Claire's," said Joe.

"Oh, hell, why didn't cha say so earlier? Sure, sure, come inside!"

The two men opened the screen and stepped into the cool darkness of the hallway. The house smelled of cigarette smoke, cabbage and mothballs. Phil Owens's widow turned ever so slowly and shuffled back into the living room, where she plopped down in a worn easy chair and pushed her walker off to the side. Then she leaned forward and pulled an ottoman closer to her feet.

"Do either of you know how to make a decent pot o' tea?"

Joe looked at Smitty, who smiled.

"Yes, ma'am," Smitty said. "Just point me toward the kitchen."

"Well, it's no mystery. Through that door on your left."

She gestured toward a small, arched doorway, through which flowed more light and a slight breeze. Smitty disappeared into the kitchen.

"You'll find everything you need on the counters," the old woman yelled. She reached down and lifted her legs, one at a time, onto the ottoman. "I always thought I'd go before my husband. His mind stayed sharp as a tack up 'til that last day when he just keeled over. Heart attack. Smoked a pack a day for four decades until the doctors—those butchers—cut out half his lung!"

With that, she reached for a crumpled pack of cigarettes on the bookshelf next to her chair. She shook one free, put it between her lips and lit it with a wooden match that flared brightly in front of her terribly wrinkled face.

"Tell me, young man," she said, turning her gaze toward Joe. "Is it true Jack Claire and his wife both died a few weeks ago? Tell me that isn't so."

Joe nodded. "I'm afraid it is."

"They were here only a year ago. God have mercy on their souls, I can't believe it!" She shook her head. "Murdered, were they?"

"We think so," Joe said, nodding his head.

"Well, Jesus have mercy, I hope it didn't have anything to do with those papers Phil left him!"

Joe's heart stopped. "You know about the papers?"

"Of course I do."

Joe wanted to call Smitty back, in case he was imagining this.

"Now, just to be clear, what papers are you referring to?"

"The Shakespeare papers, the Shakespeare papers! The ones that prove William Shakespeare was a fucking farce!"

Her voice was so loud Joe knew Smitty must have heard her, and sure enough, Smitty's head popped into the doorway.

"Did I hear you mention the Shakespeare papers?"

"Yes, dear," the woman said sarcastically. "Are you dense?"

Smitty smiled at Joe.

"We just assumed that you knew nothing about them."

"Oh, you two must be thick. Of course I knew about them. It was my idea to get rid of 'em. I didn't want those damn papers around here!"

"Why not?" asked Joe.

She directed her stern gaze toward him, blowing out a stream of gray smoke.

"They scared the be-Jesus out of me, that's why. For Christ's sakes!"

"I don't understand," said Smitty. "Why didn't your husband come forward with the papers?"

She turned and gave Smitty a disgusted look.

"Are you daft? And be the laughing stock of the whole of England? Who would believe a second-rate professor at a poor university in the tiny country of Wales, up against the likes of Mister William bloody Shakespeare?"

Smitty couldn't help but laugh.

"I guess you're right," he said.

The teakettle whistled just then and Smitty pulled himself back into the kitchen.

The old woman took another drag of her cigarette, and then strained her head to yell into the kitchen. "You'll find a package of butter cookies right next to the stove. Bring those in with the tea, will ya?"

"Yes, ma'am," Smitty called back.

"I have to ask you, Mrs. Owens. Where did your husband find the papers?"

"He didn't find them," she said, annoyed. "His father gave them to him."

"Your husband's father gave him the papers?"

"Yes, sonny boy, that's right."

"And who gave your husband's father the papers?"

She took another long drag of her cigarette and exhaled.

"His father, and his father before him, and his father before him." She smiled broadly at Joe.

"You mean, they've been passed on from one generation of Owenses to another?"

"Now you're catching on, sonny boy."

Smitty walked in carrying a tray with three cups on saucers, a teapot, a bowl of sugar, a small pitcher of milk, and a small plate of cookies.

"Here we are," he said putting the tray on top of the large dark television set. "Tell me what I've missed, lad."

Joe chuckled. "Well, according to Mrs. Owens—"

"Just call me Rosy," the woman said, crushing her cigarette in the ashtray balanced on the arm of her chair.

"As Rosy was saying, her husband got the Shakespeare papers from his father."

"Oh?" asked Smitty as he poured a cup of tea. He looked at Rosy Owens. "Would you care for cream or sugar, dear?" he asked ever so politely.

"Yes, *dear*," she said. "Lots of both. A good, creamy cup of sweet tea is my favorite meal these days, along with those butter cookies."

Smitty handed her a teacup with two cookies balanced on the saucer. Rosy Owens immediately ate one of the cookies and then washed it down with a few sips of tea.

"Not bad," she said. "You made a good pot of tea. Bless you, Dr. Smythe."

"And who, pray tell, gave the papers to Phil Owens's father?" asked Smitty.

"His father," said Joe. "And evidently his father was given the papers by his father, and so on back through several generations.

Suddenly, Smitty looked at Mrs. Owens with a very serious expression.

"Of course!" he said. "Of course!"

Taking another sip of tea, Rosy Owens nodded and grinned.

"Now you know," she said.

Joe looked from the old woman's smug expression to Smitty's inscrutable face. "What?" he pleaded. "What do you know?"

Smitty smiled at Joe. He closed his eyes, as if to savor the knowledge alone for a few seconds. Then he poured another cup of tea and turned to Joe. "Cream and sugar?"

"I don't care," said Joe. "Sure."

Smitty put a cube of sugar in the cup and stirred it slowly, grinning the entire time. Then he slowly poured milk into the cup and stirred it again. "Cookie?" he asked Joe.

Joe shook his head and laughed in frustration. "Sure, Smitty. Give me a cookie with my English tea. Why the hell not."

"There'll be no cursin' in my home, goddamnit," Rosy said sternly. "At least not by guests I don't know well enough to spit at."

"Sorry," Joe said. He glared at Smitty.

"Oh, put the poor boy out of his misery," the woman said, "and tell him the answer."

"Don't you see, lad? Generations ago, one of Phil Owens's forefathers was a scrivener."

"A scrivener?"

"Oh, dear lord!" exclaimed the old woman. "Don't tell me you don't know what a scrivener is? A copyist, for Christ's sakes!"

"Yes," said Joe, "I know what a scrivener is."

Smiling, Smitty continued. "He must have worked for Edward de Vere. Don't you see, Joe? It was he who made the copies for the playhouse, for the actors."

Suddenly, Joe understood. "And he kept the originals?"

"Yes," said Smitty. "After making copies for the theatre company, Scrivener Owens simply kept the originals."

"All these years?" asked Joe.

"All these centuries!" Rosy chimed in, after sipping her tea again. "What a bloody burden, too, let me tell you. Keeping a secret like that!"

"But why didn't one of the Owenses come forward years ago?" asked Joe.

"You must be daft, sonny boy," Rosy huffed. "A Welshman's word against the word of all those English gentlemen? Those bloody British aristocrats? Why, they'd have boiled us in oil!"

"Literally, boiled him in oil!" Smitty repeated. "So, Mrs. Owens. You're husband's ancestor worked as a scrivener for Edward de Vere, right?"

"Yes, of course, and others, like *Sir* Francis Bacon, until that asshole de Vere died."

Joe laughed. Calling these noblemen "assholes" seemed so irreverent to him.

"After de Vere died?" asked Smitty gently. "Who did the scrivner work for then?"

Rosy Owens took her last swig of tea, draining the cup.

"It's as obvious as that ugly little nose on your face," she said. "A woman. A woman by the name of—"

"Mary Sidney?" asked Joe.

Rosy Owens turned and gave Joe the sweetest, kindest look.

"So, you're not as stupid as you look," she said, still grinning.

"The Swan of Avon," said Smitty, "which accounts for the dedication in the *First Folio.*"

Rosy nodded. "Dat's right. And when the family had the *First Folio* published to honor one of de Vere's daughters on her marriage, they presented a copy to Owen Owens, too."

Smitty grinned and looked at Joe. "That explains why the leather-bound copy of the *Folio* was included with the manuscripts."

"Owen Owens?" repeated Joe.

Rosy clucked. "The scrivener, the scrivener. He retired in 1623 and moved back here. That lousy leather book was his going away gift."

Joe watched as an expression of serene satisfaction spread across Smitty's face.

"But what about Shakespeare's signature?" asked Joe. "The distinctive 'S' that looks like an 8 on his will? We saw it on some of the manuscripts."

Smitty knitted his eyebrows and watched the old Welsh woman struggle to light another cigarette. She flashed the two men a look of contempt. Exasperated, she blew out a stream of smoke.

"From what *I've* been told," she said, "the great Mister Shakespeare struggled like hell to copy young Owens's handwriting. Dumb as a stone, he couldn't put more than five sentences together! Haven't you ever read that pitiful poem he wrote for himself?"

Smitty smiled. "The one on his tomb?"

"Dat's the one," Rosy said, inhaling her smoke. "If you want a *real* sample of Mister William Shakespeare's poetry, just read that doggerel!"

Smitty turned to Joe. "We should stop at Stratford-upon-Avon, on our way back to London, Joe."

They finished their tea and said goodbye to Rosy Owens after calling a taxi from her house. The taxi took them to the station, where they found a train that could connect them to Stratford.

During the ride from Swansea to Cardiff, Smitty opened his satchel.

"What are you looking for, Smitty?"

"I just remembered something from *Henry IV*, a line that refers to a Welsh character."

Joe watched Smitty dig around in his bag. "She seems awfully bitter, doesn't she, Smitty."

The older man nodded. "Poor woman has lost her husband and her health."

"I mean, about the English."

Smitty glanced up. "You know, the English oppressed the Welsh the same way they did the Irish and the Scots. Took away their language, their sovereignty, their identity."

"Do you think I should give her some of the manuscripts?"

Smitty shook his head. "She made it pretty clear that she didn't want them. Besides, at her age and in her condition, she probably doesn't have the means to deal with them." Smitty bent down and continued looking for something in his bag.

"Still," Joe said, "I think I should send her a check, you know, to help her live out her final years. I mean, after I've sold one of the plays."

Still leaning over, Smitty glanced up. "Which play?"

Joe grinned. "How about *The Taming of the Shrew*?"

Smitty shook his head. "Oh, Joe. That was bad." He turned his attention back to the bag.

"You think *The Merry Wives of Windsor*, then?"

"Here it is. *Henry IV.*" Smitty opened an edition of Shakespeare tragedies. "Do you know the play, Joe?"

"Not very well."

"One of the characters, Edmund Mortimer, has a Welsh wife. As I recall, they aren't the happiest couple." Smitty scanned the thin pages, turning them slowly. "Here's the line. 'This is the deadly spite that angers me: / My wife can speak no English, I no Welsh.'"

Smitty looked up and stared ahead.

"It doesn't really prove much," said Joe. He looked over at Smitty, seeing the rolling green hills of the Welsh countryside out the windows. Enormous white clouds grazed the hilltops.

"No. Only that the writer was aware of the conflict between the English and the Welsh. Imagine for a moment the working relationship between Edward de Vere and the scrivener from Wales. There must have been times when the scrivener asked for more money. I can imagine the arguments, can't you, Joe? If Rosy is any indication of the scrivener's temperament, then there could have been some heated arguments."

"True," admitted Joe, grinning at the idea of a male version of that Welsh hag Rosy arguing with de Vere.

"Don't you see it, Joe? The scrivener must have cursed de Vere in Welsh, and the highly erudite de Vere couldn't understand him."

Joe laughed.

"De Vere was fluent in French, Italian, Latin and Greek, but when the Welsh scrivener got angry and cursed him, de Vere couldn't understand a word!"

Joe laughed again, trying to imagine the scene. The ornately dressed aristocrat, eyebrows knitted in anger, the young Welshman stomping out of the nobleman's chambers, swearing in a language the lordly de Vere couldn't stoop to understand. A battle of classes, a battle of cultures.

CHAPTER 50

To be once in doubt is once to be resolv'd.
From *Othello*

In Stratford-upon-Avon, Joe and Smitty toured Anne Hathaway's Cottage, also known as Shakespeare's house, moving through it slowly with the line of other tourists.

Joe leaned over. "Doesn't anyone think it odd that there were no books or unfinished plays in the house when Shakespeare died?"

"I'm sure they do. The tour guides usually say that such things were probably lost or stolen over the years."

"Right, but we read his Last Will, Smitty. He mentions no books, no plays, no manuscripts—nothing that a typical writer would bequeath his family. Even ordinary people *must* think *that's* suspicious."

"You're preaching to the converted, lad."

After the tour, Smitty led Joe down Mill Lane to the Holy Trinity Church. The gray stone structure stood on the banks of the River Avon surrounded by trees. The late afternoon sun lazed behind those sheltering trees whose leaves were already beginning to turn color. White swans floated on the gentle current of the river. Across from the Church stood beautiful full weeping willows. Dozens of tourists lined the walk to gain entry into the church. Joe and Smitty made the slow crawl to the large wooden doors.

Forty minutes later, they pushed inside with a few others. The small church, dim and cool, was noisy inside as tourists from all parts of the world pointed and chatted about what they saw. Most of the crowd moved toward the colorful bust of Shakespeare. A few stray people sat in the pews.

Joe followed Smitty, who walked down the aisle between the pews and the wall, apparently drinking in the atmosphere. Joe glanced around. There was something charming about the little church, something pleasant about the joy and wonder of the tourists. He thought about Sara and the kids. One day he'd bring them here, even if this was not the burial site of the true Bard. A smile spread across Joe's face as he glanced over at Smitty, who looked serene.

They stood under the bust of Shakespeare on the north wall of the chancel, looking up with a dozen other tourists who had gathered to admire it. A few people aimed their cameras and snapped pictures of the bust with its bulbous head and bright red shirt. In the figure's right hand was a quill pen and under his left hand was a page. Black columns framed the image. The docent—a slight man with a white toothbrush moustache—stood directly under the monument and spoke in a clear, high-pitched voice to the small crowd while Joe and Smitty listened.

"The monument was erected sometime between Shakespeare's death in 1616 and 1623 when Leonard Diggs mentions it in his poem, which appeared in the *First Folio*. Over the years, the bust itself has been taken down and repaired several times." The docent withdrew a hanky from his rear pant pocket and blew his nose loudly, wiping each nostril with dramatic flair before stuffing the hanky in his back pocket again. "An early drawing of the monument done in 1653 by William Dugdale looks a bit different in that the figure seems to be holding a sack of grain rather than resting his hands on a pillow. Dugdale's drawing does not show Shakespeare holding a quill pen or a sheet of paper, which some people find curious."

Smitty raised his hand, and the docent pointed to him and nodded.

"Weren't there some other differences between Dugdale's sketch and the bust as we see it today?"

"Yes," acknowledged the docent. "The sketch shows a gaunt face with a drooping moustache. A researcher named Charlotte Stopes discovered that money was raised in the mid-1700s to re-beautify the monument. She claims that's when substantial alterations were made—the fuller face and the upturned moustache."

"Any theory," Smitty asked, "as to why those alterations were made?"

The docent shrugged. "Simply to make it more attractive, I suspect."

"Or possibly to make it match the Droeshout engraving of Shakespeare in the *First Folio*?"

"That's another theory," admitted the docent. "Now let's move on to the grave stone."

The small crowd followed the little man, while Joe and Smitty continued to stare up at the monument.

Joe shook his head and glanced at his companion. "Is it just me, or does it seem, I don't know, less than impressive?"

Smitty smiled. "A little cartoonish, perhaps?"

He looked back up. "Yeah. Kind of gaudy."

"Joe, you realize what we're doing, don't you?"

Joe looked down from the monument and examined Smitty's face. "Proving Edward de Vere wrote the plays."

Smitty nodded. "And in doing so, we're knocking that monument off its pedestal."

Joe nodded and smiled, but he felt a pang of regret. From the corner of his eye, he noticed someone sliding toward him in one of the pews, a dowdy woman wearing a gray wool sweater almost the same color as her hair.

Her head down, she pushed herself into the aisle right in front of him, saying, "Excuse me, sonny."

"No problem," Joe said. He stepped aside and waited for the old woman to move out of his way.

Instead, she slowly turned around and looked up into his eyes, through wire-rimmed glasses. Joe glanced down as the woman unclasped her large red purse and reached inside.

"I knew you'd find your way here." Now the woman's voice was much younger. It was a voice he knew.

She faced him. Under the wig, under the heavy makeup, behind the wire-rimmed glasses stared young eyes deep within an angry face he recognized. She pulled a German Luger from her purse and pointed it at Joe.

"How?" was all he could manage as his heart raced with fear.

"How did I find you? Your secretary was kind enough to tell me you were headed to England. I knew you'd come here, to this church, eventually."

Joe saw her finger tighten on the trigger and spun away in time--the shot exploded with an awful ringing noise, but the bullet missed his gut. He heard the shot ricocheted off the wall even as the ejected shell bounced on the floor, making a succession of pings.

She aimed again.

With his left hand, Joe grabbed the woman's right wrist and twisted, while he clutched the woman's throat with his right hand.

"Let go of me!" she screamed.

Joe swung her around, a dozen screams echoing in the small church.

"Help! This man's trying to kill me!"

Joe shoved her back against the wooden pew and pushed her arms up so the barrel of the Luger pointed away from his face.

She fired again, the blast echoing against the walls of the church, bringing a new round of screams from the crowd.

Joe saw the head on Shakespeare's bust roll off its perch and hit the floor with a resounding thud. Like a bowling ball, it rolled across the marble until Smitty stopped it with his foot like a soccer player.

"Oh, dear," Smitty said. As if embarrassed, he pulled his foot off Shakespeare's dismembered head and glanced at the stunned crowd.

Releasing the woman's neck, Joe grabbed the smoking pistol with his right hand and twisted the hot metal out of the woman's slender fingers, letting it drop to the floor. The acrid smell of gunpowder burned his nostrils as he spun his assailant around, holding her in a bear-like hug.

Several men rushed toward Joe and pulled him off the woman.

"No," he said, his heart racing with adrenaline. "It's *her.* Deirdre Claire. *She's* trying to kill *me*."

The men succeeded in disentangling Joe and the woman.

"Look," the woman screamed, pointing to the floor. "He tried to shoot me with that gun."

"No," said Smitty, his voice cracking. "It was the other way around. She tried to shoot my friend."

The woman shot a fierce look of hatred at Smitty. "You're crazy," she yelled.

"Am I?" Before she could stop him, Smitty—his hand shaking—snatched the gray wig from the woman's head.

Several people gasped. A younger woman's full head of lustrous hair was piled up tightly underneath the wig.

"Call the police," said Joe. "This woman is wanted for murder back in the States."

Over the next few hours, police from Scotland Yard once again interviewed Joe, Smitty and several witnesses before handcuffing Deirdre Claire and taking her away. Several of the other tourists had captured every move on their cell phones and cameras, including the shot that had beheaded Mr. Shakespeare.

Before leaving, one of the investigators, Sergeant Digby Mills, a pudgy, pale-faced man from Scotland Yard, walked over to where Smitty and Joe were sitting. "We've gotten most of the information we need. Do you two have any questions?"

Joe nodded. "I don't understand how she managed to get a gun here in England."

"Ah. We wondered that, too. Evidently, Ms. Claire is chums with an antique dealer in London. I spoke to him just now by phone. He sold the gun to Ms. Claire a couple of days ago. Claims the Luger's firing pin had been removed and she must have found a gunsmith, but we suspect he sold her the gun intact, probably with some ammunition, too."

Sergeant Mills hesitated.

"Is there something else, Sergeant?" asked Smitty.

"My Captain tells me you two were involved with the shooting on the London Eye yesterday. Is that true?"

Joe chuckled, his face reddening. "I'm afraid so."

Mills pulled his earlobe and shrugged. "The Captain wants to know how much longer you plan to stay in England, then. Says I should inquire."

Joe glanced at Smitty, who responded, "Actually, we're scheduled to leave the day after tomorrow."

"That's good," Mills said. "The Captain hoped it would be sooner than later. Says he wonders what landmark you'll destroy next."

"I assure you," said Smitty, "we have no plans to do anymore damage."

The plump man nodded. "Please see that you don't."

With that, he turned slowly, nodded to the older gentleman—his Captain, Joe suspected—and walked away.

When calm and quiet was restored to the famous little church, Joe turned to Smitty.

"Should we head back to London or finish our tour?"

"We've come this far together, lad. Might as well complete the journey."

Before he realized it, Joe was standing over the slab that covered Shakespeare's grave.

"Look, Joe," Smitty whispered. "As far as we know, this is the only real poetry William Shakespeare undoubtedly wrote by himself. Read it with your own eyes."

Joe looked down at the stone engraved with four lines all in capital letters. As he scanned the lines, he glanced over at Smitty. "Are those misspellings typical of British English at that time?"

Smitty shrugged and grinned. "A couple are. 'Forbeare,' for example, and 'curst.'"

An elderly man had just finished a rubbing using bright purple chalk that made the indented letters stand out nicely. Looking over the man's shoulder, Joe read the lines out loud quietly:

GOOD FREND FOR IESVS SAKE FORBEARE,
TO DIGG THE DVST ENCLOASED HEARE.
BLESE BE YE MAN YT SPARES THES STONES,
AND CVRST BE HE YT MOVES MY BONES.

"It's awful!" cried Joe. "Never mind the misspellings, the cadence of the first two lines is off! And the imagery, isn't it reversed?"

"What do you mean?" asked Smitty.

"Shouldn't it read, 'Blessed be the man who spares my bones, and cursed be he who moves these stones'? Wouldn't that make more sense?"

Dr. Jonathan Smythe nodded. "Perhaps."

Joe looked back at the slab and shook his head. "Mrs. Owens was right. It's the worst doggerel I've ever read!"

He turned toward Smitty, who said, "Hard to believe that the same man who wrote Hamlet's supreme soliloquies also wrote this."

Joe remembered the opening lines from Hamlet's first soliloquy. "Oh, that this too, too solid flesh should melt, thaw, and resolve itself into a dew."

Smitty nodded. "So excellent a king that was to this—" he gestured to the tombstone—"Hyperion to a satyr; so loving to my mother, That he might not beteem the winds of heaven visit her face too roughly."

Joe answered, saying, "She would hang on him as if increase of appetite had grown by what it fed on."

Smitty's voice grew soft as he spoke another line. "A beast that wants discourse of reason would have mourned longer."

Joe turned his gaze back to the grave. "Married with my uncle, my father's brother; but no more like my father than I to Hercules."

They stood silent now as shafts of evening sunlight slanted across the slab. Then Joe read aloud the simple lines on the grave once more.

He couldn't help himself. Joe laughed. The harder he tried to stop, the harder he laughed. His laughter filled the church. As people stared at him, Smitty started to laugh, too. Their laughter echoed from the walls and high ceiling. Clutching each other's arms, like two drunks weak in the knees, they clung to each other, laughing at a hoax only they fully understood.

The End

Dedicated to THE John Smith,
Professor emeritus, friend, confidante, kind critic.

ACKNOWLEDGEMENTS

At first, this novel seemed a playful project that might capture the attention of a few readers who love murder mysteries and wouldn't object to learning a little literature along the way. To get the facts, I began doing a little research and soon found that with Shakespeare, there is no such thing as a "little" research, especially when it comes to the authorship question. While I have consulted at least fifteen books and many more articles, listed in the bibliography at the end, I've relied heavily on several sources in particular. These are Mark Anderson's insightful biography ***Shakespeare by Another Name***, J. Thomas Looney's most thorough ***"Shakespeare" Identified,*** John Michell's intriguing ***Who Wrote Shakespeare?*** Joseph Sobran's very readable ***Alias Shakespeare***, and Charlton Ogburn's comprehensive examination, ***The Mysterious William Shakespeare***. I am equally indebted to John Smith, Professor Emeritus, University of the Pacific, a Shakespeare scholar whose patience and encouragement kept me at it. I must also thank Dr. Earl Showerman, who organized the enchanting Shakespeare Authorship Conference in the fall of 2005 in Ashland, Oregon, where the actor James Newcomb's performance of Richard III thrilled us all, and Dr. Daniel Wright, who brings scholars from all over the world to the charming Concordia University, the site of the Conference of Shakespeare Authorship Studies in Portland, Oregon. Finally, I'd like to thank Dr. Georgianna Zeigler and others at the Folger Shakespeare Library in Washington, D.C. Their help and guidance enabled me to do an extraordinary amount of work in a short time in a beautiful facility.

SUGGESTED READING

Shakespeare by Another Name, The Life of Edward de Vere, Earl of Oxford, The Man Who Was Shakespeare - Mark Anderson 2005

Shakespeare Identified - J T Looney. Kennicat Press USA } 2 volume

Poems of Edward de Vere - J T Looney. Kennicat Press USA} set

Who Wrote Shakespeare? - J Michell. Thames & Hudson

The Mysterious William Shakespeare - Charlton Ogburn. EPM Publications USA

The de Veres of Castle Hedingham - Verily Anderson. Terence Dalton

The Real Shakespeare - Eric Sams. Yale University Press

A Documentary Life - S Schoenbaum. Clarendon Press

Shakespeare's Lives - S Schoenbaum. Clarendon Press

Alias Shakespeare - J Sobran. Simon & Schuster/Free Press. 1997

The Life of Henry, Third Earl of Southampton - Charlotte Stopes. Cambridge University Press

The Seventeenth Earl of Oxford - B M Ward. John Murray

Shakespeare - The Evidence - Ian Wilson. Headline Publishing

Shakespeare who was he? - Richard Whalen. Praeger. USA

Shakespeare: In Fact - Irvin Matus. Continuum USA 1994

Shakespeare's Unorthodox Biography - Diana Price. Greenwood Press 2001

Monstrous Adversary - Alan Nelson. Liverpool University Press 2003

The Mysterious Identity of William Shakespeare - Bertram Fields. Regan Books, 2005

INTERESTING FACTS:

During the winter season of 1604-5 six of Shakespeare's plays were presented at court, by command of James I. This has an air of commemoration. In 1609 the *Sonnets* were published in a pirated edition. The famous dedication describes the author as 'our ever-living', a phrase which was invariably used of the dead, and with the change of only one letter is an anagram of Oxford's motto Vero nil Verius ('nothing truer than truth', or 'than a Vere'). In 1622 Henry Peacham published, in *The Compleat Gentleman*, a list of poets who made Elizabeth's reign a 'golden age'. Unaccountably, he omitted Shakespeare but included Oxford; perhaps he knew them to be the same person.

We do not know who instigated the publication of the First Folio edition of the Shakespeare plays in 1623, but there is no mention of any executor or relative of the man from Stratford. However, of the two men who financed it and to whom it was dedicated, the brothers Philip and William Herbert, the former, Philip, Earl of Montgomery, was the husband of Oxford's daughter, Susan, while the other, William, Earl of Pembroke, had once been a suitor to Bridget. Pembroke became Lord Chamberlain, the supreme authority in the world of theatre, and thus was in a position to decide which plays were published and which suppressed. We also know that Ben Jonson, who wrote much of the introductory material, was well known to De Vere family after Edward's death. The First Folio was very much a family affair, but the family was not the one in Stratford-on-Avon.

CPSIA information can be obtained
at www.ICGtesting.com
Printed in the USA
FSHW022201181119
64250FS

9 781452 077383